BIOG
Couri
Klein, Edward

KATIE the Real Story

D0170822

KATIE

KATIE
The Real Story

BY EDWARD KLEIN

CROWN PUBLISHERS
NEW YORK

Copyright © 2007 by Edward Klein

All rights reserved.
Published in the United States by Crown Publishers, an imprint of the
Crown Publishing Group, a division of Random House, Inc., New York.
www.crownpublishing.com

CROWN is a trademark and the Crown colophon is a registered
trademark of Random House, Inc.

Library of Congress Cataloging-in-Publication Data
is available upon request

ISBN 978-0-307-35350-4

Printed in the U.S.A.

Design by Lauren Dong

10 9 8 7 6 5 4 3 2 1

First Edition

For Jack, Annalise, Nathaniel, and Ryan

I had a sort of perfect life until I was forty. Jay used to say I was born on a sunny day—everything just sort of went right for me. Everything changed when I turned forty.

—KATIE COURIC

PART I

"Let Them Know You're Here!"

Chapter One

The Stuff of Legend

KATIE COURIC WAS IN TEARS.

"I'm going to be *fired*!" she said.

It was Thanksgiving week in 1980, and Katie was in CNN's brand-new Washington bureau on Wisconsin Avenue. She was seated on a big cardboard packing box (most of the office furniture hadn't arrived yet), pouring out her heart to Jean Carper, the network's medical correspondent.

"Can you believe it, Jean?" she said. "They're going to *fire* me!"

Katie was a small fireplug of a woman (five-foot-two on a good-posture day), and from her perch on the packing box, her feet barely reached the floor. Thanks to her diminutive size, bubbly personality, and a wide mouth that revealed a set of tiny, childlike teeth, Katie could have been mistaken (and often was) for a high school cheerleader.

Nearly six months before—on June 1, 1980—Ted Turner and a handful of veteran journalists had launched the country's first twenty-four-hour-a-day cable news network, and these tough newsmen had trouble taking the girlish Katie seriously. It wasn't that she lacked the smarts or get-up-and-go. On the contrary, Katie was a ball of energy, an entry-level VJ (or video journalist) who was willing to work for $3.35 an hour—25 cents above the federal minimum wage. She came into the CNN Washington bureau on her days off and volunteered to run cameras, write scripts, and produce live stand-ups for correspondents like Jean Carper.

Jean had taken a shine to Katie and was distressed to hear that her protégée was going to be fired. The ax couldn't have fallen at a worse time. It was the beginning of the holiday season, and Katie was getting a pink slip instead of the Christmas promotion she had been hoping for. It looked as though Katie was all washed up in the television news business at the tender age of twenty-three.

"Jean," Katie pleaded, "what am I going to do?"

"Who told you you're getting fired?" Jean asked.

"Stuart," said Katie.

She was referring to Stuart Loory, the managing editor of CNN's Washington bureau.

"Why would Stuart do a thing like that?" Jean asked. "I've told him—every time you've gone out to help me produce a segment, you've been a real asset."

Katie hadn't confided in Jean Carper that she didn't want to be a producer—someone whose name flashed on the screen for a split second during the credit roll at the end of a show. She had bigger dreams. She dreamed of being a star, and not just a relatively minor star like Jean Carper, but a major star, the biggest kind of star, an anchor at a major network with a show of her own.

Katie had been obsessed with this dream since college; in fact, she once told a college boyfriend that her goal was to become the next Barbara Walters, who at the time was co-anchoring ABC's *World News Tonight* with Harry Reasoner. As soon as Katie received her degree in American studies from the University of Virginia, she talked her way into her first job in TV journalism—as a desk assistant in the Washington bureau of ABC News.

"My first day at ABC," she recalled in an interview with *Washingtonian* magazine, "Sam Donaldson came into the newsroom, jumped on a desk, and started singing 'K-K-K Katy.'"

During her brief stint at ABC, Katie was responsible for making coffee, answering phones, and getting ham sandwiches for anchorman Frank Reynolds.

"It was the most humiliating job I ever had," Katie said.

A few months later, she switched to CNN, because advancement at the fledgling cable network was likely to come a lot quicker than at ABC. Ever since then, she had been pestering CNN's Washington bureau chief, Stuart Loory, to give her a shot on-camera. But Loory, a hard-bitten newsman who had been managing editor of the *Chicago Sun-Times*, didn't think Katie had the right stuff to become a reporter.

To begin with, Katie suffered from stage fright. In front of a camera, her voice shook, her hands fluttered, her nose ran, and she stumbled over words. Her high-pitched, untrained voice didn't match the aura of grave moral authority that the startup network was striving so hard to achieve.

Her looks didn't help, either. The simple truth was, Katie didn't fit the mold of CNN's female anchors—pretty young things with long blonde hair. Katie might be cute, but she wasn't conventionally beautiful, and her mop of dark brown hair didn't add much to the overall package.

Even so, Katie had been given several opportunities to prove herself on air.

"One morning, an anchor in the Washington bureau failed to show up, and the producer running the show put Katie on in his place," recalled Reese Schonfeld, who had cofounded CNN with Ted Turner and was its first CEO. "I got a call from one of the guys on the news desk in Atlanta. 'Hey, look, they've got Katie on,' he told me. I turned on the TV and, sure enough, there was Katie, white-faced and scared stiff, and looking all of fourteen. I called the producer in Washington and told him, 'Never put anyone on the network without first asking me or the producer in Atlanta.' "

Reese Schonfeld's orders had the force of law at CNN, and everyone interpreted his words to mean: *Never put Katie on the air again.* In the face of such an edict, Katie's chances of becoming an on-air personality at CNN—much less an anchor—were nil. And now it appeared that Stuart Loory had sealed her fate by giving Katie her walking papers.

* * *

JEAN CARPER PLACED a consoling hand on Katie's shoulder.

"Let me see what I can do," she said.

"Oh, would you, Jean?" Katie said. "I'd be so grateful."

"I'll call Reese."

Jean Carper didn't waste any time making good on her promise to intervene with Reese Schonfeld, the man who ran CNN on a day-to-day basis.

"Katie's in tears," Jean told Schonfeld when she reached him on the phone in Atlanta. "She's crying because Stuart Loory's about to fire her. I think it'd be a big loss to CNN if that should happen."

Reese Schonfeld was receptive to Jean Carper's appeal. She was one of his most valuable correspondents and had broken many important medical stories that were popular with CNN's viewers. What's more, although Schonfeld was loath to admit it, he was ready to believe the worst about his Washington bureau chief, Stuart Loory.

Jealousy and competition colored the relationship between Schonfeld, the top dog at CNN's headquarters in Atlanta, and the prickly Loory, who ran the Washington bureau as though it was his independent fiefdom. From day one, Loory was a thorn in Schonfeld's side. As far as Schonfeld was concerned, Loory's background in print journalism only aggravated the situation, since it made Loory a poor judge of TV talent.

After he hung up with Jean Carper, Schonfeld was struck by a thought. He recalled that a popular CNN husband-and-wife anchor team, Don Farmer and Chris Curle, had expressed an interest in bringing Katie down to Atlanta to work as a junior producer on their afternoon show, *Take Two*, which was modeled after *The Today Show*. In fact, now that Schonfeld thought about it, *Take Two*'s talented director, Guy Pepper, was a big Katie fan, too.

And so, Schonfeld summoned Don Farmer, Chris Curle, and Guy Pepper to his office.

"Do you want Katie on your staff?" he asked Farmer.

"You bet," said Farmer, who swung a big stick at CNN because he had made his reputation in TV's big leagues—as an ABC foreign correspondent and later as ABC's Capitol Hill reporter during Watergate.

"I used to share an office with Ted Koppel and Sam Donaldson at ABC," Farmer said, "and Katie was a desk assistant who'd pitch stories to us. You know, 'This energy bill . . . maybe you need to . . . wouldn't it be great . . . blah, blah, blah.' Katie was a ball of energy, bright and cute. I like Katie because she can write and she's a one-man band: ask her to go find so-and-so, and she'll research it, take the bull by the horns, set it up, get the crew, come back, edit, and do the narration."

"And you?" Schonfeld asked, turning to Guy Pepper, who hadn't said anything up until now.

"Oh, yeah," Pepper said rather matter-of-factly. "She'd be great."

THE STORY OF how Katie Couric barely escaped being fired by CNN was the stuff of TV legend.

In the years to come, Katie would never tire of recounting how CNN's bungling bosses failed to spot her potential. Even after she became the star of *The Today Show* and was recognized as the most popular female broadcaster of her generation, even after she joined CBS as the first woman to solo anchor an evening news broadcast, even after all that, resentment and bitterness over her treatment at CNN remained fresh in Katie's memory.

"I had nobody on my way up saying, 'We're going to make you a star,' and I think that really helped me," she once told *Newsweek*. "It forced me to work."

That was part of the Katie Couric legend, too.

She had climbed to the top on her own.

But what about the people at CNN, like the director Guy Pepper, who had gone to bat for her? Normally, directors were low on the TV totem pole, but at CNN, Guy Pepper was the exception to the rule. He possessed a brilliant grasp of the electronic medium and was viewed by his bosses at the struggling cable network as an indispensable man. All that—plus his talent for schmoozing and playing office politics—had earned Guy Pepper a great deal of influence.

"Of that early CNN crowd," said Judy Milestone, a researcher on *Take Two*, "Guy understood TV best of all. He was always getting the show on the road. He had a good sense of how to put all the pieces together, and he understood the technical part. Guy could think of something and figure out which camera should be operating. He had a sense of how to stage a show. In addition, he was a warm, lovely person—a nice Jewish boy from Miami."

As CNN's chief director, Pepper supervised the other directors, but his primary responsibility was the midafternoon show *Take Two*. The show originated out of Atlanta, but it frequently went on the road in order to broadcast live from other cities, and Pepper was said to have girlfriends at several stops along the way. When *Take Two* went to Washington, the handsome director met the ambitious, irrepressible Katie Couric.

"The thing about Katie was that she was a lowly frigging VJ, for God's sake, and yet she made herself well known to everyone," said Marcia Ladendorff, one of CNN's early blonde anchors. "She was cute and assertive, with bright, sparkly eyes. I remember that particularly about her—that she knew how to use her eyes. She was very flirtatious and knew how to stroke Guy Pepper's ego."

Before long, Guy and Katie were an item. Office romances between senior managers and ambitious younger women were not uncommon at CNN, where many of the men on the fifteenth-floor executive suite (from Ted Turner on down) promoted their girlfriends' careers. And CNN was typical of the ruthless TV news business, where women eager to get ahead felt enormous pressure to sleep with their bosses. Go-getting young VJs like Katie Couric were particularly susceptible to such pressure.

"I don't know who to screw to get ahead anymore," a VJ at CNN was once heard complaining, perhaps in jest. "Last night, I made it in the backseat with a guy I thought was a vice president. It turns out he was a VJ like me."

Under ordinary circumstances, Guy Pepper's affair with Katie Couric wouldn't have attracted much attention at CNN. But Guy's circumstances were hardly ordinary. He had been hired by CNN as a twofer, along with his fiancée Denise LeClair, who had been an anchor in Hartford, Connecticut. Everyone, including Katie, knew that Guy and Denise planned to get married once they were settled in Atlanta.

"But all the glory of being the indispensable man went to Guy's head," said Marcia Ladendorff, "and after he met Katie, Guy had second thoughts about marrying Denise. I remember once having a conversation with Guy, and he was talking in the third person. 'What if you knew somebody who was getting married and didn't want to?' And I said, 'I'd tell the bride.'

"A lot of us were very upset about Guy's relationship with Katie, because it was so out in the open," Marcia Ladendorff continued. "I'm not trying to absolve Katie from responsibility. She didn't have to do that stuff—working on Guy. She was very smart. But she capitalized on her charm more than she did on her intelligence. She was young and hungry, and one of the most ambitious women I've ever met."

Even after Guy Pepper married Denise LeClair in October 1980, he and Katie continued their long-distance love affair.

"Guy was always going on business trips, always on the weekends, and Denise would question him where he was going," said one of Denise's closest friends, who requested anonymity because she was not authorized by Denise to speak to the author of this book. "He would never allow Denise to go with him. He'd always make the trip sound kind of hidden and mysterious. If she showed the slightest suspicion or concern or jealousy that he was carrying on with another woman, he'd get very angry and tell her she was crazy. And pretty soon, Denise started to doubt her own instincts."

GUY PEPPER HAD everything to gain and nothing to lose by moving Katie down to Atlanta. Such a move would please Katie, who appeared to be counting on Guy to jump-start her career. And it would pacify Denise by eliminating the need for Guy to make mysterious trips on the weekends.

However, there was one hitch: the only person who had the authority to create a slot for Katie in Atlanta was the network's CEO, Reese Schonfeld. And ever since he had yanked her off the air, everyone at

CNN was under the impression that Schonfeld had washed his hands of Katie.

How were Guy and Katie going to convince Schonfeld to transfer her to Atlanta? To some, it appeared that they came up with a plan to play on Schonfeld's competitive feelings toward his Washington bureau chief, Stuart Loory.

"Reese Schonfeld thought I was going to fire Katie because I was such a bad judge of TV talent," Stuart Loory said in an interview for this book. "But the fact of the matter was, Katie came to me and said she *wanted* to leave the Washington bureau and go work on *Take Two*, and I said okay. I *never* had any intention of firing Katie Couric."

Looking back, Reese Schonfeld agreed with Stuart Loory's version of events.

"Katie played me," Schonfeld admitted. "She set me up by making it appear that she was being fired, and that if I wanted to keep her in the company, I'd have to find another spot for her. Here I was, going to Don Farmer, Chris Curle, and Guy Pepper and saying, Do you want to have Katie on your show? when all the time it was a setup.

"It shows a side of Katie I wouldn't have guessed," Schonfeld added. "I thought she was more naïve than that. She wanted to go to Atlanta headquarters because she was in love with Guy Pepper, and she was afraid that if she came and talked to me directly and said she wanted to move for love, I wouldn't let her do it."

And so, on Thanksgiving week in 1980—just one month after Guy Pepper married Denise LeClair—Reese Schonfeld telephoned Katie Couric and told her that he was giving her a second chance. He was reassigning her to Atlanta to work on *Take Two*.

At the time, Schonfeld didn't suspect that he had been snared by Katie's crocodile tears. Nor did it occur to him until much, much later that Guy Pepper, the master of the electronic medium, had every intention of making his lover, Katie Couric, a television star.

Chapter Two

Family Secrets

Dinner!"

It was the voice of Elinor Couric, Katie's mother, calling her family to the Thanksgiving table. Within minutes, everyone was assembled in the dining room—everyone, that is, except Katie.

Elinor called out again, this time a good deal louder.

"DINNER!"

Still no response from Katie.

Elinor went upstairs and knocked on Katie's bedroom door, then pushed it open. As usual, her daughter's room was in a state of complete disorder and confusion. Everywhere Elinor looked there were discarded blouses and bras, shoes and sneakers, paperback books with torn covers, spilled makeup, half-eaten sandwiches, soda bottles, and piles of dirty laundry. In the midst of this chaos stood her daughter, Katherine Anne Couric, furiously stuffing clothes into a large suitcase in preparation for the ten-hour drive the next day to her new job at CNN's headquarters in Atlanta.

"[My father] said to someone that they could never teach me to be neat," Katie confessed years later. "That I was a procrastinator and waited until the school bus arrived to finish my homework. All true. I'm still a mess, dropping things, getting things dirty, not putting things away. . . ."

With her mother leading the way, Katie came down the stairs of her family's modest split-level house. Her parents had moved here to Arlington, Virginia, in 1957 when Katie was six months old. In those days, Arlington was one of the fastest-growing suburban communities in the United States; it attracted people looking for work in the burgeoning federal government, and during the decade of the 1950s, its population doubled every year except two—when it tripled.

The Courics' house was located in a leafy neighborhood of redbrick colonial homes. It belonged to one of several post–World War Two housing developments in northern Virginia that boasted such pretentious names as Country Club Manor, Kent Gardens, and Tara. While Montgomery County in the Maryland suburbs on the northern perimeter of Washington had a liberal tilt, Virginia's bedroom community where Katie grew up had a more conservative southern flavor and attracted families from the states of the Old Confederacy.

Waiting for Katie at the dining room table was the entire Couric clan. Katie was the youngest of four children. Her eldest sibling, Emily—ten years Katie's senior—was a willowy five-foot-nine, and towered over her baby sister. Emily was the divorced mother of two boys, Ray and Jeff, and was planning to marry the man seated next to her, Dr. George Beller, a cardiologist at the University of Virginia Medical Center.

Seated near Emily was Katie's other sister, Clara, who was called Kiki. She was six years older than Katie and married to the man next to *her*—James Batchelor, an architect.

And, finally, there was Katie's brother, Johnny, a strapping six-footer, who was an accountant and a businessman.

At their places on either end of the table were Katie's parents— John Martin Couric Sr., a southerner by birth and breeding, a gimlet-eyed journalist, a role model to his children; and Elinor Hene Couric, born and bred in Omaha, Nebraska, as bubbly and outgoing as her husband was taciturn and reserved.

When they were growing up, the Couric children were expected to appear each evening at the dinner table with a new word they had learned that day. Emily and Kiki always dominated the discussion.

Both girls went on to graduate from Smith, the exclusive women's college in Northampton, Massachusetts, and Kiki received a master's degree in landscape architecture from Harvard's Graduate School of Design.

In the Courics' competitive household, where the children were constantly clamoring for praise from their hard-to-please parents, Katie struggled to avoid being eclipsed by her older sisters. She could never hope to match Emily and Kiki in knowledge or maturity. But as the baby in the family, she could attract attention by being clever, playful, and mischievous.

"She was a cutup," Emily recalled. "Even when she was an infant, we'd put her in her plastic seat and then all sit around and watch her."

Katie followed in her sisters' footsteps and became a high school cheerleader and student leader. Unlike Emily and Kiki, however, she showed less interest in schoolwork than she did in boys. She necked in the backseat of cars in Fort C.F. Smith Park, danced the night away at Eskimo Nell's, and had pizza at Mario's on Wilson Boulevard. When she returned home after a Saturday-night date, Katie would often bounce into the living room and entertain her parents with a stand-up comic routine. No matter what the hour, John and Elinor Couric indulged Katie's craving for attention.

"She had a really outgoing personality," said a family friend, who was a frequent guest in the Couric household. "She was full of it. But she wasn't obnoxious. She was well behaved, always smiling and laughing, and seemed to be a happy kid. She and her friends would put on little plays in her home. She was very much the entertainer as a kid."

Katie was just twelve years old when Emily married R. Clark Wadlow, an attorney. Because of the big age difference between the sisters, Emily had been like a second mother to Katie, and Katie naturally missed her after she left home. Emily promptly produced two sons, which only deepened Katie's admiration of her sister. However, when Emily's marriage failed after ten years, it was almost as big a shock to Katie as it was to Emily.

Emily did not try to hide the pain she felt over the breakup of her marriage. And Katie and the entire Couric family suffered along with her.

"I can remember leaving my desk and sobbing in a back room of my office shortly after the breakup of my marriage," Emily recalled in a book that she wrote many years later titled *The Divorce Lawyers.* "I have seen other people so driven by anger and the need for revenge against a former mate that they seemed almost demoniac.... [T]he only thing I oppose more than divorce is a forced, unhappy marriage. The suffering in these homes is far greater than the pain of divorce."

Katie was determined that *she* would have a happy marriage.

OF ALL THE Couric children, Katie resembled her mother the most. Both had a perpetual twinkle in their eye and what Katie derisively described as "chipmunk cheeks."

Elinor was an outspoken feminist and a member of the local chapter of the Planned Parenthood Federation of America. She instilled in Katie the belief that being a woman was neither an excuse for failure nor an impediment to success. Nothing was beyond Katie's reach. To build character—and to gain the admiration and respect of others—Elinor insisted that Katie do volunteer work at the Western State psychiatric hospital in Staunton, Virginia, and at a summer camp run by the Columbia Lighthouse for the Blind.

"I always told the children: *Let them know you're here!*" said Elinor. "Don't just sit back in the crowd. Get out there and make your presence known."

More than the other children, Katie took her mother's advice to heart. A life in the shadows wasn't a life worth living. Years later, Katie contributed a brief introduction to a *Life* magazine book called *Life with Mother*:

My mother remains my best friend and most trusted confidant. What are the reasons for my boundless devotion? . . . Her explanation of the female reproductive system as she drove me to my piano lesson . . . Driving her station wagon over to Steve Elliot's house, knocking on the door, dragging me out and throwing my 10-speed in the trunk, when all we were doing was smooching in his basement while his mom was at work. Laughing at the slightly bawdy jokes I told at the dinner table while my father pleaded, "Please, Elinor. Don't encourage her. . . ."

Katie's mother came from a Jewish family that traced its roots to Germany. She grew up in the Midwest, where her father, Berthold B. "Bert" Hene, was a successful architect. Katie's great-grandparents on her mother's side, Isaac and Emma Frohsin, were also German Jews. One of Elinor's uncles owned the Leon Frohsin Shoppe, an up-scale women's clothing store on Peachtree Street in Atlanta, which sold gowns by Valentino, Givenchy, and Dior.

The Frohsins were prominent members of their community—so prominent, in fact, that in the 1930s, Leon Frohsin's wife served as chairman of the Red Cross campaign to eliminate pellagra in Atlanta. During the Depression, Elinor's rich uncle sent her boxes of clothing— a generous gesture that nonetheless left Elinor feeling somewhat like a poor relation.

Though Elinor came from a long line of practicing Jews, she agreed to become a Protestant when she married John Couric in 1944. At the time—the climactic months of World War Two—it was rather uncommon to hear of a Jewish woman who turned her back on her heritage. Many American Jews (especially German Jews like the Henes and the Frohsins) had lost relatives in the Holocaust, and that searing experience created a strong sense of Jewish identity. Many Jewish parents of that era would have said Kaddish (the Jewish prayer for the dead) over a daughter who married a Gentile.

The Courics attended the Little Falls Presbyterian Church in Arlington, less than six miles from the Arlington-Fairfax Jewish Congregation (now Congregation Etz Hayim), a synagogue affiliated with Conservative Judaism.

"When you're raised Presbyterian," said Katie, "you're supposed to become a member of the church in seventh grade. I had a tough time when our minister showed me a diagram of Jesus on a throne surrounded by my family. I had a tough time with the idea that Jesus was more important than them. I didn't become a member."

Even more puzzling than Elinor's religious conversion was the fact that the Courics rarely talked about her Jewish background. As a result, Katie and her siblings never entirely understood why their mother had made such a life-altering choice. Had she suffered as a girl from the anti-Semitism that was rampant in the Midwest in the 1930s? Did she feel ashamed of being Jewish? Was she eager to pass as a WASP?

In the absence of a satisfactory explanation, Katie and her siblings chose to believe that their mother's motive for leaving her faith was to make life easier for *them,* not for herself. After all, even in the 1940s and '50s, it was more comfortable growing up in the South as Christians than as Jews. In fact, Isaac and Emma Frohsin's grandson, Leon Frohsin III, was also raised as a Christian.

Katie rarely told anyone that her mother was Jewish. For instance, none of her college friends interviewed for this book ever suspected that she was half-Jewish. In fact, Katie didn't talk about her Jewish heritage in public until she was in her forties and was seriously thinking of marrying a Jew.

In the absence of more information, it is hard to know how much her mother's secret Jewish identity affected Katie. But by their very nature, family secrets—no matter how unimportant they may appear to outsiders—usually have a long half-life.

KATIE'S FATHER WAS born in Georgia, near the Alabama border, not far from his family's pre–Civil War mansion, Eufaula, where generations of Courics had owned slaves. One of his forebears was a minister; another, a cotton buyer. At one point, the family had a great deal of money, but the Couric inheritance—along with its privileges and patrician lifestyle—was long since gone.

His ancestors fascinated John Couric, who looked back on his family's faded glory with sadness and longing. Despite the Slavic-sounding last name, *Couric* was of French derivation, and John and his wife traveled to France in search of his family records.

What he found did not entirely please him. His earliest known relative, Mathuron Couric, turned out to be the illegitimate son of a French landowner from the coast of Brittany. Fleeing France in 1829, Mathuron reached the southern shores of the United States, married a wealthy French widow, and Anglicized his first name to Charles.

John Couric had a deep attachment to the conservative values of the Old South. He was a courteous, soft-spoken man with an extensive knowledge of American history. Given subjects that interested him, especially the Civil War and journalism, he could be an engaging conversationalist, though compared to his gregarious wife, he struck people as reserved and socially ill at ease.

After serving in the navy during World War Two, he secured a job as a reporter at the *Atlanta Journal and Constitution*. Later, he became an editor for the wire service United Press. In the mid-1950s, shortly before Katie was born, her father decided that he could not afford to educate four children on his meager salary as a newsman. And so, he gave up what he called the "high priesthood of journalism" for a job as head of public relations for the National Association of Broadcasters, a lobbying organization headquartered in Washington, D.C.

It was a poor fit. The introverted John Couric turned out to be ill suited for the extroverted occupation of publicist. And when Katie was in high school, he was fired from his job.

"John was a pretty laid back guy," said Dawson "Tack" Nail, a veteran reporter for the trade journal *Communications Daily*. "He was afraid of his own shadow in the PR job. He didn't have the thing a PR person needs to deal with the press. And he never got over his bitter feelings about being fired."

Just as Elinor Couric avoided the subject of her Jewishness, John Couric glossed over his firing. He tried to pass it off as a "buyout." But he didn't fool his children. They knew that their father had made a great personal sacrifice on their behalf when he gave up journalism for public relations, and as a result, they no doubt felt they were at least partly responsible for his humiliating dismissal from his job.

For a time, John Couric found work writing press releases for the Labor Department. (To make ends meet, his wife took a job as a

saleslady at Lord & Taylor.) As the months passed, the children noticed that their father was spending a lot of time alone in his den and
that he acted more withdrawn than ever.

The effervescent Katie was the apple of her father's eye and could
always be counted on to cheer him up. She loved listening to her father
talk about the famous battles of the Civil War. He was a moderately
left-leaning Democrat, an admirer of Presidents John F. Kennedy and
Lyndon B. Johnson, though he had nothing much to say about Johnson's landmark civil rights legislation. Katie also shared her father's
fascination with journalism, especially as it was presented on the TV
news shows that they watched together each night.

"As far as I'm concerned," said her father, "the number-one job in
journalism is Walter Cronkite's anchor slot on the *CBS Evening News*.
A close second are the correspondents' jobs on *60 Minutes*."

The CBS newsmagazine *60 Minutes* debuted in 1968, but it didn't
settle into its now-familiar Sunday-evening time slot until December
1975, Katie's freshman year in college. By then, thanks in large part to
the Watergate reporting of Bob Woodward and Carl Bernstein, journalism had become one of the most glamorous occupations in America.
Woodward and Bernstein's book, *All the President's Men*, was a smash
best-seller and had been adapted as a movie starring Robert Redford
and Dustin Hoffman. Suddenly, reporters were as well known as the
people they covered, and journalists (such as Walter Cronkite, Mike
Wallace, and Morley Safer) became celebrities in their own right.

Television news seemed to be the perfect fit for the daughter of John
Couric—the ideal platform for an incurable entertainer like Katie.

"I was inspired to go into journalism largely because my father
urged me," Katie said. "I thought about newspapers, then decided that
if my face didn't stop a clock, I might as well try television."

"I encouraged her to go into broadcasting because I thought it was
more promising than print, having been in print myself," said her father.

Asked why he thought TV was more promising, he replied with
one word: "Money."

If Elinor Couric was the engine that drove Katie's ambition, John
Couric gave that ambition a clear direction and focus. Eventually, all

of John Couric's thwarted hopes and dreams would come to rest on Katie's shoulders.

SINCE KATIE SOUGHT the spotlight, people automatically assumed that she possessed an abundance of self-confidence. She struck most people as the quintessential blithe spirit—cheerful, carefree, and fearless. And, in fact, that was the face she chose to display in public. In private, however, Katie often exhibited quite a different side of her personality. She was easily hurt, quick to tears, and susceptible to feelings of embarrassment and humiliation.

That was hardly surprising in view of her family history. No matter how hard Katie tried, she must have felt powerless to compete with her older sisters in the never-ending skirmishes for their parents' approval. She adored Emily and Kiki, but she undoubtedly nursed feelings of rivalry and resentment. Perhaps in an effort to deny those painful feelings, Katie romanticized her childhood.

"I had a really happy, normal childhood—idyllic in many ways," Katie recalled. "I lived in a neighborhood where there were a ton of kids on the street. We played baseball, had crabapple fights, played tag. It was really a *Leave It to Beaver* upbringing."

Of course, *Leave It to Beaver,* which premiered on CBS in 1957—the year Katie was born—was an idealized version of American family life that had never existed. It certainly did not exist in the Arlington household of John and Elinor Couric. Though the Courics were decent, loving parents, their home was permeated by an atmosphere of sadness and loss—the loss of wealth, social status, cultural affiliation, and professional identity—and the yearning to recapture a lost past.

This may help explain some of the puzzling contradictions that would become evident in Katie's personality. On the one hand, she projected the image of a strong and independent woman; on the other, she was extraordinarily needy and dependent on the support of men. One moment, she was all incandescent charm and joviality; the next, she was sunk in a dark mood. She was famous for her ability to identify with another person's feelings, yet she also had a tendency to fly into cold rages and to heap scorn on those who disappointed her.

Katie's friends insisted, "With Katie, what you see is what you get," as though she was a simple, uncomplicated person. But that assessment failed to take into account the perplexing personality mixture that defined Katie: unfathomable ambition combined with gnawing self-doubt.

LIKE HER SISTERS, Katie applied to Smith College, but she didn't have the grades to be admitted. So instead, in the fall of 1975, she headed to her father's alma mater, the University of Virginia in Charlottesville.

Consistently ranked as one of the best public universities in America, U.Va. rises on 1,800 rolling acres in the foothills of the Blue Ridge Mountains, 122 miles south of Washington. Its founder, Thomas Jefferson, called it his "Academical Village," and designed its main Rotunda building after the Parthenon in Athens. The school opened in 1825 as a gentlemen's college and didn't go coed until 1970—only five years before Katie enrolled.

In her freshman year, she lived in one of the few all-girl dorms. She was reluctant to admit people into her room because it was such a mess. When friends knocked on the door, she would step outside to talk to them.

Like many freshman girls, Katie put on a good deal of weight. In interviews for this book, several of her professors remembered Katie as a plump coed. A few pounds made a big difference on her petite frame, and she had trouble taking off the weight—a struggle that would continue throughout her life. Nonetheless, Katie was a very popular girl on campus and she easily crossed the lines that separated the various cliques—from hippies to so-called pretty socials.

"The first time I saw Katie was her picture in U.Va.'s *Face Book*," said Jack McCallie, a premed student. "I invited her to a party at my fraternity, Zeta Psi. She said she wasn't really into the fraternity scene, but agreed to come anyway."

By her sophomore year, Katie had put aside her aversion to

fraternities, and, like many other coeds, was getting smashed at rau-
cous fraternity parties. In her junior year, she dated Scott Brittain,
the president of Zeta Psi, a fraternity that boasted several members
of the student government.

"Katie was serious about her commitments and had a lot of drive,"
Brittain recalled. "She told me she wanted to get into the media. She
said her goal was to be the next Barbara Walters, who was the first
woman to anchor an evening news show.

"In her senior year—after I graduated—Katie lived on the Lawn,"
Brittain continued. "The Lawn was the oldest and most desirable part
of the university, the location of Mr. Jefferson's original buildings. You
had to make a significant contribution to the university to be invited to
live in the rooms on the Lawn. It was a big honor. If you lived on the
Lawn, you were recognized as one of the top honor students."

According to two former classmates who were interviewed for this
book and requested anonymity, Katie said that if it hadn't been for her
father, she would never have been chosen to live on the Lawn. While
she was away at college, she was in almost daily phone contact with
him. John Couric was keenly conscious of social status and lost no
opportunity to remind Katie of the importance of making friends in
high places. He urged her to be on a first-name basis with people whose
influence would extend far beyond the campus in Charlottesville and
who might be of use in her future career.

In order to stand out from the crowd, her father recommended that
Katie become a resident adviser, a role that would win her recognition
as a mentor of younger female students. He was also behind Katie's decision to join Delta Delta Delta, a sorority known as Tri-Delt, which attracted an elite group of white Protestant girls from around the country.
And he encouraged her to write a series of articles for the *Cavalier*, the
student daily newspaper, on the powers that be at U.Va.

Her father helped Katie shape her series of articles, which were titled "Professor Profiles." He advised her to include only the most powerful and influential faculty members. She wrote flattering—not to say
fawning—pieces on the dean of the college, Dr. Irby Cauthen ("the
University's Renaissance man"); the school's only married teaching

couple, Ernst and Ingrid Soudek ("in superb physical condition"); art history professor Frederick Hart ("an excellent speaker capable of moving and sensitive characterizations"); Alfred Cobb, one of the few black professors ("You work hard to please him because he is so genuinely happy to see students learn"); and Robert J. Harris, a distinguished constitutional scholar ("a veritable Mr. Chips").

"Katie could be ruthless about getting where she wanted to go," recalled one of her classmates. "She was very political about school, which I thought at the time was rather extraordinary. Most of the kids just tried to get good grades and have a decent time. With her, everything was a political calculation.

"She knew practically every member of the faculty and the administration, and knew how to charm them," he continued. "We talked about it, and I asked her why she was so political with the tweedy, pipe-smoking old academics, and she said, 'You just never know who you are going to need.'

"On the one hand, Katie would stay up all night talking to a freshman girl who was depressed over breaking up with her boyfriend. And I give her full credit for that. But on the other hand, if you were going for the same cookie, Katie might bite off your finger."

DURING HER FOUR years at U.Va., Katie deviated from her father's game plan in only one important respect. That was her friendship with the school's most eccentric oddball, Sam Schwartz. Enormously overweight, unwashed, disheveled, gay, and Jewish, Sam was the managing editor of the *Declaration*, a counterculture weekly student paper.

Katie's association with Sam Schwartz—like her sloppiness and procrastination—might have represented a sly rebellion against her father. Certainly, John Couric would not have been pleased, to say the least, if he had known about his daughter's relationship with Sam. Nor, for that matter, would he have approved of her contributions to the *Declaration*. The paper ran stories on local massage parlors; gave Anaïs Nin's infamous erotica, *Delta of Venus*, an enthusiastic review; and offered an illustrated guide to scatological messages.

"Sammy was very close to Katie," recalled Jack McCallie, the premed student who dated her in her junior year. "They spent endless hours debating the hot issues of the day, and he had a great deal of influence on her. She even wrote feature articles for the *Declaration* occasionally, though not under her own name."

Katie might have been one of the few students in whom Sam confided that he was gay.

"She was very concerned about gay bashing on campus, and that was a cause they shared," said another classmate. "They were together constantly. She seemed to be with Sammy more than her boyfriends. They were a total odd couple: a beauty-and-the-beast act. He was about the grossest-looking guy on campus, because he didn't care about attracting girls, and she was one of the cutest and neatest, a preppy dresser. But Sam was her intellectual guru. He helped her to think critically and to question everything she had always assumed was right."

Chapter Three

"A Tongue with a Tang"

The master, the swabber, the boatswain, and I,
The gunner and his mate,
Lov'd Mall, Meg, and Marian, and Margery,
But none of us car'd for Kate:
For she had a tongue with a tang,
Would cry to a sailor, "Go hang!"

—WILLIAM SHAKESPEARE, *The Tempest*

W HEN KATIE ARRIVED IN ATLANTA TOWARD THE END OF 1980,
CNN was still very much a work in progress. The network was the
brainchild of Ted Turner, the prodigal son of a prosperous Savannah
businessman who committed suicide when Ted was twenty-four. Ted
himself was hardly a model of mental stability; on any given morning, he could be seen wandering around the CNN sets, unshaven,
dressed in his bathrobe, looking for a cup of coffee.

Improvisation was the order of the day (as were constant on-air
foul-ups), and the staff referred mockingly to CNN as Chicken Noo-
dle News. Some of them had to work out of temporary trailers in the
parking lot. Others were headquartered in a former Russian-Jewish
country club, a redbrick mansion situated in downtown Atlanta.

"Inside was like a giant hangar with all these worker bees in this open space," recalled Susan Lisovicz, who broadcast from Atlanta in the 1980s and still reports for CNN from the New York Stock Exchange. "You were able to smoke and eat your lunch, and be the total slobs that TV journalists used to be. It was all very young, people who were eager to get a chance.

"CNN was unbelievably incestuous at the time," Lisovicz continued. "Ted put a former *Playboy* playmate on the air. Ed Turner, who was no relation to Ted and was in charge of the domestic bureaus for a time, also had a girlfriend on air. You tended to fraternize with people you worked with. Going out with somebody at CNN was like wearing a jacket and tie to IBM. It was really commonplace."

So commonplace, in fact, that Katie and Guy Pepper did little to hide their feelings for each other. Though Guy was living at home with his new wife, Denise LeClair, he often left her alone to go to dinner with Katie. His extramarital involvement with Katie was a topic of gossip at Harrison's, the local watering hole favored by CNNers.

"Katie and Guy's relationship was out in the open," said Mardi Waters, who served as the administrative head of CNN's graphics department and was the wife of Lou Waters, one of the network's original anchors. "It was a very stormy relationship. Lots of disagreements, ups and downs. They broke up a couple of times and got together again. Guy was a very flamboyant, feisty character, and everything he did was magnified."

One day, Denise LeClair's New York–based agent, a veteran of the TV news wars by the name of Alfred Geller, visited her in Atlanta. While wandering around, Geller spotted Katie in a darkened corner in one of the tech rooms, making out with Guy. Geller did not have the heart to tell Denise what he had seen. And as was often the case in such matters, the wife was the last to know.

"Denise was phoning me telling me that she had these suspicions," said one of Denise's friends, who anchored at a TV station not far from Atlanta. "She'd say, 'I think there's a little intern at work named Katie who won't leave Guy alone.' Or she'd say, 'The other day, I was looking out the big picture window in the commissary that overlooks the parking lot, and I saw Guy with Katie carrying tennis rackets. They were going off to play.'

"Then one night I got a call from Denise, and she was beside herself, distraught," her friend continued. "And she said, 'I really need you to be with me here. If you don't come, I don't know what I'll do that might be stupid.' I took the next flight to Atlanta, and when I landed, Denise met me at the airport. I had never seen her in the kind of state she was in.

"'Guy has left me,' she said. 'He's run off with Katie.' I spent the whole weekend with her, letting her talk and cry and getting it out in the open. I thought for sure that it would blow over. But they never worked it out. They never got back together."

WHILE HIS MARRIAGE was falling apart, Guy Pepper was doing everything in his power to make Katie a star.

"When *Take Two* went on a Texas tour, with Houston as its first stop, there was Katie on the screen once again," recalled CNN's honcho Reese Schonfeld. "This time she did a package on Gilleys, a nightclub made famous by John Travolta's movie *Urban Cowboy*, which featured a mechanical bucking bull. . . . The idea was good, the visuals were great, but Katie was still unready. She looked more frightened of the camera than [of] the bull.

"Katie and Guy Pepper had fallen in love," Schonfeld went on, ". . . and when I saw Katie on the air, I suspected the worst. I was doing my best to make sure that CNN didn't become a 'girlfriend's network.' Since I had tried to keep Ted Turner's girlfriends off the air, I couldn't put Guy Pepper's on. So I sent a note to Pepper, Farmer, Curle. It said: 'No more Katie till further notice.'"

But Katie seemed to have nine lives at CNN. Before long, another senior executive appeared on the scene to pluck her from obscurity. He was Ted Kavanau, the network's head producer, and a man known around the office for having an eye for pretty young women.

"[Management wasn't] into the material sent by our affiliates," Kavanau said. "They thought it was too local, I guess. I found some of the features fascinating. I created a half-hour show, *Real Pictures*, which played stories from around the country. I'd sit in a chair and lead in to the pieces. It was pretty boring.

"And one day I walked past the assignment desk, and saw this very cute girl there. I was attracted to her, and my hormones started working, and so, showing off, I said to her, 'How would you like to be a star?' The old cliché. She said, 'Sure I'd like to be a star.'

"That's how Katie Couric became my cohost. My first impression was that she was a very sweet, innocent little girl. And then she started ad-libbing these little cutting insults that weren't good for my ego. I took a completely different look at this girl, and decided she was a tough little cookie. And I said, 'Katie, if you keep putting me down, I'm going to do the same to you.' And that's what happened. Then one day, Reese Schonfeld came to me and said, 'Ted Turner wants this show for his girlfriend,' and that was the end of that."

TED TURNER LOVED being a famous media baron. In 1981, he flew to Havana with his girlfriend, Liz Wickersham, to go duck hunting with Fidel Castro. They bagged a couple of ducks and struck up a friendship. The easily flattered Turner returned to Atlanta singing Fidel's praises. As a result, several months later CNN was allowed to broadcast live from Havana, a first for an American network since the Cuban revolution.

The project was entrusted to Guy Pepper, who by then had managed to push out the executive producer of *Take Two* and get her job. Pepper took with him the anchors of the show, Don Farmer and Chris Curle; Mike Boettcher, a veteran foreign correspondent; a talent booker named Gail Evans; producer Calvin Houts; and his girlfriend, Katie Couric. They flew down to Puerto Rico and then chartered an old DC-3 to shuttle them to Havana.

When they checked into Havana's Hotel Nacional in early April

1982, the manager at the front desk informed the CNN team that most of the old U.S.-manufactured toilets did not have seats. The American embargo of Cuba made it impossible to import replacements for the broken seats. It turned out that Katie's room was the only one with a toilet seat, and it was in that room that she and Guy Pepper spent a good deal of their downtime.

Guy Pepper and Gail Evans, Jewish and spending Passover in Cuba, had packed several boxes of matzoth, or unleavened bread. Given the sorry state of Cuban cuisine at the time, the CNN crew feasted on matzoth with peanut butter.

Katie's primary responsibility was to produce the daily live feeds from Havana, no mean feat in a poor Third World country with a crumbling communications infrastructure.

"I have a vivid picture of Katie, sprawled on the floor of a dilapidated hotel room in Havana with research books around us, trying to put on a three-hour show, talking in halting Spanish to these local technicians," recalled Don Farmer. "She had them eating out of her hands. She was her cute self, yet very tough. And it was just great how she charmed these macho Cuban guys."

Guy Pepper encouraged Katie to do some broadcasts of her own from Havana. They turned out to be lively and fun, certainly different from the usual sober CNN fare. One of her pieces featured a coming-out party for young women in Marxist Cuba.

"One night at two in the morning, two Cuban officials knocked on the door of the room that Guy and Katie were sharing," Reese Schonfeld said. "They said, 'We have something from Fidel for you.' Then they brought two giant boxes into the room and said, 'This is a gift for Ted Turner from Fidel. Please take it back with you.' The boxes contained two stuffed ducks that Ted had shot when he went hunting with Fidel."

NINETEEN EIGHTY-TWO WAS also the year of a major management shakeup at CNN. After a series of bitter quarrels, Ted Turner fired Reese Schonfeld and replaced him with Schonfeld's deputy, Burt

Reinhardt. Reinhardt was known for his solid judgment, but his first major decision was widely considered to be a blunder. He named Ed Turner, a notorious womanizer, as *his* deputy.

"Ed Turner . . . had a hard time around women," Reese Schonfeld wrote in his memoir, *Me and Ted Against the World*. "He said things he shouldn't, and they came back to haunt him. . . . Ed was working as Burt [Reinhardt's] vice president when Katie came to see him about becoming a correspondent. He was sitting at the head of a conference table, surrounded by a number of other people. He greeted Katie with something to the effect of, 'Come on in here, Katie, and let me look at those beautiful boobs.' Katie felt humiliated, but mostly angry with herself, because she just stood there and took it."

Ed Turner rarely promoted a woman he hadn't slept with. He was jealous of Guy Pepper's relationship with Katie and tried to woo Katie away. When she refused to go to bed with him, he turned nasty and made her life miserable.

Despite that, Katie was still determined to become an on-air talent at CNN. She convinced Guy Pepper to send her on the road for *Take Two* to do profiles on candidates in the 1982 off-year elections. And she did stand-ups at the 1984 Democratic National Convention in San Francisco that nominated Walter Mondale.

From the perspective of Burt Reinhardt, who was now running the network, Katie didn't look, act, or sound like a serious journalist. It wasn't that Reinhardt had anything against women covering presidential politics. In fact, as *60 Minutes'* Lesley Stahl noted in her memoir, *Reporting Live,* "[W]omen covering the campaign had reached a critical mass. Most of the barriers in political reporting were down . . . it was at last a co-ed activity."

Reinhardt simply felt that Katie did not have reporter's chops. One day, he called Ed Turner into his office and told him to take Katie off the air—*permanently.* Ed Turner was only too happy to oblige.

"At lunchtime . . . I went to the Side Dish, a place between the Headline News and CNN newsrooms, where people could go for coffee and donuts," John Baker, vice president for operations, wrote in an unpublished memoir. "Katie Couric and Guy Pepper were sitting at a table. . . . Katie's eyes were red, not with sorrow, but with hatred. She was so angry you could feel her electricity. I thought the forks and spoons were going to fly up from the table.

"I couldn't stand it," Baker went on. "Finally, I walked over. Katie looked up.

"'They told me I can't report anymore,' she hissed. 'I'm not authoritative enough. Not CNN enough.'

"People at other tables were beginning to listen. I couldn't believe what I was hearing.

"'I can't believe that,' I said.

"Self-righteously trying to right a wrong, I marched up to the executive offices.

"'Why?' I asked Ed [Turner].

"'Katie doesn't fit with our style and with our other reporters,' Ed said.

"Then I went to Burt.

"'She makes things look frivolous. That's not CNN,' he told me."

FOR THE NEXT several months, Katie was in a pout. Her colleagues urged her to leave CNN. But where would she go? And who would hire her? Once again, Guy Pepper came to the rescue. He put together a video résumé of Katie's best work and sent it to news directors at several stations.

While she waited for a response to her video reel, Katie worked with Guy on improving her television technique—the pronunciation of her words (she had a habit of saying "git" instead of "get," and "ta" instead of "to"); the rhythm of her speech (she talked too fast); the movement of her head for emphasis (she raised her eyebrows too often); the placement of her hands (she didn't seem to know what to do with them); her makeup; and her hair.

Then, to her great relief, she was called for an interview at Miami's NBC affiliate WTVJ. After saying good-bye to Guy Pepper (not, she hoped, for the last time), Katie threw her belongings into a suitcase; stowed her cats, Lucy and Desi, in the backseat of her car; and took off on her next great adventure in the TV news business.

"But she never forgot that I reacted negatively to her on camera," Reese Schonfeld said. "Katie keeps the hurts."

Chapter Four

Shattered Dreams

In the fall of 1985, Katie Couric was approaching her twenty-ninth birthday. By her own admission, she was still struggling to lose her baby fat and find a more mature look. She had four years of experience in the TV news business, yet her whole career could be summed up in four discouraging words: *Nobody took her seriously*.

As she pulled out of Atlanta and pointed her battered secondhand car down Interstate 95 toward Miami, she was hoping to change her luck. Her dream was to become a star at WTVJ Channel 6, Florida's leading television station, then return to Washington in triumph as a network correspondent.

In that regard, she was no different from any other young TV journalist in a local market who yearned to be discovered by a network. In the mid-1980s, two local markets provided the best exposure for talented young people: Hartford (because many network executives had first or second homes in Connecticut), and Miami (because Florida was a vacation destination for a lot of network brass).

Katie's arrival in Miami could not have come at a better time. There she would work as a night-beat reporter for the eleven o'clock news. The city crackled with violence. "If it bleeds, it leads," as the saying goes in local TV news, and Miami produced a gusher of blood-and-guts stories that led the newscasts night after night.

Not long after Katie started work, the FBI announced that the Miami-Dade metropolitan area had surpassed Detroit as the most dangerous city in America. The popular *Miami Vice* TV series, starring Don Johnson and Philip Michael Thomas as undercover police detectives, was a pale imitation of the real Miami vice.

"What a place for a young journalist to learn her craft, for Pete's sake," said Al Buch, the WTVJ news director who hired Katie. "Miami was a news town like no other. One day, a drug house would blow up. Another, one hundred people would drown off the coast of Florida trying to come to the U.S. illegally. Cigarette boats running drugs off the coast got busted. You'd go to the airport and watch the Feds find millions of dollars' worth of cocaine. Police officers were being arrested for murdering traffickers in cold blood and then stealing their drugs."

WTVJ was located in downtown Miami in the historic Capitol Theater, a landmark structure that had been built in the 1920s. The actual broadcast studios for the news and sports departments were housed next door in a more modern facility, which was across the street from a lot where Katie parked her beat-up old car.

"[Katie] was on the team captained by Ralph Renick, the leading voice of Miami TV news for 35 years, who so dominated the ratings that he would later make an unsuccessful bid to become governor of Florida," wrote *The Hollywood Reporter.* "It really meant something if you made the grade as a reporter on *The Ralph Renick Report.*"

WORKING THE NIGHT shift, Katie witnessed a sad army of female prostitutes and transsexuals soliciting customers along Biscayne Boulevard. What especially caught her attention were reports of young male prostitutes, many of them teenagers, working the area. She sold the idea of a story to Al Buch, the news director, and dragged John Lang, a young cameraman whom she had befriended, through the seedy late-night streets.

"She was absolutely determined to find these boys, no matter what," recalled Lang. "So, night after night, we went out looking. But she couldn't find one. Katie really believed she was on to something and tried her best. She put herself under a lot of pressure over it, and she wasn't the easiest person to get along with when she was frustrated."

Katie refused to give up the search for underage male prostitutes. She approached numerous young men who happened to be out by themselves or with male buddies. She asked them if they were hookers. The replies she got ranged from bafflement to hilarity to outrage. Eventually, her boss, Al Buch, ordered her to drop the story.

Katie had more luck finding people to back up her special report on global warming, which aired on August 12, 1986. She interviewed several environmentalists who fretted about greenhouse gases and holes in the ozone. In a voice-over, Katie agonized about "stepping on mother nature in the name of progress," and wondered whether the residents of Miami would be able to breathe the air and drink the water by the year 2000.

Then, over a recording of Ringo Starr singing "Octopus's Garden" ("I'd like to be under the sea/In an octopus's garden in the shade . . ."), Katie described an underwater hotel in the Florida Keys where visitors could "feel how the fish feel."

Later that same month, she did a story that won even more attention. It was called "Street People." Katie dressed up as a homeless person—and a rather perky one at that. She chirped merrily to passersby as she begged for money, squeegeed car windshields, and waded into the fountain of the Intercontinental Hotel to fish out pennies. However, under the brutal Miami sun, her thick theatrical makeup buckled and ran down her face, and the alarmed street people mistook her for a burn victim instead of one of their own.

That winter, when the University of Miami was invited to the Sugar Bowl for the first time in the fifty-two-year history of the annual college championship event, Al Buch dispatched Katie to New Orleans to provide color backup.

"She came with me to do a story on tarot card readers and palm readers," said Tony Segretto, the station's chief sports reporter. "It was a moviemaker's dream. We had fedoras on, and had an absolute blast. We'd walk down these eerie, deserted cobblestone streets, and Katie said, 'I can't believe you're getting me in this; I'd rather not be here.'

And on one of these streets, we found a tarot card reader who would tell us if Miami would win the game.

"Katie did another story on how to shuck an oyster," Segretto went on. "When she finished a feature like that, she had the ability to go and do a hard news story. Whether hard or soft, she always made you feel comfortable, because she was comfortable in her own skin."

KATIE WAS FINALLY beginning to find her voice.

After years of trial and error, she dropped the pretense that she was a traditional newswoman—serious, solemn, and detached—and began to relax and let her true self shine through. Almost immediately, some important people took notice.

"The keys to [Katie's] success are not just her personality and smarts," said Fred Francis, NBC News' former Pentagon correspondent, "it's her ability to make people able to relate to her. I first saw it when I saw her in Miami; I was visiting my parents there and saw her doing a cop story. I called the cop and asked him about her, and he said, 'She's good. She's dating another cop.'"

"I had my eye on Katie," said Donald Brown, who at the time was the NBC bureau chief in Miami. "She was a terrific general assignment reporter, gutsy and good. She had network correspondent written all over her."

The *Miami Herald*'s TV critic Steve Sonsky agreed that Katie had learned to relax on camera and come across as more natural and authentic. "Katie had clearly improved," he said. "She popped off the screen in some appearances. She was developing star presence."

KATIE LIVED IN a one-bedroom apartment at 2855 Tigertail Avenue in the area known as Coconut Grove. Her modest flat was in a three-story group of apartments with exterior hallways overlooking a small kidney-shaped pool. It was within walking distance of the Grove's bustling bars and restaurants, which catered to a predominantly young singles crowd.

John Lang, the WTVJ cameraman, visited Katie's apartment, and recalled that it was strewn with clothes, papers, and old pizza cartons.

"She was always late, because she couldn't find the keys in her purse, couldn't find her briefcase, couldn't find the cup of coffee she had just sat down with while searching for the keys. Her life appeared chaotic."

Another visitor to Katie's apartment was Hank Goldberg, WTVJ's florid sports commentator, who was seventeen years her senior. Known as "The Hammer" or "Hammering Hank," Goldberg introduced Katie to the sporting life—Hialeah, jai alai frontons, and dog tracks. His world was peopled by millionaire sports moguls such as George Steinbrenner, politicians, and cardsharps.

"We dated," said Goldberg, who, like Guy Pepper, was Jewish. "We went to a lot of concerts together, and I'd take her out to dinner. . . . Sometimes we'd go out with my father, who was a retired sports columnist, and they got along great.

"Katie was the kind of person who wanted to be good at what she did," Goldberg continued. "She used to call me after one of her stories or features ran, and talk about it. She'd spend hours in the editing room making sure whatever she put on the air was right. She wanted to make the network."

"Hank was kind of a strange guy, but he and Katie had a good time together, and he certainly knew the television business," said John Lang. "He was helpful to Katie in a lot of ways."

Goldberg was soon replaced in Katie's life by a more serious romantic interest. His name was Bill Johnson, and he was a veteran cop who was twelve years older than Katie. Johnson was the media spokesman for the Metro Dade Police Department, a position that put him in the know, and made him a source par excellence for an ambitious young journalist like Katie.

Tall and lanky, Johnson was a sharp dresser with premature gray hair and sad, intense eyes. As his public profile grew, he spiffed up his look and grew a full mustache. He and Katie were seen together all over Miami.

If Bill Johnson was the first to know what was going on in the real world of Miami vice, Katie was the second. Soon, he became a regular on her features and news spots. And although he was also interviewed by other journalists, it was his relationship with Katie that prompted winks and sarcastic comments in the local newsrooms.

"The joke was that Katie was on top of the big crime stories in Miami because she was on top of Bill Johnson," said a journalist who did voice-overs for Johnson's police training tapes.

Katie and Bill Johnson had met at the Coco Range, a dark tavern around the corner from WTJV that catered to cops and reporters. At the time, Johnson was married and the father of two. But his marriage was on the rocks, and he made no secret of the fact that, once he got a divorce, he hoped to marry Katie.

"I was with Katie one day when she was talking about how she met Bill," said a friend and former colleague. "She said, 'Bill's separated from his wife.' *Separated?* That's married to me. He wasn't divorced yet.

"Katie's an extremely ambitious woman, and always had a vision of where she wanted to go and what she wanted to be, and everything else was peripheral to that," this colleague continued. "There was an incredibly soft, funny, loyal side to Katie with her friends. But there's also a steely edge. She wouldn't let anything get in her way."

Ralph Renick Jr., son of the famous Miami anchorman, recalled inviting Katie and Bill Johnson to be his guests on his thirty-foot yacht, *Miss Liberty*, during a charity fishing tournament.

"It was actually a near disaster," Renick said. "We were pretty far into the Florida Straits and a sudden storm came up. It was some of the biggest seas I had ever seen—waves breaking high over the bow and plunging us into deep troughs. They were big enough to swamp a boat bigger than mine.

"Katie was a sailing novice and pretty scared," he continued. "Bill took her into the cabin and comforted her. She was just on the edge of panic, but managed to keep it together thanks to Bill. They had a very good relationship. That was always obvious. But he was also a great contact for her."

A former cop, who was a close friend of Johnson, put it more succinctly: "Bill was getting divorced and looking for love. Katie was looking for a big story."

IN LATER YEARS, Katie would claim that she had covered immigration, the overarching issue in Miami during the 1980s. But the Louis Wolfson Moving Image Archive in Miami, where WTVJ broadcasts from the period are stored, holds no Katie Couric segments on immigration.

The summer of 1980 had seen a flood of 125,000 so-called Marielito boat people, many released by Fidel Castro from Cuban prisons and mental hospitals. The result of El Jefe's mischief—and President Jimmy Carter's paralysis in dealing with the crisis—was a tsunami of crime and the rise of Miami's cocaine culture, which was so memorably rendered in Michael Mann's *Miami Vice* and Brian De Palma's *Scarface*.

Yet, judging from the aired segments of Katie's work in the Louis Wolfson Moving Image Archive, she dodged the issue of immigration, concentrating instead on reports that would have been just as appropriate in Duluth or Toledo.

But it wasn't for lack of trying that Katie missed out on some of the big crime stories of the day. For instance, when she was tipped off by Bill Johnson that the FBI was in a blazing shootout with two desperados in South Miami, Katie called the news desk and begged to be put on the story. Though Katie said she could get to the scene in a few minutes, another reporter—who was more than forty minutes away—was dispatched to cover the melee. It was the kind of story that made a reporter's reputation, and Katie was furious about being shut out.

"She worked her butt off, but she just couldn't get a break," said Lu Ann Cahn, who worked with Katie in Miami. "They always saw her as the cub reporter, because she was so cute and looked so young."

"Another time," Lisa DePaulo wrote in *George* magazine, "Couric got a shot to fill in for the noon news anchor. Couric was so excited she dragged her two close girlfriends at the station—Cahn and Lisa Gregorisch, now executive producer of *Hard Copy*—to help her find a suit. 'I remember this big shopping trip for "Katie's new outfit,"' says Cahn. But again, Couric tried too hard. 'I mean, she didn't bomb,' Cahn remembers. 'But you didn't go, "Wow! She's our next Katie Couric." I don't think they ever let her anchor again after that.'"

Tammy Leader, another close friend, recalled that Katie was terrible at doing live stand-ups.

"She didn't know how the earpiece worked, she didn't know how to address the camera," said Tammy Leader. "She screwed up all the time. She was smart and knew how to put stories together, but her presentation was terrible."

It wasn't only Katie's presentation that held her back. She also had an irritating know-it-all attitude.

"She didn't get along great because she was smart and had a lot of ideas," said Tammy Leader. "She would always jump in with 'Why don't we do it this way?' and would tell the guys when she thought they were wrong. And when they *were* wrong, she would rub it in their faces. She never got great stories because she didn't play the game really well. . . . Her attitude was 'Screw all of you. I know I'll be fine when I leave, and you'll still be here.'"

One day, while having lunch with her girlfriends at a sub shop in Fort Lauderdale, Katie broke down in tears.

"I'll kill myself if I can't make it," she said.

Her friends worried that she wasn't simply using a figure of speech.

"She took it all terribly seriously and acted like her life depended on her success," said one of her friends. "I think it's fair to say she wouldn't have thought her life worth living if she didn't get where she wanted to go in the business. She had an incredible emotional investment."

Her friend Hank Goldberg blamed the station's news director, Al Buch, for Katie's desperate state of mind. Goldberg believed that Al Buch had it in for Katie from the start.

"Al Buch didn't give her a shot to anchor," Goldberg said. "He didn't know any better. He didn't have an eye."

Ira Lazernik, a WTVJ news photographer, agreed.

"The station tried out people to anchor the news at noon," he said.

"Katie wanted a trial, but Al Buch told her she didn't have the presence to be an anchor."

As might be expected, Al Buch had a very different version of events.

"My office was near the exit door to the street," he recalled. "After a newscast, I'd often see Katie walking toward the exit, looking really upset. And I'd get up and go to her, and see that she was in tears. And I would ask her, 'What's going on? What's the matter? What happened?'

"I'd usually end up walking her across the street to her car in the parking lot," Buch went on. "And I'd finally get the story out of her. There were people in the newsroom who were giving her a hard time. They teased her unmercifully about her dreams of becoming a network correspondent. They didn't think she was good enough. They were shattering her dream."

Chapter Five

Mother Teresa

In the summer of 1986, Katie's contract with WTVJ had only a few more months to run, and she was eager to leave Miami. She was still using Katherine as her professional signoff; she and her father (who continued to guide her career from behind the scenes) thought Katherine gave her an "air of dignity," and made her more appealing to the powers at the NBC network in New York.

"Katie said she was talking to people in New York who were grooming her and giving her advice," recalled a colleague in Miami. "People were orchestrating the best place for her to go after Miami. She was kind of mysterious about it, and didn't name any names, but I knew she was still in touch with her old boyfriend, Guy Pepper.

"By this time, Guy had left CNN and was working for NBC News in New York," Katie's colleague continued. "He was a fill-in director, working on both *The Today Show* and *Nightly News*, and he promised to put in a good word for Katie. At least, that's what he told *Katie*. But he confided to *me* that he was discouraging his network bosses from taking Katie on. Maybe he was angry with her for ditching him. Maybe he was jealous of Bill Johnson. Who knows why Guy did what he did?"*

---

* When contacted by the author, Guy Pepper refused to comment.

In any case, the network did not come calling, and Katie was left wondering where to turn next. Her agent sent Katie's tape résumé to Jim Van Messel, the news director of WRC-TV, NBC's owned-and-operated affiliate in Washington. Van Messel, in turn, forwarded the tape to his boss, John Rohrbeck, the general manager of the station. Rohrbeck liked what he saw.

"She was probably at that time one of the most natural and spontaneous people on television," Van Messel said. "We were looking for someone who could do live shots at eleven P.M.—doing something live in the field, reporting a story. She was just a natural. She could do a serious story; she could do a funny story. She was warm; she was friendly. She exuded the personality we were looking for.

"I made a deal in August or September, and tried to get the WTVJ news director in Miami, Al Buch, to let Katie out of her contract early," Van Messel continued. "He said no, because he needed her for the November sweeps. And so, he kept her through most of December, and by the time she started at WRC-TV in Washington, I had made my own deal to go to *Entertainment Tonight* in L.A.

"Incidentally, I recall that after she agreed to come to Washington, and before I left for Los Angeles, her father telephoned me and said he wanted to visit the station to check the joint out. He was serious, he made no bones about it, and I gave him a tour. Also, the following summer, Katie came to visit me in L.A. and indicated that Mary Hart's job, as host of [*Entertainment Tonight*], might be a good next move for her. I guess things worked out for her without getting Mary's job."

As Christmas approached, Katie packed her bags and prepared to say good-bye to her boyfriend, Bill Johnson. By all accounts, he was crushed.

"We were in the Coco Range, the tavern around the corner from WTJV, and Bill and I were talking," said a WTJV reporter. "He was 'Katie this, Katie that.' She dumped him and broke his heart. He was talking like a person who was still hurting, still wistful. He'd say things like 'Katie never cooked; we'd go out to eat a lot.' He had nothing but nice things to say about her. He was still very much in love with her."

ONE OF KATIE's first assignments in Washington was the crash of a Conrail freight train and an Amtrak commuter train in a suburb of Baltimore. Several people were killed in the crash, and the Conrail engineer was later found to be high on marijuana. The press briefer for the National Transportation Safety Board used a lot of complex railroad jargon, but Katie was a quick study, and did an outstanding live shot.

It soon became clear, however, that Katie was best at doing features about ordinary people struggling to overcome adversity. These heart-wrenching stories might have appealed to Katie because they reminded her of the struggles and sacrifices that her parents had endured. To the degree that that was true, Katie's choice of subject could be seen as a way of paying back her parents for all they had done for her.

Such stories played to Katie's strength—her ability to portray the emotions of empathy and compassion on camera. One of Katie's features, on a dating service for the handicapped, won a local Emmy and an Associated Press award, and her colleagues at WRC-TV "NBC 4" began calling her "Mother Teresa."

While Katie was struggling to develop her own distinct style of broadcasting, she came to the attention of George Michael, who anchored the sports desk at WRC-TV. A former disk jockey and an avid equestrian, Michael was a larger-than-life figure with a natural, seemingly off-the-cuff delivery that had made him one of the most popular media personalities in the Washington area.

"Katie was a delight—a bundle of vibrancy and enthusiasm," George Michael said in an interview. "She would go out and do stuff and light up the screen. But she didn't have a rabbi at WRC. Not only didn't she have a rabbi; she was disrespected because no one gave her the credit she deserved.

"Katie would say things like 'George, why don't they like me here; why don't they give me a chance to anchor?'" Michael continued. "I went to Brett Marcus, who had replaced Jim Van Messel as the station's news director, and told him, 'Brett, if you don't give her a shot, you're going to lose her.' But he didn't care."

Katie also struck up a friendship with George Michael's producer, Bob Peterson. Though Peterson worked at the local level, he was known at the NBC network (along with Katie's old boyfriend Guy Pepper) as one of the most creative people in the business. Katie learned a great deal by watching Peterson work, and eventually she would make him her so-called look producer—the person in charge of all visual elements—at *The Today Show* and the *CBS Evening News*.

Katie telephoned her father after every broadcast. He was her biggest booster and thought she was ready to anchor. But Brett Marcus, the news director, had other ideas. He did not think Katie was particularly good at reading the teleprompter. And when she approached Marcus and asked him for the chance to anchor, he told her she needed more experience.

"If I were you and wanted to anchor," said Marcus, "I'd look for a really small market somewhere."

"Like where?" Katie asked.

"Like Casper, Wyoming," he said.

BRETT MARCUS COULD be excused for failing to see that a wholesome Doris Day type like Katie Couric was the future of television news.

After all, Marcus and men like him had come of age in television at a time when news was still defined by the serious mien of Edward R. Murrow. Then, journalists viewed news as a sacred calling, not a business. Journalists were commanded to be impartial observers, reciting the facts and staying out of the way of their stories.

This time-honored journalistic tradition paid bountiful dividends with viewers. By 1979—the year Katie Couric graduated from college—

nearly 120 million Americans tuned in to the three network news shows
every night.

As Lesley Stahl noted, "We were so predominant and influential
that our deadline at six-thirty P.M. Eastern Time became the deadline
of the entire federal government. . . . Television had surpassed newspapers, magazines, and radio as the major source of news in the
country."

Though the news divisions of CBS and NBC had always turned a
small profit, their value was not predominantly financial. News was
the glue that bonded the network to its affiliates, which couldn't afford their own national and foreign newsgathering operations. Men
like CBS chairman William Paley loved being associated with the
news, because it gave them status in society and made it easier for
them to deal with the Federal Communications Commission, which
regulated radio and television "in the public interest, convenience and
necessity."

"The creation of CBS News," wrote Alan Weisman in *Lone Star:
The Extraordinary Life and Times of Dan Rather,* "was in fact a sop to
the government so that stations could continue to reap profits from entertainment programs."

However, sometime in the mid-1970s, *60 Minutes* began making so
much money that all three networks suddenly woke up to a new reality: their news divisions could contribute substantially to the bottom
line. At about the same time, the very nature of television viewing was
shaken by a technological revolution. In a universe of twenty-four-
hour-a-day cable news, instant satellite feeds that allowed local stations to scoop the networks on their own stories, and VCR taping
machines that permitted people to watch whenever they pleased, the
television universe became fragmented, and the networks' audience
for the nightly newscasts was in a freefall.

Alarmed, TV producers embarked on a search for a new definition
of news. All at once, Ed Murrow's basso profundo was considered to be
outdated, and heart-tugging emotional "moments" were hip and cool.
Now, TV journalists were urged to make *themselves* as important as the

stories they covered. To survive, they had to become actors, celebrities, even sex symbols.

Perhaps the most startling example of this change in attitude was Diane Sawyer's vampish photo shoot by Annie Leibovitz for the September 1987 issue of *Vanity Fair*. After the provocative photos appeared, Diane's boss at CBS, News President Howard Stringer, privately told colleagues that she had besmirched her reputation as a serious newswoman and would never recover from her display of poor judgment.

He was wrong. Indeed, not long after the *Vanity Fair* photos appeared, ABC's Roone Arledge snatched Diane away from CBS, promising to create a new primetime show for her and make her the backup for both Ted Koppel on *Nightline* and Peter Jennings on *World News Tonight*.

BY THE TIME Katie arrived in Washington, news was viewed less as a sacred calling than as part of the overall race for ratings and advertising dollars. The race was spurred on by new corporate owners like Laurence Tisch (the hotel magnate and fabled Wall Street investor) at CBS, and Jack Welch (General Electric's brilliant chairman) at NBC.

"As GE and Laurence Tisch found," Brandon Tartikoff, the former head of NBC programming, wrote in his memoir, *The Last Great Ride*, "television bears little resemblance to the consumer electronics or hotel businesses."

Under the directives of Larry Tisch, the CBS newsgathering budget was cut to the bone. For the first time in the history of CBS News, profit—not public service—was king, and the line between hard and soft news began to blur. This blurring required a new type of journalist—someone who punched through the screen like a movie star, seemed as trustworthy as a best friend, and who was as compassionate as a family member.

In short, the new era of television news was tailor made for Katie Couric. And the men who came to power in television in the late

1980s discovered that Katie's so-called disabilities, the very things that up until then had held her back—her ordinary looks, her lack of sophistication and style, her wicked and playful ways, the audacity with which she treated powerful people—that those "weaknesses" were actually Katie Couric's strengths.

Chapter Six

The Hardcore

L IKE MANY SINGLE CAREER WOMEN IN THEIR THIRTIES, KATIE HAD never found time to get married. Her mother constantly reminded Katie of her ticking biological clock and pestered her to start a family before it was too late. But first, her mother said, Katie had to make a genuine effort to find the right man.

"All you have to do is let them know you're here!" Elinor Couric said.

Katie wasn't so sure about that. Could she really have it all—a high-octane job, a husband, and children?

"I thought that I wasn't going to have children because I came of age at the height of the feminist movement, where women wore little bow ties and suddenly doors were opened that hadn't been before," she said.

During the summer of 1988, while Katie was covering the Democratic National Convention in Atlanta, she ran into an old college friend.

"Hey, Beth," she shouted over the din of the delegates on the convention floor, "are you married yet?"

"No," Beth replied.

"Oh, good," Katie shot back. "Neither am I."

Several months later, early in the new year and just after her thirty-second birthday, Katie attended a party in Falls Church, Virginia. This time, she was determined to follow her mother's advice and let the eligible bachelors at the party know that she was a presence. She chose a tight black miniskirt and slipped on a pair of four-inch high heels.

"What do you do?" one of the men asked Katie.

"I'm a reporter at WRC-TV," she replied. "What do *you* guys do?"

"We're lawyers," they responded, almost in unison.

"Oh," said Katie. "Washington lawyers—that's fascinating."

At which point, she stuck a couple of fingers down her throat and pretended to regurgitate.

Without missing a beat, one of the attorneys stepped forward.

"I'm a painter," he said.

He was tall, thin, handsome, well spoken, and elegantly dressed—just the image Katie was looking for in a husband. She knew he was joking about being a painter, but she decided to play along with his white lie.

"Do you want to have lunch with me?" she said, seizing the initiative.

"I'll think about it," he said.

"Well, who do you think you are—Heathcliff?" said Katie.

His name was John Paul Monahan III (Jay to his friends), and, unlike Heathcliff, the character in Emily Brontë's novel *Wuthering Heights*, he did not take a perverse pleasure in other people's suffering. After waiting a decent interval, *he* asked *her* out for a date.

She didn't know much about him other than the fact that he was a litigator at the prestigious Washington, D.C., law firm of Williams & Connolly. A trial lawyer had to be pretty smart and aggressive to make it at Williams & Connolly. And it didn't hurt that litigators made a handsome living. But Katie's sister Emily was divorced from a successful lawyer, and Katie had heard stories about how attorneys at top law firms were so overworked that they often ignored their wives and kids.

Thus, despite her attraction to Jay Monahan, Katie wasn't sure that he was going to be the right fit. Before their first date, Katie left word with the WRC news desk to beep her—just in case she needed an excuse to make a quick exit.

She needn't have bothered.

"They had great chemistry—two very smart, well-rounded, well-educated people," said Mandy Locke, a former news reporter in Washington. "For both of them, family was always the most important thing. They both played the piano, sometimes together, and we'd all sing. They were both interesting and quick witted; Katie was more outgoing and gregarious, he had more of a dry wit."

"They were dedicated to each other, and so similar in so many ways," said Sara Crosman Kane, one of Katie's childhood friends. "They . . . both enjoyed politics, issues, history. Her personality is so outgoing; he was not quite so outgoing, but he did like to perform, especially on the piano. He was a southern gentleman, like Katie's dad."

Actually, Jay Monahan was raised about as far from the Old South as you could get. He came from a large middle-class Irish Catholic family in Manhasset, a New York City bedroom community located on the north shore of Long Island. Over the years, Manhasset had produced a great many lacrosse players, and Jay was a gifted athlete who was one of the better players in his class. The game required expensive equipment and easy access to broad green fields; when Jay was growing up, lacrosse still had an Eastern private school snob appeal.

In his late teens, Jay developed into a good-looking, above-average young man with considerable ambitions. He was eager to put Manhasset and his narrow Irish-Catholic background behind him and enter one of the professions, such as law or banking, that were associated with the WASP establishment. Along the way, he acquired a fascination with the antebellum aristocracy of the Old South, and when it came time to choose a college, he enrolled at Washington and Lee University in the Shenandoah Valley community of Lexington, Virginia, where both Generals Robert E. Lee and Stonewall Jackson are buried.

Washington and Lee University had a superb lacrosse tradition, and Jay made the team. While at school, his interests in the southern side of the Civil War deepened, and he began to acquire those characteristics—an attachment to family, home, and chivalry—that would define him as a southern gentleman. Later, during his three years at Georgetown Law School, he took his hobby one step further and became a Civil War "reenactor"—someone who dressed up in a Civil War uniform and participated in reenactments of battles.

Jay dressed in the uniform of a Confederate officer for these mock battles. He didn't like the term *reenactments,* because the word suggested politically incorrect racist redneck shoot-'em-ups. Instead, Jay called himself a Civil War "interpreter"—someone who interpreted the daily life of Confederate cavalrymen. As he told Katie on one of their first dates, in order to achieve the greatest degree of historical accuracy, he had become a so-called hardcore.

"Hardcores didn't just dress up and shoot blanks," wrote Tony Horwitz in *Confederates in the Attic: Dispatches from the Unfinished Civil War.* "They sought absolute fidelity to the 1860s: its homespun clothing, antique speech patterns, sparse diet and simple utensils. Adhered to properly, this fundamentalism produced a time-travel high, or what hardcores called a 'period rush' . . .

"Losing weight was a hardcore obsession, part of the never-ending quest for authenticity. . . . Southern soldiers were especially lean. So it was every Guardsman's dream to drop a few pants sizes and achieve the gaunt, hollow-eyed look of underfed Confederates."

Jay Monahan had that look. At first, Katie found it hard to take his intoxication with the Civil War seriously. She laughed out loud when he told her that some hardcores actually soaked the buttons of their gray wool jackets in a saucer filled with urine in order to oxidize the brass and give it an authentic patina.

"I used to tease him about it," Katie said. " 'If you think I'm gonna be following you around in a hoop skirt and snood, you've got another think coming.' "

But Katie soon learned that Civil War reenactments were more than an amusing hobby to Jay. They constituted a way of life—and a time-consuming, expensive way of life at that. If he and Katie were going to be serious about each other, he expected her full support.

"I can see Katie in the chill of an October morning, a hood pulled over her head, watching Jay on a horse, riding up and down the fields in a reenactment of the Battle of Cedar Creek," said Michael Gore, the former director of Virginia's Belle Grove Plantation, a member of the National Trust for Historic Preservation. "Jay was dressed as a Confederate officer under the command of General Jubal A. Early."

During their brief courtship, Katie and Jay double-dated with Lea Thompson, an anchor at WRC-TV, and her husband, who, like Jay, was a lawyer.

"I was struck by Jay, because he was so supportive of Katie, and took great pride in whatever story she was working on," Lea Thompson recalled. "Our husbands hit it off, too. They both had an extensive knowledge of Civil War battles in the Shenandoah Valley, and had these intellectual conversations about the Civil War. Katie tried to be understanding of Jay's hobby, but we both had to laugh about it."

When they attended parties, Jay would often seek out men who shared his interests.

"At a party in Virginia," said Peter Cook, a member of the Belle Grove board of directors, "Jay tried to persuade me to become a Civil War reenactor. He had a specific character in mind for me. You see, I'm British, and there was a British Army officer who was attached to the southern forces as an observer, and was reporting back to London on the latest tactics and weaponry. Jay thought I should play this British colonel. I politely turned down his invitation."

IN THE FALL of 1989—just ten months after their first date—Katie and Jay visited her home in Arlington so that Jay could formally ask John Couric for his daughter's hand in marriage.

John Couric was enthusiastic about Katie's choice of a husband. He found many things to like about Jay: the courtly quality of Jay's personality, which made him seem so southern; the fact that Jay, like Couric himself, had served in the U.S. navy; Jay's down-to-earth priorities, which made him put Katie's happiness above his career as a criminal defense lawyer.

"Is there anything I should know about Katie?" Jay asked, half in jest.

"Oh, yes," John Couric replied in all seriousness. "She can be a pouter."

PART II

America's Sweetheart

Chapter Seven

The Hardest Beat
in Washington

WHEN KATIE MARRIED JAY, SHE HAD BEEN WANDERING IN THE wilderness of local television for ten years. But all that was about to change.

It just so happened that the studios of WRC-TV and the Washington bureau of NBC News occupied the same building on Nebraska Avenue. This automatically put Katie on the radar screen of Tim Russert, the network's newly minted bureau chief, who was looking for a number-two at the Pentagon.

"When she was at WRC," recalled Fred Francis, NBC's senior Pentagon correspondent, "and I saw her on the air here [in Washington] doing a story on the bodies of servicemen killed in the USS *Iowa* explosion live from Dover, Delaware, I told Tim Russert I wanted her as my backup at the Pentagon."

"New York was sending me tapes from all around the country," said Russert, who screened more than fifty tapes of prospective Pentagon correspondents. "But every night I'd watch local here [and] I would see this Katherine Couric doing a variety of reporting. I was impressed by her presence, intelligence, and poise, and I went to see the general manager of WRC [John Rohrbeck] as a courtesy and asked, 'Do you mind if I interview Katherine Couric?'"

As general manager of the station, John Rohrbeck was aware that his news director, Brett Marcus, had advised Katie that she would be better off in a smaller market. But Rohrbeck didn't tell Tim Russert that. After all, if one of Rohrbeck's people was considered good enough to make it "upstairs" at the network, it would be a feather in his cap.

"[Katie] came down and told me it was her dream to work for the network," Russert recalled.

One meeting was all it took for Russert to size up Katie's enormous potential. He was to become the first boss who didn't underestimate her.

Though they came from vastly different backgrounds (Katie was solidly middle class; Tim Russert's father was a garbage collector), they soon discovered they had a lot in common. Both grew up discussing politics with their fathers in front of the family television set. Both telephoned their fathers after every show for a no-holds-barred critique of their on-air performances. And both tended to idealize their childhoods, comparing them to the same TV show, *Leave It to Beaver*.

Russert offered Katie the Pentagon job. Though the position represented a giant leap in status, it meant only a small step in salary.

"Let me think about it," she said.

After she left Russert, Katie phoned her old friend Don Brown, the NBC bureau chief in Miami, who had been one of her earliest admirers.

"I was riding down North Bay Road in Miami, and I got a call from Katie," recalled Brown. "She said, 'I want your opinion. I've got an offer to be number-two at the Pentagon. It's not much money. Is it the right move?' And I told her, 'Katie, go for it.'"

"The Pentagon is the hardest beat in Washington, no question—any reporter will tell you that," Fred Francis said. "The way you deal with it and be successful is you have to work the hallways, make the rounds a couple times a day in the biggest office building in the world. I told [Katie] this is how it's done, this is how you'll be successful, and she never batted an eyelash and worked the hallways. She had about two or three dozen contacts in all—the air force, international relations, the navy. She broke stories and got news because she was a good reporter.

"On her third day there—a Wednesday—she was leaving the Pentagon and couldn't remember where she had parked her car in that huge parking lot and was standing in the mall entrance and noticed two women her age who worked at DOD [Department of Defense] standing next to her," Francis continued. "She asked them where the press parking lot was, and they walked her out to show her. They hit it off and stood there chatting for about ten minutes.

"The next morning the phone rings—it's one of the women. Katie puts her hand over the mouthpiece and asks me if we do espionage stories and puts me on the phone. This woman gives us the story of an air force captain who had been arrested in Berlin for spying for the Soviets. I got confirmation, and Katie's piece led the *Nightly News* on Friday. Right after it airs, our competitor at CBS, David Martin, comes out of his office and says to me, 'Tell me you gave her that story.'

"She's still friends with that woman, and that's a perfect example of what a good reporter is—a relationship with sources. She had a great personality, and it didn't hurt her that she was so good-looking. Some admiral once left her flowers. David Martin went nuts!"

When Fred Francis was sent by *Nightly News* to cover the United States' invasion of Panama, Katie got another big break. She was seen by millions of viewers practically every night doing live stand-ups from the Pentagon.

"The military has a chain of command," Katie said. "People don't like to talk. They like to follow orders. They're very wary of the press. . . . [But] I think covering the Pentagon elevated me in the eyes of a lot of people. You can't be an airhead and cover F-14s."

Chapter Eight

Doogie Howser

WHEN TOM CAPRA ARRIVED IN NEW YORK IN 1990 TO TAKE OVER as executive producer of *The Today Show*, the program was facing the worst crisis in its history. The most visible cause of this crisis was a thirty-one-year-old leggy blonde by the name of Deborah Norville. The media blamed her for driving Jane Pauley (whom they dubbed "the older woman," though she was only thirty-nine) from the bosom of *The Today Show* "family."

The appointment of Deborah Norville as Bryant Gumbel's co-anchor had, in fact, been a terrible mistake. All at once, *The Today Show*'s ratings headed south, toward second place after *Good Morning America*. And this collapse of NBC's profitable news show drove everyone at the Peacock Network crazy.

Bryant Gumbel sent out an incendiary memo in which he called one producer a "lazy broad" and blasted weatherman Willard Scott for holding "the show hostage to his assortment of whims, wishes, birthdays and bad taste." Bob Wright, the president and CEO of NBC, fired the network's highly regarded news president, Larry Grossman, and replaced him with Michael Gartner, a print man (the *Wall Street Journal* and the *Des Moines Register*) who had a prickly personality and no experience in the world of broadcast news.

In fact, the underlying problem with *The Today Show* was not

Deborah Norville; it was the NBC News front office, which was run by neophytes who had little or no experience producing a television news show. This cast of characters included Michael Gartner's number-two, Donald Brown (Katie's old friend from Miami days), a bureau chief who had recently been brought to New York and put in charge of newsgathering for the network.

To make up for their lack of experience in the highly technical and star-studded world of television news, Bob Wright, Michael Gartner, and Don Brown became apostles of cost cutting.

"They believed the road to profitability was controlling costs," said William Wheatley, the well-regarded executive producer of *Nightly News with Tom Brokaw*, "whereas in TV news, the way to profitability is in creating successful programs."

Flailing around for a solution to NBC's problems, the ill-tempered Michael Gartner fired two executive producers of *The Today Show*, and then offered the job to someone who promptly turned him down. Finally, Gartner hired Tom Capra, the son of legendary Hollywood director Frank Capra and a veteran news director of KNBC in Los Angeles.

It was against this bewildering background of corporate incompetence, personal backbiting, and creative anarchy that Tom Capra stepped onto the ground-floor set of *The Today Show* at 30 Rockefeller Plaza on January 29, 1990. He was the eleventh executive producer in *The Today Show*'s thirty-eight-year history, and he had some very nervous bosses looking over his shoulder.

Chief among them, of course, was Bob Wright.

"Wright was engaging, extremely smart, a quick learner, and very confident when it came to talking news," recalled a journalist who lunched with him at the Four Seasons restaurant, "though he seemed on less-sure ground on what NBC News ought to be about. He seemed quite taken with what he called TV tabloid journalism."

Another person Capra had to worry about was Brandon Tartikoff, the president of NBC's profitable entertainment division, which was headquartered in Los Angeles. Tartikoff was a favorite of Jack Welch, the chairman of GE, and as a result, Tartikoff's power reached well beyond entertainment all the way to New York and the news division of the network.

Whether they wanted to admit it or not, these executives understood that Deborah Norville was not, as widely trumpeted by the NBC publicity department, the network's Great Blonde Hope. The corridors at NBC News were abuzz with references to Deborah Norville as "the Stepford anchor." A ranking news executive at a rival network spoke for many when he said that he found it hard to take her journalistic credentials seriously.

"If the president of the United States were shot at nine in the morning, and Deborah Norville had to go on and give the facts to the nation and the world," he said, "there is no reason to believe that she would be qualified to do that. She isn't Phyllis George [the former anchor of the *CBS Early Show*], but she sure as hell isn't Diane Sawyer either."

Deborah Norville seemed to be plagued by some of the same doubts as everyone else. In fact, she sounded increasingly like a woman on the verge of a breakdown.

"I don't know what I'm all about," she told the author of this book during an interview for the January 1990 issue of *Vanity Fair*. "I work so hard. I come from a background where as a reporter you don't get in the way of the story, but now I'm on *The Today Show*, which is clearly unlike any other product produced by NBC News, and I've got all these people saying, '*Reveal* yourself. Give me more, Deb, give me *more!*' "

As Tom Capra saw it, NBC had no choice but to stick with Deborah Norville for the time being. *The Today Show* had been so battered by bad publicity that it could not afford another upheaval in its dysfunctional family. More important, Capra didn't have an obvious replacement for Deborah Norville waiting in the wings.

One of his first tasks, then, was to conduct a search for someone to fill the high-profile job of *The Today Show* "girl," the traditional distaff role once played by Barbara Walters. Several NBC women were considered as candidates, including Faith Daniels, *The Today Show*'s newsreader, and Jamie Gangel, a correspondent in the Washington bureau.

But it soon became apparent to Capra that Katherine Couric (as she was then still known) was everyone's favorite choice.

Katie had made many friends in high places, just as her father had taught her to. Brandon Tartikoff, the entertainment czar, thought Katie had an energy that was otherwise missing in the reporting ranks of NBC News. Michael Gartner was impressed by NBC's internal research, which showed that Katie was "a girl men like who doesn't threaten other women."

Another influential Katie supporter was Don Brown, the new executive vice president of NBC News.

"I saw Katie do a live shot from the Pentagon during the invasion of Panama," said Brown. "It clicked in my mind to give her that shot she had always wanted, and I had her substitute as the anchor on the weekend *Nightly News*. After that, she picked up the telephone and called Brett Marcus, the guy who had once told her to go to a small market somewhere, like Casper, Wyoming. It was a classic moment. Katie asked him, 'Hey, Brett, is this the right market?'"

In point of fact, Katie did not impress her bosses at NBC as a born anchor. Her let-it-all-hang-out personality wasn't suited for the tightly scripted ambience of the evening news. And she looked uncomfortable reading the teleprompter. On the other hand, she possessed a spontaneity that made her a natural for a personality-driven program like *The Today Show*.

No one had to twist Tom Capra's arm to hire Katie Couric. As the son of movie director Frank Capra, Tom had grown up in an atmosphere where careers were made or broken at the box office. He understood that it was stars who attracted the audience. He was looking for someone who could make love to the camera, draw millions of viewers, and pile up millions of advertising dollars for NBC.

"Katie has that sort of extra little thing," Capra told the author of this book. "The camera really likes her. She's unafraid. I always liked the way she asked questions—that disarming way she had of asking the tough questions. . . . TV news has a star system, which makes it different from print. Stars make big money. It's more like Hollywood than the *Washington Post*."

To introduce Katie to *The Today Show*'s viewers, Capra appointed her as the national correspondent in May 1990, just five months after he had arrived at NBC.

"That was a position we invented," he said. "What we needed at that point was a signature reporter, a field person who could just work for our show. She did it perfectly."

THERE'S A SAYING in television that no matter how great your talent—whether you're Oprah Winfrey, Barbara Walters, or Katie Couric—you can't succeed without a great producer. To serve as Katie Couric's producer, Tom Capra named Jeff Zucker, a short (five-foot-five), twenty-five-year-old Harvard graduate who looked like everyone's idea of a nerd. In Jeff Zucker's case, appearances were wildly misleading. He was a consummate office politician, and a genuine TV genius, whose precocious talents earned him the nickname "Doogie Howser," or "the Doogster," after the teenage doctor on the then-still-popular TV series *Doogie Howser, M.D.*

"He had on this gray sweatshirt, bluejeans and white Keds that I thought only girls wore," Katie recalled. "I thought he was the cockiest guy I had ever met. I wasn't that excited about it. He was so young, and so cocky. And I thought he was a bit of a dweeb."

But Zucker's appointment was an inspired choice. He belonged to a new generation of producers who believed that TV reporters had to establish an intimate rapport with their viewers and reveal more of themselves. He had worked as Jane Pauley's Washington producer for the past couple of years, and had found her a bit chilly for his taste. Katie Couric was another matter; she was warm and bubbly and accessible. Zucker had no trouble transferring his allegiance from Jane to Katie overnight.

"Jeff hitched his wagon to Katie's star," said Tom Capra. "As she rose, he rose. They're both quite ambitious, and he saw that potential in her."

Jeff Zucker had an ego to match his outsized talent. He never let people forget that he had been president of *The Harvard Crimson* (though he didn't mention that he had failed to get into Harvard Law School). As time went on, his boasting didn't bother Katie. She was tickled that this intense, hotshot producer had dedicated himself to making her a star.

Next to her husband, Jeff Zucker became the most important man in Katie's life. In fact, judged by the hours he spent with Katie, Zucker was even more important than Jay Monahan. Zucker and Katie huddled in the studio at the crack of dawn, lunched together at noon, and talked on the phone late into the night.

"Zucker was like Katie's Svengali," said a colleague who worked closely with both of them. "He would advise her that she needed to do something this way or that. Or, wasn't this an interesting way into a story? Or, you need to be shot against this backdrop. He was into the minutiae of everything she did, and of course she loved that."

Katie had to go to the Pentagon very early and she often gave a junior producer a ride in her car.

"I was usually bleary eyed, and one time I apologized for biting my nails," the producer recalled. "'Don't worry,' she told me. 'I used to bite my nails. In fact, I still do. I bite my toenails, too.' She was wearing sandals, and when I looked down at her feet, I saw that she wasn't kidding.

"As we rode along, she would give me advice on my future career in journalism. I know from talking to her that she thought she had had a very rough time early on, and that she had made some huge mistakes. She kept telling me, 'Whatever you do, you have to start out in a small market, because you want to make your mistakes in a small market. If I had made my mistakes in a big market, I'd be finished by now.'"

Chapter Nine

Capra-Corn

In August 1990, Saddam Hussein invaded and annexed the tiny, oil-rich kingdom of Kuwait, and President George Herbert Walker Bush responded by dispatching the 82nd Airborne and several fighter squadrons to the Middle East. The looming desert war would be fought by the nation's all-volunteer army, and the miles of videotape showing fresh-faced young American men and women tramping off to war were tailor-made for *The Today Show.*

The show's executive producer, Tom Capra, had learned the art of melodrama at the knee of a grand master, his father, Frank Capra, whose sentimental movies (*Mr. Smith Goes to Washington*, *It's a Wonderful Life*) were known in Hollywood as "Capra-corn." Under Tom Capra's guidance, *Today* pulled out all the stops, portraying America's crusade against Saddam Hussein as a battle between good and evil.

"One Friday, the show closed with a montage of GIs in the sand that was shown over a soundtrack of spouses saying how proud they were of their husbands and wives who were serving in the desert," reported *FineLine: The Newsletter on Journalism Ethics.* "It was moving stuff— in the same way Ray Charles singing 'America the Beautiful,' with Ronald and Nancy Reagan and all those red, white, and blue balloons at the close of the 1984 Republican National Convention in Dallas was moving stuff. The close of *The Today Show* was a direct descendant of the great propaganda films the elder Capra made for the government during World War II."

That summer, as war fever captured the media's attention, Capra sent Katie Couric to Shaw Air Force Base in South Carolina. There, she donned a flight suit and clambered aboard an F-16 for a televised demonstration of the air force's most advanced fighter jet. At the conclusion of her report, Katie presented her airsickness bag, and, flashing her trademark grin, revealed that she had used the bag twice during the supersonic flight. It was a classic Katie performance: simultaneously intrepid *and* self-deprecating.

Before the full-scale American bombardment of Baghdad commenced on January 16, 1991, Capra dispatched Katie and Jeff Zucker to the Middle East to do up-close-and-personal features on America's fighting troops. On the second day of the air war, Katie broadcast a report on how U.S. Patriot missiles were easily knocking Iraqi Scuds out of the sky.

"Three miles above Dhahran in the early-morning hours, a U.S. Patriot missile meets an Iraqi Scud missile," Katie told the audience. The screen then filled with a shot of triumphant U.S. anti-missile troops telling correspondent Couric, "We are the first Patriot battery in the history of the world to knock down a Scud."

Katie's report was filled with great TV images, but unfortunately it turned out to be wide of the mark. The army was never able to provide reliable evidence in support of any Patriot warhead kills. Back at NBC headquarters in New York, no one seemed to mind, and Katie instantly became the network's Scud Babe.

She was also the target of some spiteful gossip at 30 Rockefeller Plaza, where NBC News staffers snickered about the "bond" that had developed between Katie and Jeff during their three weeks together in the Arabian desert. Some people insinuated that the newly wed Katie and the bachelor Jeff were having an affair. But although Katie and Jeff Zucker were forced by circumstances to live in intimate proximity covering Desert Storm, there was never evidence that their relationship was anything but professional.

*   *   *

TOM CAPRA WAS having the time of his life airing special editions of what *The Today Show* called "America at War." These specials were solo-anchored by Bryant Gumbel without his cohost, Deborah Norville, who often didn't appear until the show's second half hour, and who was instructed not to speak unless spoken to by Gumbel.

"Bryant and Deborah's relationship got very bad," said one of the show's producers. "He felt he was out there all alone. Sometimes Bryant's comments would go over Deborah's head. Bryant turned on her. Sometimes he wouldn't even say good morning on the air."

Deborah Norville's situation was complicated by the fact that she was struggling through a bad pregnancy. She had a potentially fatal medical disorder called preeclampsia, or toxemia of pregnancy, which is characterized by hypertension, and, in severe cases, can cause liver and kidney failure, and convulsions.

She was torn over what to do. On the one hand, she knew that she should follow her doctor's advice and stay in bed for the remainder of her pregnancy. But she was terrified (with good reason) that if she went on hiatus, she would never be invited back to *The Today Show*.

In the end, the decision was not hers to make. Fred Francis, NBC's chief Pentagon correspondent, and Tim Russert, the politically adroit Washington bureau chief who was Katie Couric's rabbi, helped persuade NBC News President Michael Gartner that Katie was the ideal choice to fill in for Deborah Norville.

"I absolutely knew Katie would be a good co-anchor," said Fred Francis. "I talked to Tim Russert, Tim agreed, and when Bryant was in town after some event here—he and I are old friends—I asked him out to dinner and asked him to let me bring my new partner from the Pentagon. We had dinner at [Ristorante] i Ricchi, had about three bottles of wine, and they really hit it off. I called Don Brown and said, 'I think I have a solution to your problem.' "

Generally, Gartner was a poor judge of TV talent, but in this case, he bowed to the judgment of others. Still, Gartner expressed one reservation: he was concerned that an abrupt change in *The Today*

Show "family" would be seen as a replay of the Jane Pauley–Deborah Norville fiasco and set off a media storm. And so, he asked Russert to sound out Katie to see whether she was prepared to handle the heat.

When Katie returned from the Persian Gulf, Russert invited her to his office.

"I told her, 'This is a meteoric rise, from local to the Pentagon to national correspondent and now co-anchor,' " Russert said. " 'Are you comfortable with that?' She stood up and she said, 'I can do it.' I will always remember that, her saying, 'Tim, I can do it.' "

Over the next few days, however, Katie seemed to develop cold feet.

"Katie started to question whether she should take the *Today* job and go to New York," said Lea Thompson, Katie's friend at WRC-TV, the local NBC affiliate in Washington. "She was born and raised here, and she got married here in this little chapel next door to this building.

"At the time, Katie was a couple of months pregnant with her first child, and she was concerned about the lifestyle in New York," Thompson continued. "She was also concerned about ripping Jay out of his prestigious law firm. This opportunity caught them when they hadn't been married very long. If she went, would Jay go with her?"

Of even greater concern to Katie was her father's reaction. How would he feel when he saw his daughter on *The Today Show* cavorting with chimpanzees and rating electric juicers with the Gadget Guru? That was definitely not what John Couric had in mind when he preached the gospel of News with a capital *N*. He had urged Katie to set her sights high—on Walter Cronkite's anchor chair, or on *60 Minutes*, not on a show that was one part news and three parts show biz razzle-dazzle. Would he be ashamed of her?

After talking it over, John Couric gave Katie the green light. She could not pass up this once-in-a-lifetime opportunity. *The Today Show* would instantly elevate her to the first rank of television news personalities. And it could prove to be a steppingstone to greater things. Just as her series of articles in the University of Virginia's student paper, the *Cavalier*, had earned her a coveted place on the Lawn, *The Today Show* might eventually earn her a place in an evening-news anchor chair. Who knew? Maybe even in Walter Cronkite's chair.

And so, Katie told Tim Russert that her answer was "yes."

Meantime, Michael Gartner and his number-two, Don Brown, were working on Deborah Norville. They insisted she make an on-air announcement that her medical condition required her to take a maternity leave. After much resistance, Deborah caved in. She was leaving the show voluntarily, she told the viewing audience, adding that Katie Couric would substitute for her during her brief absence.

No one in the media bought the story, not even when Deborah Norville insisted, "This was my decision. . . ."

As things turned out, it really didn't matter whether people believed her or not. For shortly after giving birth to a boy (she named him Karl Nikolai "Niki" Wellner), Deborah Norville made the public-relations faux pas of posing for *People* magazine breast-feeding her baby.

"Network brass," said an NBC source, "found the photo self-serving and embarrassing."

Deborah Norville broke down in tears when Michael Gartner informed her that she would not be welcomed back to *The Today Show*, and that NBC was buying out the remainder of her $5 million contract. But her former *Today* colleague, Bryant Gumbel, did not feel her pain.

"Katie," he said, introducing the woman who had been known to the audience as Katherine Couric, "Katie is now a permanent fixture up here, a member of our family, an especially welcome one. Deborah Norville is not. . . ."

"PUTTING KATIE ON *The Today Show* with a guy like Bryant Gumbel, who's a pretty imposing anchor, was a huge risk," said Donald Brown, the executive in charge of newsgathering. "And I remember the buildup the first time Katie nervously settled into her seat, and the producers were counting down the show . . . five . . . four . . . three . . . and we were holding our breath, not knowing what was going to happen.

"It was probably about twenty seconds into the show," Brown continued, "and you go, 'Oh my God, there's a chemistry here, a naturalness here.' A lot of people in the control room felt something good was happening. She was a natural. Even the rough-around-the-edges part worked well.

"In my view, one of the main reasons Katie succeeded was she has a unique personality. Unlike other young talents who were groomed to be anchors, Katie was never homogenized and manufactured. She was forced to be in the street, among people, forced to be out getting a sense of the real world. That was what made her so credible."

Katie, who was five months pregnant when she made her debut, had a different recollection of her first day on *The Today Show.*

"I had the worst cold in history," she said. "I was miserable, pregnant, with terrible sinuses, and I think I even had thrown up that morning."

To sandpaper some of Katie's rougher edges, Don Brown moved Jeff Zucker into the control room and made him the program's supervising producer.

"There was some skepticism among some of the producers about whether I was old enough or mature enough to handle it," Zucker admitted. "After the first show, I went home and threw up."

Jeff Zucker knew how to bring out the best in Katie. As he talked into her earpiece, leading her through the show, he could see her confidence visibly improving.

"He eats, sleeps, and drinks *The Today Show,*" Katie said. "His youth is an asset in many ways. We all have to look ahead, and who better to run things than someone with a fresh outlook. We'll be on the cutting edge. . . . With Jeff talking in my ear, I know where we're going. He guides me."

As supervising producer, Jeff sat in the dimly lit, freezing control room, his sleeves rolled up, facing a wall of television screens, yelling to cameras: *"Get the shot! Get the shot! Get the shot!"*

"There's a difference between producing a piece and producing an entire show," Don Brown said, "and Jeff and I talked about that. When it came to learning the basics and protocol of the control room, he was the quickest study I've ever seen in my life."

"Jeff Zucker worked hard with her," said a *Today* staffer. "After every show, Jeff and she would sit and critique tapes. He would show her how to be better. He would say, 'Look at how Bryant did it.'

"Jeff was a hell of a TV producer," this person continued. "He had imagination and intelligence, he loves TV, and he's not afraid of it. He'd routinely kill commercials when there was good stuff on air. And he helped Katie to have the courage to push beyond what it said in the anchors' printed daily lineup."

Among Zucker's many talents was his mental agility.

"If Whoopi Goldberg didn't show up for an interview, then he'd call her up so we could talk to her while she was stuck on the Brooklyn Bridge," Katie said. "He was always excited about every story, and gave us wings to do a great job."

ZUCKER WASN'T THE only person who was happy to be working with Katie. From day one, she was popular with members of the crew. Most of them were eager to forget the fourteen months of contention and strife between Deborah Norville and Bryant Gumbel. In contrast to Deborah, who had been earnest to a fault, Katie played the wisecracker—the same role she had played while growing up in Arlington. She joked with the cameramen and janitors, and belted out karaoke.

"I kinda pretend I'm like a lounge lizard around here," she said, producing an echo mike from her office cabinet. Then, she would croon: "Looove, so precious and new, come on board—we're expecting you—YEAH!"

Katie proved to be a terrific shot in the arm—not just for *The Today Show*, but for the entire NBC organization. Even the bristly Bryant Gumbel found it hard to resist her girlish charms. At last, he had someone to play with on camera, someone who was smart enough and quick enough to pick up on his patter. A perfectionist who drove everyone as hard as he drove himself, Bryant was impressed by Katie's work ethic.

"Katie worked hard at being a better interviewer," said a producer. "Writers do pre-interviews and write questions for the anchors, plus they write a summary of what each segment's about. At first, Katie would stick to the list of ten questions. She wasn't a very good interviewer at the beginning. For Bryant, you'd write ten questions, and you'd feel honored if he used one of them. But Katie worked hard to where it was a conversation between her and the subject, which let her personality come through."

"I try to make people feel like there's no glass between us," Katie explained. "I used to be terrified that I would draw a blank in the middle of an interview, so I'd write out every question and memorize them. Now I just trust my instincts, which makes it much more spontaneous."

ON JULY 23, 1991, Katie gave birth to Elinor Monahan. The baby was named after Katie's mother. During her maternity leave, Katie, Jay, and little Ellie lived in Old Town Alexandria in Alexandria, Virginia, not far from Katie's parents' house in Arlington. This peaceful family interlude was short-lived, however. Six weeks after Ellie was born, Katie boarded a plane with her infant and a nanny, and flew back to her job on *The Today Show*.

"Being apart [from Jay] is really rough and definitely not what I had in mind when I got married and decided to have a family," she said. "I don't think it's healthy; I don't think it's good for Ellie. I think there's going to be a point when Jay will be up here [in New York] and possibly take some time off, so we can be together."

That, however, was not what Jay Monahan had in mind. He was making $200,000 a year as a litigator at Williams & Connolly and wasn't ready to give up his career at one of the best law firms in America just because Katie had a higher public profile and made more money than he did. Instead, Jay insisted on commuting to New York a couple of days a week. On the weekends, Katie and Ellie flew down to Virginia.

"It was very difficult," Monahan said. "I [miss] Katie and the baby. . . . We're tired all the time."

John Couric had warned Jay that Katie could be a pouter when she didn't get her way. And, sure enough, when Jay balked at spending more time in New York, Katie went into a sulk. Why couldn't Jay take cases in the New York area so they could be together? Didn't he realize the pressure she was under? Did he appreciate that she had to get up at five o'clock in the morning for *The Today Show,* and that after putting in a fourteen-hour day, her bosses sometimes asked her to substitute for Tom Brokaw on *Nightly News*? And who was going to cook the turkey while she was hosting Macy's Thanksgiving Day Parade this year?

Friends began to notice a change in Jay. He seemed to be sunk in deep thought. It wasn't clear whether he was preoccupied by work or unhappy in his personal life. Some of these friends thought that Katie was making a big mistake by casting Jay in the role of second fiddle. After all, no man liked to feel that he was less important than his wife.

But other friends dismissed such talk as poppycock. Jay was a proud guy, they said, and it was perfectly normal for a man like Jay to have trouble adjusting to the demands of his wife's pressure-cooker life.

Surely, Jay and Katie would work things out. At least, these friends *hoped* that Jay and Katie would work things out.

Chapter Ten

Breaking the Mold

Reviewing Katie's first day back at *The Today Show*, Tom Shales, the *Washington Post*'s award-winning television critic, wrote:

"The hard part is finding a flaw. She's the everything gal. She's an apple a day. She's real, she's natural, she's totally at home on the air. She's a godsend, that's what she is."

Shales was not alone in his adoration of Katie. Television critics from all over America lined up to welcome her back from maternity leave. The NBC publicity machine, noted *USA Today*, treated Katie's return to television with all the hoopla accorded General Douglas MacArthur's return to the Philippines at the end of World War Two.

And with good reason. In the fall of 1991, the network's news division was in desperate shape. *Nightly News with Tom Brokaw* seemed permanently mired in third place, behind ABC and CBS. And the once-bright spot on the news schedule—*The Today Show*—had been leaching ratings (and millions in advertising dollars) during Katie's six-week maternity leave.

The top news executives at 30 Rockefeller Plaza—Michael Gartner and his deputy, Donald Brown—were well aware that their jobs depended on turning things around as quickly as possible. And they were counting on their bright new star, Katie Couric, to work the magic.

Katie's producer, Jeff Zucker, who rivaled Tim Russert as an accomplished office politician, was quick to grasp the meaning of all this. During the time that Katie had been on leave, her value to NBC had skyrocketed. As Zucker saw it, that put Katie—and him—in the catbird seat.

Zucker was not one to leave things to chance. During the summer of 1991, while Katie was still living in Virginia, presumably warming baby formula and changing diapers, she and Jeff spent hours on the phone planning their next move. They needed to convince Gartner and Brown that the survival of *The Today Show* depended on making Katie an equal partner with Bryant Gumbel. Just as important, their plan called for Jeff Zucker to replace Tom Capra as executive producer of the show.

On Katie's first day back on the set—September 9, 1991—she offered a small sample of what was in store for Bryant Gumbel. That morning's show was devoted to a welcome-back party for Katie, complete with a montage of photos showing her with her newborn baby.

"Is it true that baby Elinor sleeps through *The Today Show*?" asked Bryant, playing along with the theme.

"Only during *your* interviews," Katie shot back.

Over the next few weeks, these zingers continued to fly in Bryant's direction, and many of them found their mark. He tried to give as good as he got.

"He doesn't talk about my hair and clothes too often," Katie said, "but when he does, it kind of bugs me, to be honest. I think he does it in good fun, but I don't want too much attention paid to my looks— it's sexist. I don't think Bryant would think it was funny if I'd said his recent hairstyle made him look like Bart Simpson."

There was something that irritated Bryant even more than Katie's mockery and derision. The NBC publicity department was sending out press releases giving Katie virtually all of the credit for improving *The Today Show*'s ratings since her return from maternity leave.

Given his standoffish personality, Bryant could never hope to challenge Katie when it came to wooing women viewers. She was an irresistible draw for women between the ages of eighteen and forty-nine—the very demographic most sought after by advertisers.

Katie's assignments reflected her focus on women. That fall, she interviewed Hillary Rodham Clinton, the embattled wife of Arkansas' womanizing governor, Bill Clinton, who was seeking the Democratic Party's presidential nomination. After the interview was taped—but before it was aired—Katie called Frank Radice, the senior vice president for NBC advertising and promotion.

"For a long time," Radice recalled in an interview, "people in the news department looked at the promotion department as a necessary evil. When I worked at ABC, Peter Jennings never picked up the phone to tell me how he wanted to do the promos on his show. And when I came over here to NBC, Tom Brokaw didn't used to call me, either. But Katie was at the leading edge of understanding the need for promos.

"On the Hillary interview, for instance," Radice continued, "Katie came down to the edit room where I was doing the promo to talk to me about how I was going to do it. She was very involved in promotion. She played a big role in creating promos when she was attached to a product."

Other NBC insiders noticed that Katie didn't exactly go out of her way to share the glory with Bryant.

"I can handle all the minutiae of my generation," Katie told the *Washington Journalism Review*. "I'm just up on the trends and what is happening. My finger is on the pulse of movies and television shows."

Off camera, there was talk among the crew of bitterness between *The Today Show*'s cohosts. But according to Tom Brokaw, one of Bryant Gumbel's closest friends, such talk was exaggerated.

Bryant "genuinely likes [Katie] and is intrigued by her," said Brokaw. "And she can handle him—and he is not always easy to handle. He is still first among equals. It is in his interest to get along with Katie."

And indeed, whatever their private feelings about each other, Katie and Bryant made an attempt to project a positive chemistry while they were on the air.

"There was a freshness and vitality between Katie and Bryant," said Don Brown. "The *Today* ensemble was developing while I was there. . . . It was one of the positive stories at NBC News. They were on the come. There was a good feeling around NBC and the affiliates that we had found the right combination."

Katie agreed with Brown.

"We just have fun together," she said. "Yes, [Bryant] can be intimidating, if you let him be. If he senses weakness, I think he sort of chews you up and spits you out—and I say this all in a flattering way. He makes me crazy sometimes, and I think I probably make him crazy. But it works."

ON A TYPICAL day, Katie would arrive at the studio at 5:45 A.M.—an hour or so later than the obsessively punctual Bryant Gumbel. She would kick off her shoes, throw her clothes on the back of a chair or on the floor, and don a pair of slippers and a threadbare terry-cloth robe. Then she would pad into the brightly lit makeup room, make funny faces at her reflection in the mirror, crack some off-color jokes about her love life with Jay Monahan, and surrender to the magic of the show's hair stylist and makeup artist.

Then, with her hair and makeup plastered in place—but still dressed in slippers and a bathrobe—Katie would wander into the newsroom. There, bent over a computer screen, she would be joined by Jeff Zucker, her producer and mainstay. Together, they would review her list of questions for that morning's interviews and talk about the most interesting news of the day.

Though Jeff was a member of the MTV generation, he always encouraged Katie to let her hard-news segments run long if they warranted it. Of course, the longer Katie's segments ran, the less airtime there would be for Bryant Gumbel.

Shortly before 7 A.M., Katie appeared on the set, generally dressed in a sweater, jacket, and skirt. She would greet Bryant Gumbel with a few pleasant words, which he made sure to reciprocate for the benefit of those within earshot. For the next few minutes, sound engineers would scurry around, adjusting the wires on Katie's and Bryant's lavaliere microphones, and just before the countdown to the show, the two of them would settle into chairs before the bank of cameras.

"Bryant and I spend more time together during the week than I do with my husband," Katie once told a writer for the *Saturday Evening Post*. "I used to laugh thinking that Ellie was going to come out of the womb thinking Bryant was her father."

Nonetheless, people who worked on the show noticed that Katie was continuing to rub Bryant the wrong way, as though she was purposely trying to provoke him. For instance, Bryant was appalled when Katie interviewed Gwendolyn Florant, an AIDS counselor at New York's Harlem Hospital. Displaying an anatomically correct plastic model of a penis, Florant unrolled a condom and demonstrated the correct way to slip it on.

"Couric says that viewer reaction [after the show] was about evenly divided between those who approved of how NBC played the segment and those who disapproved," wrote Edwin Diamond, *New York Magazine*'s media critic. "Among the negative callers was [Katie's] father, who phoned from Arlington, Virginia, to complain that she had gone 'over the top.'"

Katie tried to placate her father. She reminded him that when he served in the navy during World War Two, sailors were often given graphic demonstrations on the proper use of condoms.

"Yes," said John Couric, "but they used a broom."

BEHIND THE SCENES at *The Today Show*, Bryant and Katie were headed for a showdown. Though there was still no hint of this looming confrontation in the media coverage of the show, the battle lines were obvious to those who worked on the set.

On one side were Katie and Jeff Zucker; on the other, Bryant and *his* producer, a bright and talented TV newsman by the name of Robert Wheelock. Caught in the middle was Tom Capra, the executive producer who was supposed to be the man in charge but wasn't.

"Bryant was used to being the big kahuna on the set," Capra told the author of this book. "And here comes this disarmingly funny, bright, intelligent, and cute woman, who also is adored by the camera. And so, all of a sudden, Bryant's got a real person sitting next to him, and not someone he can kick around.

"The atmosphere between Katie and Bryant got very tense," Capra continued. "A lot of the time, I felt like a basketball referee in an NBA game, where everybody's bigger than you are."

As relations between Katie and Bryant went from bad to worse, Capra asked his boss, Michael Gartner, to intervene. But Gartner wasn't up to the task. Unlike Roone Arledge, who ran ABC News with the mastery of an old Hollywood studio boss, Gartner didn't have the impresario's skills to keep his stars in line. While NBC News lost traction under Gartner, ABC surged ahead, becoming the dominant news network under Arledge.

"Yes, I think the record is clear," Arledge told the author of this book during an interview for *New York Magazine* shortly after he had lured Diane Sawyer away from CBS in 1989. "Peter Jennings is now only a half a rating point away from Dan Rather on the nightly news. We have Ted Koppel, Barbara Walters, David Brinkley, Sam Donaldson, Jeff Greenfield. And now we have Diane Sawyer."

None of this was lost on Bryant Gumbel. He was fed up with Katie Couric, he informed Roone Arledge during a confidential chat, and he wouldn't have minded joining ABC's murderers' row of news stars. Bryant and Roone spoke a common language—sports. Bryant had begun his career as a sports announcer, and Roone was president of ABC Sports as well as ABC News.

However, Roone had no interest in tinkering with the winning combination of Charlie Gibson and Joan Lunden on *Good Morning America,* which continued to edge out *The Today Show* in the ratings. What's more, it turned out that Roone was less interested in Bryant Gumbel (who seemed to be on the verge of burnout) than he was in Katie Couric. In fact, Roone had been tracking Katie's career for the past several years and had hinted (in a series of hush-hush conversations with Katie) that he would consider creating a primetime program for her if she jumped ship and came over to ABC to become the eighth member of his network's murderers' row.

While all these clandestine talks were going on, *Today* continued to close the ratings gap with *GMA*. And this encouraged Katie to demand more say in how the show was run. She made it clear that she did not want to be relegated to women's segments, such as parenting and cooking. As she pointed out, she had grown up around Washington, D.C., and had been a Pentagon correspondent, which earned her the right to do important political stories.

Challenged by Katie for the big stories, Bryant became more and more bad tempered—not only with Katie, but with other women on the staff. Bryant had earned the reputation of being a male chauvinist on a show that was staffed predominantly by women. He treated women as inferiors and frequently made them cry with his crude remarks.

No MATTER HOW hard Tom Capra tried, he was powerless to smooth things over between Katie and Bryant. And as Capra's star faded, Jeff Zucker's star burned ever brighter.

Thanks to Jeff's skills as a producer and world-class schmoozer, he had become the fair-haired boy of Bob Wright, the CEO of the network. He had unfettered access to Wright, and he convinced Wright that *The Today Show* was headed for a crackup. It is not known what Bob Wright told Jeff Zucker during their private conversations, but after one such talk, Jeff returned to the set and confidently told staffers:

"When Tom Capra says something in the control room, we're just going to ignore him."

Bob Wright finally forced Michael Gartner to act. Gartner signed Katie to a five-year, $1-million-a-year contract, which formally named her cohost and guaranteed her the right to open the show every other morning. To keep Bryant on the reservation, Gartner doubled his salary to $2 million a year. Most important of all, Gartner fired Tom Capra as executive producer and replaced him with Jeff Zucker.

Before Zucker was formally offered the job, he met with Bob Wright.

"I've heard that you have the reputation for being tough and demanding," Wright said, according to someone who was present at the meeting.

"Okay," Zucker said, accepting Wright's assessment as a compliment. "That's okay."

When he was appointed executive producer of *The Today Show* in December 1991, Jeff Zucker was all of twenty-six years old.

"DOES IT BUG [Bryant] that I'm getting so much attention?" Katie said in an interview with *TV Guide*. "I don't think so, and if it does, he's never let on to me that it does. And I think it's very apparent to anyone watching that Bryant is a very crucial part of the show. Without him it wouldn't be *The Today Show*.

"I think we complement each other," she went on, apparently not realizing how condescending toward Gumbel she sounded. "I'm not at my best when Bryant isn't next to me, and I don't think he's at his best when I'm not there to give him a hard time or make fun of him or make sure he's not taking himself oh-too-seriously.

"When they talked to me about this job, I said I didn't want it unless it was a shared partnership with Bryant. If I was doing lead-ins to style pieces or fashion shows or all Martha Stewart stuff, I'd rather be a reporter. An equal split was extremely important to me."

Once Jeff Zucker became executive producer, however, the split was no longer quite so equal. Katie became *the* star of the show. She demanded that she be given at least half of the big "gets"—interviews with major newsmakers.

"In the television news business," said a veteran agent, "if you allow any other person in your shop to get a prominent story, they can outshine you. In that sense, Katie became like Barbara Walters and Diane Sawyer: she was in a position to kill anyone else on her show, including Bryant, from getting the big story."

Jane Pauley agreed.

"In the Bryant-Jane combination," she said, speaking of herself in the third person, "Bryant had the electricity. In the Bryant-Katie team, she has more. . . . He seems more mellow these days, doesn't he?"

When Katie heard what Jane Pauley said, she couldn't resist adding sarcastically: "After the show, Bryant goes into his office, turns on his music, and lights his incense. At night I think he plays golf in the dark."

During 1992, while Bryant nursed his wounds, Katie scored a number of big gets in which she displayed her interviewer's chops.

To Chrysler Chairman Lee Iacocca, Katie said, "You can get [your cars] into the market, you can have the product there. But can you make people buy them?"

To former Ku Klux Klansman David Duke: "What makes you think you're qualified to be president?"

To Republican presidential hopeful Pat Buchanan: "Are you trying to drive the president crazy? Or are you just on a big ego trip?"

To political consultant Ed Rollins: "When it comes to [your former client] Michael Huffington, you basically say, 'There was no *there* there.' If there was no *there* there, why were *you* there?"

Katie made her biggest splash in October. While conducting a live TV tour of the White House with Barbara Bush, the president suddenly appeared—unscripted and unannounced—with Ranger, his springer spaniel, on a leash.

"Ranger and I want equal time," President Bush joked.

He was probably "figuring on a few seconds of genial banter," *Time* magazine reported. "But Couric figured differently. For nineteen minutes, she grilled him with unscripted questions on topics from his tax policy to the Iran-Contra scandal. When the interrogation paused, Bush seemed frazzled."

Executives at NBC headquarters in New York were over the moon. No one—not even Tom Brokaw—had ever gotten nineteen unscheduled minutes with the president of the United States. More than ever, Katie was the toast of the network.

"It was like being in an Olympic race," she said of the interview. "And afterwards I walked around like a zombie for two hours. It wasn't a moment I relished, but looking back, I think it's a moment I was proud of."

Several months later, however, Matea Gold of the *Los Angeles Times* uncovered quite a different story about Katie's "spontaneous" interview with George H. W. Bush. While Katie was in the White House grilling the president, Jeff Zucker was outside in a satellite truck parked in the White House driveway.

"[Zucker] shouted questions into her earpiece," reported Gold, "helping [Katie] turn the chance encounter into a newsmaker interview."

"JEFF WAS ALWAYS in Katie's ear," said an NBC insider, referring to the earpiece that connected Katie to the voice (and, in many ways, the brain) of her trusted executive producer. "She never wanted to make a mistake."

Though some people snickered at the Svengali-Trilby relationship between Jeff and Katie, it worked brilliantly. By early 1993, *The Today Show* had not only recovered its sea legs; it was in a dead heat with *Good Morning America*. That February, Bob Wright rewarded Jeff Zucker by making him the executive producer of *Nightly News with Tom Brokaw*. And, in an unprecedented move, Wright allowed Zucker to keep his day job at *Today*.

"Does [Jeff] have the energy, stamina, and organizational skills to handle both?" said Michael Gartner, toeing the NBC corporate line. "Absolutely."

Less than a month later, the hapless Gartner was fired, forced to take the fall for a *Dateline* scandal involving the use of simulated explosions to discredit GM trucks. Following the exploding-truck fiasco, there was talk that GE's Jack Welch was so upset over the embarrassment to his company that he was thinking of selling NBC. In an effort to save the network, Bob Wright reached out beyond the ranks of NBC to a veteran CBS producer, Andrew Lack, to replace the unpopular Gartner.

As news president, Andy Lack brought a brash, aggressive energy to NBC. His role model was Roone Arledge, who wielded unchallenged power at ABC News. Given a free hand by Bob Wright, Lack immediately took Jeff Zucker off *Nightly News* and *The Today Show*, and made him the executive producer of *Now*, a newsmagazine coanchored by Tom Brokaw and Katie Couric. When that seemed to throw Katie off stride at *The Today Show*, Lack didn't hesitate to move Zucker back to *Today*.

Both Lack and Zucker had their eye on Bob Wright's job. But Lack didn't let his ambition overwhelm his judgment. He encouraged the creative partnership between Zucker and Katie Couric. In an interview with the author of this book, Lack described himself as "a huge Katie fan."

"She's a super-talent," he said. "Very few people in my years in TV have her range, her depth of skills, her work ethic, flexibility, curiosity, spontaneity, and her seriousness of purpose. Listen, Don Hewitt started offering Katie jobs on *60 Minutes* the day she appeared on *The Today Show*. She was—and is—the most talented person in the news business."

Under Lack's leadership, Katie changed the very nature of morning television.

"Katie broke the mold in terms of what it meant to be an anchor on a morning show," said the respected media analyst Andrew Tyndall. "Until Katie came along, all previous anchors conformed to sexual stereotypes as to the division of labor. The man did the hard news and sports, and the woman did the women's sphere—child rearing, clothes, and food. Katie smashed those stereotypes. She and Bryant shared everything. They were a unisex anchor team. She was the first modern woman on morning TV."

Katie was such a hot property, in fact, that rumors began circulating that she was going to replace Tom Brokaw as the anchor of *Nightly News*.

"There's nothing to the story," insisted Jeff Zucker. "It wouldn't utilize her skills to the best. But I don't think she's going to stay on *The Today Show* forever."

* * *

ZUCKER WAS IN a position to know, for he and Katie had quietly begun to explore their opportunities beyond the traditional confines of *Today* and *Nightly News*.

Their interest was piqued by a conversation that Katie had had with late-night talk show host David Letterman, who was represented by Michael Ovitz, the Hollywood super-agent. Ovitz and his friend CBS Broadcast Group President Howard Stringer had recently engineered Letterman's move from NBC to CBS.

Stringer was on the prowl for talent. He had wanted Letterman so much that he sent him "a special videotape of CBS correspondent Connie Chung, for whom Dave has jokingly lusted for years," *People* magazine reported. "In a low voice, [Connie] vowed that if Letterman signed with CBS, whenever she made love with her husband, talk-show host Maury Povich, she would moan, 'Oh, Dave! Oh . . . Dave!'"

In the end, Ovitz and Stringer agreed on a precedent-shattering deal: CBS would pay Letterman $42 million over three years, cede ownership of *The Late Show with David Letterman* to Dave's production company, Worldwide Pants, and guarantee Dave the opportunity to produce a follow-up program at 12:30 A.M.

Fascinated by the Letterman deal, Katie and Zucker met with Ovitz several times to discuss their options as a producer-anchor team. None of the principals—Katie, Jeff, or Mike Ovitz—would comment on these meetings. But according to a source who was familiar with the talks, Katie and Jeff sought Ovitz's advice on whether they could do better—both creatively and financially—at another network or in syndication. At one point, Ovitz took Katie to a meeting with Howard Stringer, who charmed her with his wit and sophistication.

"Ovitz gave Katie some very sage advice," this source said, "but the sticking point was her husband. Jay Monahan inserted himself into the discussions, and started to basically second-guess everything that Ovitz was doing. Jay fancied himself as knowing a lot about everything, and it became clear that he thought he knew more about deal making than Ovitz.

"By then," the source continued, "Jay was ready to give up his job in Washington, move to New York, and take a bigger role in raising their daughter Ellie. He had a lot of time on his hands, and was playing the role of an agent, trying to change Katie's image outside the morning-show sphere. He was a very difficult husband to deal with."

Chapter Eleven

"Ego, Ego, Ego"

On a frosty October morning in 1993, Jay Monahan put on a Confederate uniform, mounted his horse, and rode off into battle shouting the Rebel Yell: *"Who-who-ey! Who-ey! Who-who-ey! who-ey!"*

He was participating in a reenactment of the Battle of Cedar Creek—a crushing defeat for the Confederacy in the waning days of the Civil War. Riding alongside Jay on the cavalry charge was his friend and Civil War mentor Todd Kern.

"Jay was head of the Stonewall Brigade Foundation in the Shenandoah Valley," Kern explained. "He kept his horses at my stables in Winchester, Virginia, and was a pretty good rider. When people like Jay portrayed the South as anything but a bunch of ignorant slavers, some called it a racist thing. But it wasn't. Through our interpretive activities, Jay and I helped preserve some important Civil War battlefields from being developed for housing and industrial parks."

As Jay Monahan and Todd Kern dashed across the open field toward the booming Union cannons, dozens of spectators watched from the sidelines. Among the shivering crowd was Mrs. John Paul Monahan III, aka Katie Couric.

Katie could be excused if her mind was on something other than the re-creation of a 129-year-old battle. She had recently signed a five-year contract with NBC that made her co-anchor with Tom Brokaw on the primetime newsmagazine show called *Now*. Between her responsibilities to the new program and her ongoing duties on *The Today Show*, Katie no longer had time to commute on weekends to Virginia to visit Jay. In fact, she barely had time to show up for his Civil War reenactments like the one that day.

The mounting demands of Katie's career posed a serious dilemma for Jay. If he stayed in Washington and continued his trial work with Williams & Connolly, he would see even less of his wife and daughter than he had up to now. On the other hand, if he moved to New York to be with his family, he would forfeit a lucrative legal career and cut himself off from the Civil War battlefields and his preservation work in the Shenandoah Valley.

Ultimately, Jay settled for an unsatisfactory compromise. He and Katie purchased an old tobacco farm in Middletown, Virginia, as a weekend retreat where Jay could pursue his Civil War interests. In return, Jay resigned from Williams & Connolly. One month after the launch of *Now*, Katie's new primetime show, Jay moved into his family's four-bedroom Manhattan apartment overlooking Central Park.

The move entailed a significant loss of status and income for Jay. It also meant that he had to abandon his dream of someday running for political office in Virginia. While he hunted for a job in New York, he began writing a history of the Shenandoah Valley, a project he would never complete. Eventually, he landed a position in the Manhattan office of Hunton & Williams, a large law firm headquartered in Richmond, Virginia.

To decorate their Central Park West apartment, Katie worked with Mary Gilliatt, an interior designer and contributing editor of *Ladies' Home Journal*. The living room was done in Katie's favorite blue-and-white color scheme and had a floral area rug. A photo Katie had seen in a decorating book inspired the textured, blue-washed walls in the dining room. And the master bedroom had a wicker sleigh bed and pale salmon wallpaper with a green paper border.

Jay displayed his collection of Civil War artifacts, including several rare bugles. Neighbors could hear him practicing bugle calls early in

the morning. After breakfast, he would leave the apartment and walk
a few blocks to the Claremont Riding Academy.

"He used to come in early—six-thirty or seven o'clock in the
morning—and I would give him private lessons," said Karen Feldgus, a senior riding instructor at Claremont. "He wanted to learn to
ride better, so that he could participate in mounted Civil War reenactments. He used to walk the streets with his riding helmet on, so when
he came in, he was already dressed. I asked him why he chose the
Confederate side. I thought he was a slave to fashion, because the Confederate uniforms were more beautiful than the Union uniforms."

THE MOVE TO New York seemed to knock some of the stuffing out of
Jay. It was nearly impossible to maintain his own identity in a city
where his wife was a huge celebrity and he was "Mr. Katie Couric."
Not only did he find it personally demeaning; it created a huge strain
on their marriage.

As usual, it was Katie who came up with a solution to their problem. In the past, Jay had enjoyed making guest appearances on Court
TV, where an old friend, Jack Ford, anchored a show. Why not look
in to television again? Katie asked. After all, Jay was handsome and
articulate, and he seemed comfortable in front of a TV camera. To
make her point, Katie enlarged a photo of Jay's face and pasted it on
the TV screens in their apartment.

"See how great you look on TV," she said when Jay came home.
"Spend some time with me, kiddo, and I'll make you a star."

Several months later, Katie bumped into Jack Ford at the NBC studios at Rockefeller Center. By then, Ford had left Court TV and
joined NBC News as its chief legal correspondent and cohost of *The
Weekend Today Show*. Katie asked Jack if there was more he could do
to help Jay with a career as a TV legal analyst.

"After I switched over to NBC News," Jack Ford said, "MSNBC
got started, and I was hosting a show covering the O. J. Simpson trial.
And I asked Jay to cover the trial with me. Eventually, he ended up

doing a lot of TV stuff on both MSNBC and CNBC. He did a mar-velous job explaining things to a general public. And he enjoyed it."

OF COURSE, JAY couldn't hope to compete with Katie. Few men could. Television news—once the exclusive province of serious male journalists—now depended on attractive women to drive ratings and advertising.

"While television has been as male-dominated as any other big business, it's women who are leading the charge to Nielsen Nirvana," Lloyd Grove wrote in the August 1994 issue of *Vanity Fair*. "These female superanchors, with their multimillion-dollar salaries and high Q ratings, are phoning, writing, and sometimes showing up on doorsteps in order to book the great 'get'—newsmagazine shorthand for the big exclusive with headliners ranging from master spy to can-nibal murderer to tragic tennis prodigy. . . . For tens of millions of newsmag viewers (60 percent of whom are women), tuning in pro-vides the guilty pleasure of video rubbernecking."*

There were seven newsmagazines on the networks' primetime sched-ules, and three more in the works. These programs were cheap to pro-duce and comfortably profitable, which made them attractive to the cost-conscious executives who ran the networks. Bob Wright, the NBC president, was particularly pleased with the performance of Guy Pepper, Katie's old boyfriend, who had developed the creative design, national branding, and business plan for the launch of *Dateline NBC*. Such shows, said Wright, would be "our main area of focus over the next few years."

In this world of infotainment, where show-biz values trumped hard news, female stars were the dominant force. First among the super-anchors was Barbara Walters, the doyenne of ABC's *20/20*, who was considered to be in a category of her own, without peer. But close behind Barbara Walters in the down-and-dirty scrimmage for the big

* Q scores are calculated twice a year by the firm Marketing Evaluations. They measure the public's familiarity with—and positive feelings about—a personality.

get were two youthful contenders, who were quickly emerging as archrivals: Katie Couric and Diane Sawyer.

The confrontation between Katie and Diane would become one of the longest-running rivalries in television news. It began in earnest when Andrew Lack, who had replaced Michael Gartner as the president of NBC News, tried to woo Diane Sawyer away from ABC's Roone Arledge. Lack offered her several million dollars a year and the chance to anchor her own primetime newscast four or five nights a week.

During Andy Lack's public courtship of Diane Sawyer, Katie bit her tongue and maintained an outward composure. When asked for a comment by a reporter, Katie said she would welcome Diane to NBC with open arms. Of course, no one believed her for an instant. Diane's arrival at NBC would almost certainly have meant the cancellation of Katie's ratings-challenged show, *Now*. Perhaps even more important, in a medium that depended so heavily on surface impressions, Katie would have been eclipsed by the far more glamorous Diane.

In the end, Diane chose to stay at ABC and use the marathon negotiations as a lever to pry more money out of Roone Arledge. But as Gail Shister, the TV critic of the *Philadelphia Inquirer*, put it: "NBC's loss in the Diane Sawyer Sweepstakes is . . . Katie Couric's gain."

Indeed, Katie demanded that her contract—on which the ink was barely dry—be shredded, and that NBC draw up a new one to take into account the perks offered by Andy Lack to Diane Sawyer. NBC had no choice but to meet Katie's demands.

"It's probably NBC's way of saying, 'We were very interested in Diane, but we appreciate you as well,'" Katie said. "It doesn't have to be an either-or thing."

The Diane Sawyer episode, which left Katie feeling bruised, marked one of several turning points in her career. She no longer felt she could place her trust in the people who ran NBC and who were supposed to guide her career. The only person she could count on was Jeff Zucker. Otherwise, she was on her own. From now on, she would behave as though she knew better than anyone what was right for her.

* * *

IT WAS ABOUT this time that people began to notice a change in Katie's personality. When they tried to put it in words, they fell back on such phrases as "less relaxed," "carried away with herself," and "high-handed." Mary Ford, one of Katie's oldest friends, noticed the same things.

"Katie became a star," she said, "and a lot of responsibilities go with being a star. Katie didn't have time for everybody, only a close circle of friends. She stopped carrying a purse. She had people pay for her when she went into a store. She wanted her assistants to do everything. She wasn't Katie anymore. She became a personality.

"I remember having dinner with Katie and her husband, Jay," Mary Ford continued. "Peter, my husband, is a TV news guy, and he and Katie were talking about their work. They were incredibly self-centered individuals. For instance, one of them would say to the other, 'Did you notice when I dropped the pencil on air?' Or, the other would say, 'How about where my elbow was on the desk. What did you think of that?' It was all about the appearances, not the substance. And that was a thread that would continue to wind through Katie's career."

"She became more demanding and self-absorbed," said a producer who worked closely with Katie on *The Today Show*. "She was surrounded by people who told her how great she was. Money and success changed her."

But money and success didn't bring Katie much contentment. No matter how high her Nielsen ratings, she never felt satisfied with her own performance. She could always do better. In a strange twist of psychology, success only seemed to make her more insecure, and her insecurity only made her more competitive and passionate about beating rivals such as Diane Sawyer at the other networks.

KATIE'S BEHAVIOR AT work seemed to be affecting her relationship at home with Jay. Some of their friends noticed that Katie was constantly challenging her husband to work harder, to strive to become more famous. They sensed that Katie's goading irritated Jay and made him feel that she was a nag.

Even when Katie and Jay went on vacation and played what was supposed to be a friendly game of tennis, she acted as though her life depended on winning.

"You would think it was the finals of Wimbledon, Katie was so intense," Jay said.

"Jay beat me and I got so aggravated at losing that I gave him the cold shoulder for three hours," Katie confessed. "Jay refused to play tennis with me again."

Katie even competed with Jay over his O. J. Simpson trial commentary on MSNBC.

"Jay and I got into a cab and the driver started looking at us," Katie said. "I expected him to recognize me from *The Today Show*. But he recognized Jay instead and asked him a question about the Simpson trial. I remember saying, 'Hey, what am I, chopped liver?'"

IN THE FACE of this constant badgering from his wife, Jay began to change, too. In the past, when Katie threw her clothes on the floor, or drank milk straight from the carton, or left a bowl of half-eaten breakfast cereal on their bed, Jay didn't complain. Her messiness hadn't bothered him; in fact, he had found it to be part of her girlish charm. Now, however, Katie's slovenly behavior got under Jay's skin.

"Katie was always a bit of a slob and would even wear her underpants inside out when she ran out of clean pairs," said someone who was frequently in her apartment, but was obviously not a true friend. "When Jay gave her a hard time about her sloppiness, she laughed it off."

But Jay no longer found it a laughing matter. He was bursting with resentment and needed someone who would listen to him vent. Unwisely, he chose to complain about his wife to their $700-a-week nanny, Nancy Poznek.

Nancy Poznek had been nannying for thirty years and had worked for such celebrities as Diana Ross and Mick Jagger. But in some ways, her role in the Monahan household was unique. In addition to looking after three-year-old Ellie (who was known as Peepeye after Popeye's nephew), Poznek served as a gal Friday to Katie. She arranged

Katie's closet, took her clothes to the cleaners, balanced her checkbook, and tried to keep her on schedule.

"[Katie] needs more care than the baby," Poznek joked. "The baby is pretty neat, but when the phone rings, Katie gets distracted, and all the toys are left on the floor. It looks like a tornado."

As Katie became increasingly dependent on Nancy Poznek, she treated her more as a confidante than as a nanny. When *People* magazine ran a reader's letter questioning Katie's qualifications as a mother, she viewed it as an attack that could harm her image in the eyes of millions of TV viewers. Katie drafted a letter for Poznek to sign and sent it to *People* as a rebuttal.

"As Ellie's nanny since she was a newborn," the letter said, "I can say without hesitation that Katie is there for her daughter at the important and not-so-important times in her daily life: taking her to dance class, being up at night, daily playground visits, mealtime, watching *Barney,* tantrums, and quiet time."

Katie left little notes for Nancy around the house, and signed them "XOX Katie." She wrote Nancy to thank her for "being my friend." One holiday season, when Nancy informed Katie that she couldn't have Thanksgiving and Christmas with the Monahans, Katie begged her to reconsider, because Nancy was a member of the family, and "families are together on holidays."

In response to this treatment from her employer, Nancy Poznek began to display an inflated sense of self-importance. She saw herself as indispensable. She came to believe that her role was to protect Katie not only from outsiders, but even from Jay.

Nancy began to badmouth Jay, telling Katie the things that Jay had said about her behind her back. When Katie confronted Jay with these hurtful things, he exploded in rage against Nancy. He refused to have someone in his house who poisoned his relationship with his wife. Nancy had to go. That's all there was to it.

Nancy said she would resign.

Katie was beside herself. How could little Ellie possibly get along without her beloved nanny? The child would be devastated. It would leave a lasting scar on her psyche.

Katie sat down and wrote Nancy Poznek a remarkable letter, calling her a "wonderful person" and "a real pleasure to live with," and describing her husband in less-than-flattering terms.

> *Yes, Nancy, Jay can be very difficult. If he's had periodic episodes of obnoxious, selfish behavior, I think it's a deviation. My success has been hard on him. To have this be a workable situation, Jay will try to control his temper and his anger.*
>
> *I will be so so so sad if you leave. I love you like a sister, Ellie adores you,*
> *Love,*
> *Katie*

This letter, which Katie wrote in July 1994, seemed to paper over her problems with Nancy Poznek. But the truce between Nancy and Jay proved to be short-lived. Within a month, they were again at each other's throats, and by the end of August, Nancy was gone—"fired for cause."

In retaliation, Nancy Poznek sold her story to the supermarket tabloid *Star*, in which she dished the dirt on her former employers. Among her milder charges: "Whenever we'd eat out, people would always come up to our table to talk to Katie. Jay and I would just be ignored. Jay would lean over to me and whisper: 'Ego, ego, ego.'"

Chapter Twelve

Coming of Age

For MILLIONS OF AMERICANS, THE HEART OF *THE TODAY SHOW* was its streetside studio in Rockefeller Center. There, crowds of tourists gathered every morning in front of Studio 1A's glass-enclosed fishbowl set to observe Bryant Gumbel and Katie Couric grill book authors and other famous guests. At the same time, the TV audience at home watched the tourists outside the bulletproof windows mugging for the cameras.

It was a daily happening on the streets of New York—a tourist attraction that rivaled the Statue of Liberty in popularity. It was also a reminder of *The Today Show*'s beginnings, when the program was still part of the Entertainment Division rather than the News Division, and Dave Garroway, the show's original host, performed in front of a window with a diaper-wearing chimpanzee named J. Fred Muggs.

By 1996, *The Today Show* had been on the air for forty-four years, but neither the tourists in Rockefeller Center nor the TV viewers at home had ever seen the true heart of the show. That was hidden deep within the control room, where a bald little man sat in the flickering light from a bank of television screens, his necktie thrown over his left shoulder to get it out of the way, and choreographed the two-hour program with all the precision of a ballet master.

That man, Jeff Zucker, had become a legend among his colleagues in television. Perhaps Zucker's most important talent was the skill with which he molded the show to match the minute-by-minute changes in its demographics. From seven o'clock to seven-thirty, the audience was composed of many professional people, a majority of them male, and Zucker went heavy on news and analysis. Then, between seven-thirty and eight-thirty, after the breadwinners had left home, and the male viewing audience fell off sharply, Zucker softened the show by highlighting homemaking features.

In the last half hour—8:30 to 9:00 A.M.—"practically the only people still watching [were] old enough to be . . . Katie's parents," noted *Newsweek*, and Zucker emphasized "health-oriented pieces on heart attacks, memory and staying 'forever young.'"

"Really we are programming to our flock," said Zucker. "And the way we have to think about it is: Who is watching when? Its news, sports, entertainment, politics, popular culture, lifestyle, all in one two-hour block. The beauty of *The Today Show* is that it's a microcosm of television and life."

The success of *The Today Show*, which had finally pulled ahead of *Good Morning America* in the ratings' race, was also due to Zucker's talent for exploiting his stellar repertory company—Bryant Gumbel, Katie Couric, weatherman Willard Scott, and newsreader Matt Lauer. But there were other factors as well. Chief among them was a monumental public-relations blunder committed by *The Today Show*'s chief competitor, *Good Morning America*. When that show's cohost, Joan Lunden, started dating Kevin Costner and hanging out with celebrities, viewers felt she had gotten too big for her britches. And once Joan Lunden lost the loyalty of her housewife fan base, *GMA* had a hard time recovering it.

TODAY's SURGE IN ratings and advertising revenues made Jeff Zucker a favorite of GE chairman Jack Welch and NBC president Bob Wright, who heaped praise and money on their wunderkind. They also counted on Zucker and his boss, NBC News President Andy Lack, to carry out a new strategic plan, dubbed "news convergence," to counter the challenge from CNN and other cable outlets.

Welch and Wright wanted to lighten up *Nightly News* with more tabloidlike features and harden *Today* with more solid news, especially in its first half hour. This "convergence" of news menus would allow NBC News to make more frequent use of its far-flung correspondents and amortize their salaries over several shows and timeframes—*Today, Nightly News*, and primetime news magazines like *Dateline NBC*. The ultimate goal was to accustom TV viewers to turn to NBC, rather than to cable, in times of high-intensity news.

As far as Andy Lack and Jeff Zucker were concerned, Katie Couric embodied everything that Jack Welch and Bob Wright dreamed of when they talked about the power of convergence. Katie could do it all—hard and soft, tough and tender, somber and silly—and she could do it with a panache that was unmatched by any other television personality.

"Being a morning anchor is the hardest job on TV," remarked Andrew Tyndall, whose *Tyndall Report* monitors television news. "It requires wearing a multitude of hats. One, a hard-news hat, which shows assertiveness and self-confidence. Two, a human-interest hat, which shows empathy. Three, a celebrity-interview hat, which shows that you have the sizzle and heat to cover glamorous subjects. And four, a household-features hat, which shows that you can make fun of yourself.

"These attributes are mutually contradictory," Tyndall continued, "but Katie's skill is such that she can shift from one register to the next seamlessly and authentically. Nobody has ever been able to do four out of four in the morning except Katie."

Katie instinctively knew how to strike the perfect emotional note. For instance, during a touchy-feely interview with Diane Keaton about her role in the movie *Marvin's Room,* Katie began to cry—and Jeff Zucker made sure that the camera grabbed a close-up of every one of those tears as they streamed down her cheeks.

With Republican presidential candidate Bob Dole, on the other hand, Katie morphed into a relentless inquisitor on the subjects of Dole's acceptance of campaign contributions from the tobacco industry and his absurd claim that nicotine was not addictive.

The Dole interview, which exposed the Republican candidate as an angry, mean-spirited man, was one of the many defining moments in Katie's career. Once and for all, it established her credentials as a hard-news journalist—as tough as the toughest men around.

To HER MANY fans, Katie appeared to be living proof that a modern woman could have everything—a fulfilling career, tons of money, a happy marriage, and a beautiful, healthy child. She had achieved this reputation for perfection through the careful cultivation of her image. But there was a painful disconnect in Katie's life between appearances and reality.

For starters, the relationship between Katie and Bryant Gumbel had become poisonous. They were sniping at each other off camera and undercutting each other on the air. Alarmed, Andy Lack, the news president, and Jeff Zucker, the executive producer, tried to convince Bryant to treat Katie as an equal.

"But Bryant wanted to steer the car," said a high-ranking NBC executive. "He wouldn't share the steering wheel with Katie. He was stuck in doing the show the way he had done it fifteen years ago. We couldn't get him past that. He insisted on selecting stories that were stale, that were born out of the same sensibility of years past, and that were repetitive. He wanted to do more sports rather than less. There was too much chitchat about his golf games and locker room talk. We couldn't get him to do a show that was a little more balanced and growing in a new direction. Jeff [Zucker] felt that Katie could grow without Bryant.

"And so, Bryant left us no choice," this source continued. "We told Bryant that we were not going to renew his contract. We decided to let Bryant Gumbel go because we came to the conclusion that *Today* couldn't grow with him."

Bryant had always been interested in doing a Sunday political program like *Face the Nation* or *Meet the Press*, or a *Nightline* type of show. Once again, he turned to Roone Arledge to discuss opportunities at ABC. But Arledge had nothing for him.

As much as Katie secretly wanted Bryant to go, she also feared that his departure might destabilize *The Today Show* and provide an opening for *Good Morning America* to regain its ratings dominance. But Jeff Zucker convinced her that she could make it without Bryant.

KATIE'S PROBLEMS WITH her husband were not so easily solved. She and Jay had grown so far apart that he frequently felt the need to vent about his wife to friends.

"He loathed her," reported a friend who was included in one of Jay's I-hate-Katie sessions.

However, others pointed out that it was impossible to know whether Jay truly hated Katie or was just letting off steam.

Perhaps in an effort to save her marriage, Katie got pregnant again, and on January 5, 1996—two days before her thirty-ninth birthday—she gave birth to a second daughter, Caroline Couric Monahan.

Katie lived by her mother's motto: "Let them know you're here!" From childhood, she had been determined to control events, rather than allow events to control her. So in addition to having a second child to help prop up her marriage, she bought a third home, this one in Dutchess County, about an hour-and-a-half's drive north of New York City, where she tried to establish a weekend refuge for her family.

And then, just when she thought she had a handle on her problems, things completely fell apart. In October 1996, Jeff Zucker was diagnosed with colon cancer.

"I got everything at an early age and I got that too," Zucker said.

He was thirty-one years old.

ZUCKER HAD SUSPECTED something was wrong.

Shortly after he married Caryn Nathanson, a producer on *Saturday Night Live*, he began experiencing a tingling sensation in his abdomen. His doctors discovered that he had a walnut-sized tumor in his colon.

"I had never thought about death or anything like that," Zucker said. "I felt worse for Caryn. I felt terribly for her."

When he came out of surgery, his wife was by his side.

"Am I okay?" he asked.

"They got it all," Caryn said.

But they hadn't. A few days later, his doctors informed Zucker that the cancer had spread to his lymph nodes. For the next seven months, he went for weekly chemotherapy treatments at Memorial Sloan-Kettering Hospital.

"He's sort of been to hell and back," Katie said.

Zucker's absence from Studio 1A's control room marked the first time that Katie had done a broadcast on *The Today Show* without her trusted producer. Zucker was no longer there to speak into her earpiece and provide her with questions for an interview. Nor was he around to give her an honest postmortem about what she had done right or wrong.

But to Katie's surprise, Jeff's absence turned out to be a blessing in disguise. Though neither of them was probably aware of it, their relationship had become as much a rivalry as a partnership, with each one jockeying to get credit for *The Today Show*'s success.

"Without her Svengali," said a *Today Show* producer, "Katie's confidence swelled. For the first time, she realized she could do the show without Jeff. Without the boy genius in the control room pulling the levers, she started acting like it was *her* show, not his. Katie came of age when Jeff had cancer. *She had the juice.*"

WITH NBC REFUSING to renew his contract, Bryant Gumbel set Friday, January 2, 1997, as his last day as cohost of *Today*. To mark the occasion, Katie read a farewell poem titled "Ode to Bryant."

> *Perspicacious, pugnacious, persistent and proud;*
> *You may not be a smoocher, but you sure can work a crowd . . .*
> *You're a hard nut to crack, but inside you're like butter.*
> *You can be a sweetheart, and an annoying brother.*

Bryant was not amused. In fact, when they were off camera, he told Katie that he found her "Ode" a "cheap-shot poem" that was meant to embarrass him. Not long after that, the true story of their toxic relationship started appearing in the media.

Katie fired the first shot. She told *USA Today* that she and Bryant "were never really close. There was a lot of creative tension. Well, there was tension. I don't know how creative it was."

Bryant returned the fire.

"We worked together—period," he said. "That isn't to say we didn't get along. But was she as close to me as Matt Lauer? No. I don't think that I would characterize Katie as being close to anybody over there."

Asked by a reporter how she felt about Bryant's departure, Katie didn't pull any punches.

"I feel like it's more my candy store," she said. "Bryant opened up every show. He threw to commercials. Basically, Bryant always spoke first. The things I'm talking about are primarily cosmetic. But they are symbolic in terms of the position of the anchors on the show. I think his philosophy was that somebody had to guide the ship. But I saw things a bit differently."

Later, in an interview with a writer for *The New York Times Magazine*, Bryant unleashed a blistering personal attack against Katie. Defending himself against criticism that he was hard to work with, Bryant said: "I've had one assistant for years. Somebody who shall remain nameless went through five in five years. I had one makeup and hair person the whole time I was at NBC. Somebody who shall remain nameless went through three or four."

THOUGH KATIE WAS now the show's top banana, she was given remarkably little say in the choice of Bryant's replacement. Jack Welch and Bob Wright made that decision at the very top. In their view, there was no contest. Matt Lauer, the show's newsreader, had a lock on the job.

Over the years, Matt had impressed Welch and Wright with his charm and humor. He dated the prettiest women (Elle Macpherson and Willow Bay, among others), read the trendiest books, told the latest jokes, and made himself the center of attention at NBC gatherings. Moreover, he and Bryant were best friends and frequently played golf with Welch and Wright. Those hours spent on the golf course paid off for Matt when it came time to pick a cohost for Katie.

Matt would not have been Katie's first choice.

"The truth of the matter was that Matt looked up to Bryant, and Bryant hated Katie," said one of Matt's former girlfriends who, out of whatever motive, didn't have a good word to say about Katie. "Matt told me that the staff hated her. She terrorized them, calling them at three o'clock in the morning. At a Christmas party at Bryant's house in South Salem [New York], Katie wasn't even invited. Nobody socialized with her. And when Matt filled in for Bryant, he and Katie hardly spoke to each other."

Katie lost no time in putting Matt in his place. He was given the secondary role on the show, the one that had traditionally been occupied by such *Today* "girls" as Barbara Walters, Jane Pauley, Deborah Norville, and Katie herself.

"Katie was a bit of a bully with Matt," said an NBC cameraman who worked with them on the road. "One time, Matt was in Hong Kong about to deliver a stand-up in front of fireworks. Katie was interviewing Condoleezza Rice, and she knew full well that the producers were going to Hong Kong for the fireworks. But by the time she got through with her questions, it was too late. The shot had to be killed. And Matt was seething mad."

ON APRIL 7, 1997—three months after Matt joined *The Today Show*—the program originated from Las Vegas, where the National Association of Broadcasters was holding its annual convention.

"There are people in the casinos here at seven in the morning when we walk through," Matt said on the air. "Hey, but we're here for a very good reason. We're being honored, kind of."

"We are," Katie said. "Actually the program is being honored. We are being honored by a big convention in town. The National Association of Broadcasters is inducting this very program into its Hall of Fame."

Katie did not mention the fact that her father had once worked as PR director of the National Association of Broadcasters. After the show, one of her father's old friends, Dawson "Tack" Nail of *Communications Daily*, buttonholed her in the Las Vegas Hilton.

"Gee, Katie," he said, "I thought your daddy would come to Las Vegas for your induction into the NAB Hall of Fame."

"No," Katie replied, "he's still so bitter about being fired by the NAB that he refused to show up even for me."

Like Katie, John Couric kept the hurts.

Chapter Thirteen

No "Woe Is Me"

THE FIRST INKLING JAY MONAHAN HAD THAT SOMETHING WAS terribly wrong came in January 1997. While covering the O. J. Simpson civil trial as a legal analyst for MSNBC, he noticed that he was tired and achy all the time. What's more, no matter how much he ate, he kept losing weight.

He chalked up his exhaustion to a punishing work schedule, which required him to travel back and forth between his home in New York and California, where the Simpson trial was being held. He just needed some rest, that was all.

However, even after the trial ended, his troubling symptoms persisted. Still, he didn't give it much thought.

In March, MSNBC sent him to cover another trial, this one of Timothy McVeigh, who had masterminded the bombing of the Alfred P. Murrah Federal Building in Oklahoma City, the deadliest act of terrorism in U.S. history up until then.

"I remember at one point, Jay and I were sitting on our live set outside the courthouse [in Denver]," recalled Jack Ford, who anchored the coverage for MSNBC. "And I looked at Jay and said, 'Are you feeling okay?' And he said, 'You know, I'm feeling crummy. I think I'll see a doctor when I get home.'"

But when he returned to New York, Jay forgot to make the

appointment. He had other things on his mind. His marriage to Katie appeared to be on the rocks. According to several people interviewed by the author of this book, Katie acted as though she had fallen out of love with Jay. She was snappish and high-handed, and made Jay feel as though he wasn't good enough for her.

It is, of course, impossible for anyone to know what really goes on inside someone else's marriage. Be that as it may, Jay's friends and colleagues said that, rightly or wrongly, he had come to believe the only thing that stood between Katie and divorce was her fear of negative publicity.

JAY FELT THAT Katie looked askance at his TV gig on CNBC's *Rivera Live*, because he was an *unpaid* guest on that show. Money meant a great deal to Katie. As her family's main breadwinner, she always worried about keeping her job and, with it, her comfortable nest egg. So Jay started shopping around for a television agent who could get him more money.

In late April, he was scheduled to accompany Katie to a cancer benefit at which she was to speak. That afternoon, he suddenly started experiencing stomach cramps that were so severe they made him double over in pain. The babysitter called Katie at NBC to inform her that Jay was taking himself to the doctor.

"So we met at the doctor," Katie recalled during an interview with Larry King. "And [Jay] was, you know, a young, healthy, athletic guy, so he didn't really have regular checkups, which is something that everybody needs to do, no matter how young they are, how good they feel. So he came to my internist, and I remember the internist saying, 'Don't worry, it's not cancer.' And I love my doctor, he's wonderful, but he, himself, couldn't fathom this healthy forty-one-year-old man having advanced colon cancer."

Nor could Jay. He didn't have a family history of colon cancer, or any of the classic symptoms of the disease—rectal bleeding and a change in bowel habits. But after Dr. Mark Pochapin, a noted gastroenterologist at New York Hospital, examined Jay, all doubts were dispelled. Not only did Jay have colon cancer, but it was in an advanced stage, and had already spread to his other organs.

ONCE KATIE GOT over her initial shock, she had to deal with her guilt. On more than one occasion, she had confided to friends that her marriage was kaput, and that she wished Jay would just go away. Now, if Jay should die, that dreadful wish would come true.

As much as Katie might not be in love with Jay anymore, she certainly didn't want to see him suffer or die. Even a woman who no longer loved her husband could still feel compassion for him in the face of a life-threatening illness. And, of course, his death would deprive her children of their father.

In fact, after giving it some thought, Katie decided not to burden Ellie, six, and Carrie, one, with the horrifying truth about their father's medical condition. After all, Jeff Zucker had survived a bout with colon cancer, and there was always a chance, no matter how slim, that Jay would pull through, too.

If there was no need to tell her children right away, Katie couldn't keep the news of Jay's cancer a secret from the people she worked with at NBC. At first, however, she confided in only three colleagues—Jeff Zucker, Matt Lauer, and Al Roker.

Zucker's first instinct was to put out a press release explaining that Jay Monahan was battling colon cancer and that Katie Couric would be taking an extended leave of absence from *The Today Show* in order to be by her husband's side. But Katie had no intention of taking time off from work.

For one thing, Katie was about to plunge into contract negotiations with NBC, and she didn't think she could afford to be off the air during the critical May "sweeps."* In the cutthroat world of television

---

* Television advertising rates are based largely on four Nielsen ratings sweeps, or audience measurements, that take place in February, May, July, and November. The May sweeps coincide with the annual TV "upfronts" when the networks present their fall schedules and lock in millions of dollars in commercial time.

news, absence did not make the heart grow fonder; it only made the greedy men who ran the networks forget how much they owed you. For another thing, Katie's friends (and perhaps even Jay himself) thought that it would be good for her, both mentally and emotionally, to keep busy during these trying times.

Katie might have had yet a third motive for playing down Jay's condition. She had reason to fear that once the print media got wind of Jay's cancer, they would start snooping into his marriage to Katie. The story of their moribund marriage would deal a body blow to Katie's image at the very moment that Alan Berger, her agent, was trying to convince NBC that she was the Second Coming.

DESPITE HIS ILLNESS, Jay continued to work, and in late May, MSNBC sent him back to Denver to cover the closing arguments and jury verdict in the government's case against Timothy McVeigh.

"During his long and tragic illness," said his MSNBC colleague Jack Ford, "Jay and I would talk. During that time, the treatment seemed so long and drawn out, but it really was fairly quick from the time of diagnosis to surgery."

In June, just as Dr. Pochapin was ready to operate on Jay, the *Washington Post* and *Star* magazine broke the story that Katie had managed to keep secret until then. Though silence on the subject was no longer possible, Katie still insisted that NBC not disclose the exact nature of Jay's illness.

At this point, no one knew why she didn't want NBC to use the words *colon cancer*. Perhaps it was to protect her children. Whatever her reason, on June 7—the day after Jay's operation—NBC issued a brief statement that said: "Jay Monahan is taking a short medical leave from MSNBC. He is having surgery on Friday. His prognosis is excellent and he is expected to return to the legal beat in a few weeks."

There was nothing in the statement about cancer or Katie. But Jeff Zucker, whose political instincts were always sharper than most others', worried about Katie's missing name in the NBC release. That omission, he felt, would only raise suspicions about her relationship with Jay. And so, Zucker took it upon himself to add a clarification.

"Katie," he was quoted as saying in the *Washington Post,* "is going to take a few days to help Jay in his recovery."

In fact, Katie took off one week. During her absence, Ann Curry, *The Today Show*'s newsreader, sat in for her. When Katie returned on Monday, June 16, Ann and Matt welcomed her back, but neither of them mentioned the reason she had been gone.

IN THE FALL of 1997—while he was still undergoing chemotherapy treatments—Jay was invited by his friend Geraldo Rivera to appear on TV to discuss the latest twist in the JonBenet Ramsey murder case.

"We were all thrilled he was doing so well," said Geraldo. "Jay was going to be my cohost and designated substitute host on *Rivera Live.* But in November he told me the cancer had come back. It had metastasized behind his eye. He woke up one morning and couldn't see.

"He went for radiation, and his vision returned—but now there was hair loss," Geraldo continued. "Yet Jay was always optimistic, talking about the future. He never complained, there was no 'woe is me' with Jay."

In November, another friend, O. J. Simpson lawyer Barry Scheck, met Jay for lunch.

"I could tell that he was in great pain," Scheck said, "but he had terrific courage. He was talking about working."

Meanwhile, Katie did not cut back on her grueling schedule. But while Jay was lauded for his courage and fortitude, Katie was roundly criticized by many of her colleagues for what appeared to be her curious detachment toward her dying husband.

Deeply concerned by this criticism (and its potential for inflicting serious harm to Katie's reputation), her friends rallied to her defense. They sought to cast her behavior in a positive light. After all, they pointed out, Katie was in an impossible position. She had to juggle several demanding roles at the same time—mother to two young, vulnerable girls; daughter to aging, needy parents; caregiver to a dying husband; star of NBC's biggest money-making news show; and sole breadwinner of her family.

In a word, *cut her some slack*. Katie was doing her best.

But few of Katie's critics bought this argument. In fact, there seemed to be no limit to the bitterness and hatred they directed at Katie.

"Before Jay became ill, I'd heard stories about Katie's indifference to her husband," an NBC reporter said in an interview for this book. "It wasn't her finest hour when Jay got cancer. The idea that she put on a brave front and came to work was bullshit.

"In fact, she would come into the studio and say how much effort, how much trouble it was that Jay was sick," this person continued. "His illness seemed to be more of a bother than anything. I've been through my mother's pancreatic cancer, and you sit there and spell people, and you stay by the sick person's side if you really love them. Katie didn't stay with Jay."

AFTER MONTHS OF suffering, Jay became so weak that he had to be admitted to the hospital. During his stay, the hospital staff noted that Katie was an infrequent visitor.

"The doctors and nurses thought Jay was a goner," said a hospital employee. "We tried to talk to Katie about it, but she didn't want to hear. She'd come in with her daughters, and leave them at the hospital with the social worker, and go to work. The social worker took these girls through to their father's end."

In January 1998—just two weeks before Jay's death—Katie flew off to Paradise Island in the Bahamas with a group of girlfriends to celebrate her fortieth birthday. Lori Beecher, a close friend who booked Katie's interviews on *Dateline NBC*, absolved Katie of responsibility for leaving her husband as he neared the end of his life.

"It had been a difficult period," said Lori. "We decided it would be a good thing to take her away. We're fond of saying that we kidnapped her, so she had no choice in the matter."

On January 24, Jay collapsed on the bathroom floor in his apartment. He was rushed by ambulance to the hospital, where he died.

"People in the office immediately started betting on how long it would take Katie to capitalize on Jay's death," said an NBC reporter. "Some said seventy-two hours; others, just twenty-four hours."

JAY MONAHAN'S FUNERAL was held at St. Ignatius Loyola Church, an imposing stone edifice on Park Avenue where Jacqueline Kennedy Onassis's funeral took place in 1994.

Katie asked Judy Collins to sing "Battle Hymn of the Republic," the Union marching song that was performed at the funerals of Senator Robert Kennedy and Presidents Richard Nixon and Ronald Reagan. Katie's choice must have raised a few eyebrows among her husband's friends, since Jay's Civil War interests were with the Confederate, not the Union, side.

Katie wrote a eulogy and asked her older sister Emily to read it to the 1,800 assembled mourners.

"Jay was so sharp, so alive, whether he was beating contestants as he watched *Jeopardy!*, reciting the names of the characters and actors in old movies, or studying in law school to the sound track of *The Wizard of Oz*," Emily read.

"He did not go gently into that good night. He fought until the bitter end."

Chapter Fourteen

Hand-to-Hand Combat

On January 24, 1998—the very day that Jay Monahan collapsed and died—the veteran television journalist Max Robins broke a bombshell piece of news in his *TV Guide* column. He reported that Jeffrey Katzenberg, who, along with Steven Spielberg and David Geffen, ran the upstart entertainment company DreamWorks SKG, was making an all-out effort to lure Katie Couric away from *The Today Show*.

"... Katzenberg," Max Robins wrote, "is courting Couric to see if she has any interest in trying to be the next Oprah Winfrey or Rosie O'Donnell. If Couric were to succeed in the syndication market, she could easily have a payday 10 times her estimated $2 million a year wage as *Today* co-anchor."

In classic Hollywood mogul style, Katzenberg, Spielberg, and Geffen put together a lavish $100,000 video presentation just for Katie. It featured people waving signs saying We Love You, Katie, and was aimed at showing Katie the kind of glossy talk show that Dream-Works was eager to produce for her. Katie was flattered and impressed. She had long felt underpaid and underappreciated at NBC, and believed that she was worth at least as much as fellow NBC Newser Tom Brokaw and ABC's Diane Sawyer, each of whom then made $7 million a year—more than three times what Katie was earning.

"She's the heart of *Today*," said a rival network executive, "and it makes the network tens of millions. She's in her early forties, and she could easily become as big or bigger than Barbara Walters, who's making more than ten million."

By now, Katie and Barbara had established a mutual admiration society. In a conversation between the two women that took place not long after Jay's death, Katie confided to Barbara that she might be ready to leave *The Today Show* if she could find something more interesting—and lucrative—in Hollywood. In fact, said Katie, she was thinking of exploring a whole new career—as a movie star.

"What do you think?" she asked.

"I think you should call my agent, Alan Berger," Barbara said.

Alan Berger, who ran the television department for the International Creative Management talent agency in Hollywood, had negotiated Barbara Walters's contract, the richest in TV news. At Barbara's urging, Katie met with Berger, and then hired him as *her* agent.*

"Alan Berger knew that Katie was the most talented person in the news business," said a high-ranking NBC executive who participated in the contract negotiations. "There was no dispute over Katie's value. The only question was how seriously Katie wanted to pursue her Hollywood dreams versus how big a check Jack Welch and Bob Wright were willing to sign to keep her."

NBC News President Andy Lack was convinced that, in her heart of hearts, Katie did not want to go into show business. He believed that she saw herself, first and foremost, as a serious journalist, and that, handled properly, she would stay at NBC News. His major concern was that Katie might have her eye on Tom Brokaw's anchor job on *Nightly News*.

---

* Her previous agent, Robert Barnett, was a partner at Jay Monahan's old law firm, Williams & Connolly, where he represented such media biggies as Tim Russert, Sam Donaldson, Jeff Greenfield, Brit Hume, and Andrea Mitchell.

To find out, Lack invited Katie for lunch at Le Grenouille, New York's renowned French restaurant.

"What do you really want to do?" Lack asked Katie, according to someone familiar with the discussion.

"I don't know," she said coyly. "What do *you* want me to do?"

"I hope you don't want to be the next Tom Brokaw," Lack said, "because I've already promised that job to Brian Williams."

"I don't want to replace Tom," Katie replied.*

Lack returned from lunch to report to Bob Wright that negotiations with Katie should be manageable. But as things turned out, it wasn't that simple.

To begin with, Katie entered contract talks with NBC from a position of strength. The network was in a serious programming bind; it had just lost *Seinfeld*, its most important primetime franchise, and had also failed to renew its deal to broadcast National Football League games, which generated gargantuan ratings. It could hardly afford to lose Katie, too.

What's more, when NBC executives sat down at the negotiating table with Alan Berger, they discovered that his client was in no mood to compromise on her demands. A big part of Katie's problem was her hurt feelings. During her leave of absence after Jay's death, she had canceled a scheduled interview with First Lady Hillary Rodham Clinton, and the producers had given Matt Lauer the plum assignment in her stead. When Hillary accused her husband's critics of being part of "a vast right-wing conspiracy," Matt scored headlines all across America—a coup that enhanced his reputation and left Katie feeling upstaged by her junior partner.

Perhaps even more telling, Jay Monahan's untimely death had transformed Katie into an iconic figure unlike any that NBC had ever dealt with before. TV viewers no longer saw Katie merely as the

---

* That was not what Katie was telling her agent Alan Berger. Far from rejecting the idea of becoming Tom Brokaw's successor, Katie had instructed Berger to keep that option open.

lovable, perky morning host. Now she was the grieving widow, the single mother, and the symbol of suffering womankind all rolled into one. Condolence letters poured into NBC on a scale that began to rival the flood of sympathy notes for Jackie Kennedy following her husband's assassination.

On her first day back on *The Today Show*, Katie wore a somber black suit and her husband's wedding ring on a gold chain around her neck. She squeezed Matt Lauer's hand, and, with tears filling her eyes, told viewers: "Words, of course, will never describe how devastating this loss has been for me and my daughters and for all of Jay's family as well."

"Some viewers with a tougher approach to privacy thought Couric's emotional statement upon her return was excessive, unnecessary," wrote Monica Collins in the *Boston Herald*. "Why burden us? Why exploit your personal situation for ratings gain. Just give us the news and the weather. But, in the morning hours, when so much is at stake, the personal touch is not part of the act, it's the key to success."

It soon became apparent to executives at NBC that they couldn't push around a woman in widow weeds. On the other hand, nothing inhibited Katie from playing rough with NBC. In a campaign that appeared to be designed to unnerve Andy Lack, stories suddenly began appearing all over the media about Katie's negotiations.

Three weeks after she returned to the show—on March 16, 1998—*New York Magazine* ran the following item in its widely read Intelligencer gossip column:

"No sooner had Katie Couric come back to work than rumors of her imminent departure from NBC started to circulate. Couric, whose contract is up in July, is being courted by at least two syndicators, ABC and CBS, several industry insiders report."

A week later, a piece appeared in the *Globe* supermarket tabloid claiming there had been "a secret plot" at NBC to oust Katie and replace her with either Jodi Applegate or Ann Curry. The article, which many thought bore Katie's fingerprints, was an effort to cast NBC in the worst possible light.

"And now," wrote the *Globe*, "the widowed *Today Show* host may repay [NBC executives'] betrayal by accepting one of a flood of offers she's received from competitors anxious to snag the popular personality when her contract expires in July."

On June 17, 1998, the *Wall Street Journal* ran a story on its Marketing & Media page under the headline 'Today' Co-Anchor Expected to Enter TV Bidding Wars. "Ms. Couric has become a juicy target for NBC's competitors," the *Journal* reported. "CBS Corp. has said Ms. Couric could be considered for a slot on *60 Minutes*—particularly if the program is extended to a second night—while at least one studio has courted Ms. Couric for a possible syndicated TV program."

That same day, Verne Gay, *Newsday*'s TV critic, proclaimed: "And now [begins] the Battle for Katie Couric . . ."

The next day, June 18, the *New York Daily News* told its readers: "The 'Today' host is prepared to walk away from the morning show if the network doesn't increase its offer."

The unrelenting barrage of press leaks proved to be too much for NBC, and the network caved in to Katie's demands. Even then, Katie conceded nothing; she demanded the right to choose the time and venue of the announcement of her huge new contract. Her choice: *Newsweek*. In the last week of June 1998, the newsmagazine broke the story that Katie had agreed to sign a four-year contract that "puts her up there with Tom Brokaw, giving her $7 million a year and a major role in NBC's election coverage."

The *Newsweek* story was accompanied by an extraordinary interview—Katie's first since Jay's illness—in which she sought to defuse charges that she had exploited the sympathy generated by her husband's death.

"Under the circumstances, I'm very conscious of not exploiting something that's been very difficult," she told *Newsweek*. "Not sharing things that I feel are not appropriate to share with the public."

Then why did she agree to do the interview with *Newsweek*?

"I had very mixed feelings about it," said Katie. "You don't want to be celebrated because something bad happened to somebody you love.

But Jay wouldn't want what happened to him to affect me professionally. He'd want me to do it, to keep going for me and for the children."

Then, *Newsweek* and Katie had the following exchange:

Q: You were on the air just two days before your husband died. . . .

Katie: I'm not gonna go there. That's so personal, if that's okay? I'd be glad to talk about him as a person, but I don't really want to talk about his illness.

Q: Why are you worth $7 million a year?

Katie: You want me to justify my salary? I thought you might ask me about that. Because I'm one of those people who wonders about the distortion in salaries in this country—why pro-basketball players make this outrageous sum of money and teachers don't make much at all. But having said that, the network makes a lot of jack off us. My personality plays a role in the show's success, not that it would collapse if I left. But people have this strong connection to you and form these bonds with you that are almost familial. It takes a long time to win the audience's trust and affection. Maintaining that continuity I think accounts for the way I'm compensated.

KATIE HAD A point.

When she joined *The Today Show* as the junior host in the summer of 1991, it was making only a modest profit and running a poor second to *Good Morning America*. Eight years later, when she signed her $7-million-a-year contract, *The Today Show* had become *her* show—and it was generating hundreds of millions of dollars in revenue. What's more, it was so far ahead of *Good Morning America* in ratings that it looked as though Katie and Matt, along with weatherman Al Roker and newsreader Ann Curry, had a permanent lock on first place.

That, at least, was the conventional wisdom. But not everyone accepted that view. One person who didn't was Shelley Ross, a senior producer with ABC's *PrimeTime Live* and *20/20,* who saw an opportunity to cut Katie Couric down to size.

A brash dynamo of a woman, Shelley Ross had cut her journalistic teeth at *The National Enquirer* and was not at all defensive about the years she had spent in the down-market field of celebrity journalism.

"I don't call it tabloid journalism," she said; "I call it popular journalism."

At ABC, Shelley had headed the coverage of the O. J. Simpson trial. Her unit was responsible for many exclusive stories, including Diane Sawyer's interviews with Detective Mark Fuhrman and the family of the slain Nicole Brown Simpson.

In December 1998—at a time when *The Today Show* seemed impregnable—Shelley wrote a remarkable memo to David Westin, the president of ABC News, that took the unconventional view that *Today* was vulnerable. Her memo was titled "Why I Want to Leave PrimeTime Live and Do the Morning Show." In it, Shelley outlined a bold plan designed to topple *The Today Show* from its ratings perch and make *Good Morning America* number-one again.

"My vision of *GMA* builds upon the traditional two-hour format," she wrote. "I personally do not believe in a radical format change. I do believe in a new way of thinking on content and presentation. . . . One key to success is providing irresistible news and information as people begin the day. A second key to success is building an appealing TV family."

To build such a family, Shelley recommended bringing back Charlie Gibson, who had only recently left *GMA* after twelve years as host. However, Gibson did not want to be paired with the current female host, Lisa McRee.

"While flying in from the West Coast, I realized that Charlie needed a better prom date," Shelley recalled in an interview for this book. "And I thought, wouldn't Diane Sawyer be amazing. It would shake up the morning TV world.

"I called Diane from the airplane," Shelley continued. "I said to her, 'There's no reason why people have to think of you as an ice princess. I know you're funny and warm.' And in the middle of our conversation, the pilot made an announcement that we were over Kansas City. And I said, 'Diane, we're in Kansas City, Toto!'"

* * *

At first, David Westin was annoyed with Shelley Ross for propos-ing a scheme that, in his view, would unnecessarily expose one of his top stars, Diane Sawyer, to the vagaries of morning television.

"Absolutely not!" Westin told Shelley. "In the game of chess, you never expose your queen."

That sounded sharp and perceptive. But Westin talked a better game than he played. He had come up the ranks at ABC through its legal department, not news, and through inexperience and indecisive-ness, he had squandered the legacy handed down to him from Roone Arledge, who had made ABC the dominant network in news.

Westin had never developed Arledge's deft talent for handling high-maintenance news stars, and he had no idea that Diane Sawyer had grown bored with *PrimeTime Live* (which was running out of ratings steam) and was hankering for a fresh challenge. As a result, he was taken by complete surprise when Diane came to him and said that she endorsed Shelley Ross's proposal.

Diane ranked right up there with Jeff Zucker and Tim Russert as a giant of office politics. She was driven by unfathomable ambition and was not shy about going over a boss's head, if necessary, to get what she wanted.

" 'Calculated' is an adjective that is often used to put down Diane Sawyer," the author of this book wrote in a cover story on Diane that appeared in the March 13, 1989, issue of *New York Magazine.* "When TV people get together over drinks, they swap stories about her [of-fice] exploits."

One such story concerned Diane when she was still at CBS. "She began to court [*60 Minutes* honcho] Don Hewitt socially," said some-one who worked with her. "And let me tell you something, as far as Don or the rest of us knew, she was *dating* [CBS founder] Bill Paley. She'd be in a meeting and someone would stick their head in and say, 'Mr. Paley's on the phone for you.' *That* didn't hurt her chances of get-ting on *60 Minutes.*"

Now at ABC, Diane was still playing the same games. She saw an opportunity to jack up *GMA*'s ratings and become the savior of the network's news division. If she was successful, she would be in a position to ask for a lot more money—perhaps millions more than Katie Couric was making over at NBC. In addition, a dramatic success in the morning would bring Diane closer to her dream of being the leading candidate to succeed Peter Jennings when he stepped down at *World News Tonight*.

With heavyweights like Diane Sawyer and Charlie Gibson willing to host *GMA* until permanent replacements could be found, David Westin could hardly say no. He made Shelley Ross the executive producer of the show, which debuted with Diane and Charlie as its new hosts on January 18, 1999.

Within less than a month, Diane and Charlie had performed the astonishing feat of adding one million new viewers to *GMA*'s ratings. In addition, they attracted a chorus of praise from TV critics all across America. The same Tom Shales who had once described Katie Couric in his *Washington Post* column as "the everything gal" and "a godsend" now had nothing good to say about her and *The Today Show*.

"They've become awfully self-congratulatory over there [at *The Today Show*]," wrote Shales, "and each day they seem to be celebrating their success rather than doing a show."

On the other hand, said Shales, "Sawyer and Gibson are making beautiful music together."

AT FIRST, KATIE dismissed such comments as coming from clueless print journalists. The visual medium of television, unlike print, was all about presentation, packaging, and personality, and print journalists failed to appreciate how hard it was to make it in such a business—and to stay on top.

What's more, print journalists were under the illusion that they were on intimate terms with the people they watched—and critiqued—on television. But they weren't. They didn't understand the first thing about Katie Couric. They assumed that a star like Katie, who was paid a fortune of money, had a lot of power and autonomy. But the truth was quite the opposite: Katie was at everyone's beck and call—the show's bookers and producers, the network's bosses and their wives, the affiliates' owners and general managers, and the advertisers and their agencies. She had no time for a life—or for her children.

And there was another thing that print journalists were slow to grasp. The days were long gone when TV news people were insulated from the tyranny of the ratings. Newspaper reporters and magazine writers could talk all they wanted to about the good old days of Walter Cronkite and Winston Burdette and Marvin Kalb, but such talk was beside the point. The economics of television had changed, and Katie was just as susceptible to the economic fundamentals of the business as were Jay Leno and David Letterman. They were all prisoners of that little red eye staring at them from the top of the television camera.

Chapter Fifteen

High Voltage

Wᴴᴱɴ, ᴀᴛ ʟᴀꜱᴛ, ɪᴛ ᴅᴀᴡɴᴇᴅ ᴏɴ Kᴀᴛɪᴇ ᴛʜᴀᴛ *Gᴏᴏᴅ Mᴏʀɴɪɴɢ America's* surge in the ratings was no fluke, she went into one of her characteristic pouts. For the first time in a long time, she was beset by her old childhood fears of public embarrassment and humiliation.

"Katie is obsessed with how Diane looks and how she's doing," a *Today Show* source told the *New York Post*'s influential Page Six gossip column. "She's driving the hair and wardrobe people crazy, and asking everyone about Diane."

Until Diane Sawyer joined the morning TV wars, Katie had been content with her girl-next-door image. If Diane was the embodiment of the untouchable blonde goddess, Katie represented the sensible Everywoman who had her feet firmly planted on the ground. She wore Gap sweater sets and a string of pearls, and didn't bother to tinker with her boyish hairstyle and natural brown hair. She went light on the makeup in the morning and heavy on the pasta at night, with the result that her face was lined (especially across her forehead) and her waist was one or two inches too big.*

---

* In the months after Jay Monahan's death, the five-foot-two-inch Katie weighed 130 pounds.

When Katie returned to daily television after Jay Monahan's death, she looked even frumpier than before. And as the first anniversary of Jay's death approached, she still appeared weighed down by grief.

"Grieving doesn't do nice things to faces," explained Joan Kron, an editor at *Allure*, the beauty magazine.

"How can you look good if you feel angry and disrupted?" agreed Phyllis Zilkha, a New York psychiatrist. "The mourning process takes a year. You go through several stages, starting with disbelief and then anger, and eventually you are able to grapple with the fact that you are left with this void, and that you have to move on or be stuck where you are forever.

"This is especially true for someone who is young," she continued. "Katie has her whole life ahead of her, even though it is a terrible, cruel, and unfair thing that has happened. If you don't feel good, you can have the most fabulous makeup and clothes on and still feel disgusting."

However, once Diane Sawyer and *Good Morning America* began taking substantial bites out of *The Today Show*'s ratings lead, Katie sprang back to life. In an effort to get into shape, she asked Jill Rappaport, the show's celebrity correspondent, for the name of a physical trainer. Jill recommended a former go-go dancer and fitness fanatic named Kathie Jo Dolgin, who went by the professional moniker High Voltage.

"People call me High Voltage because I have the energy of a kid," Kathie Dolgin, who was fifty-three years old at the time she met Katie, told the author of this book. "Jill Rappaport saw me on the *O'Reilly Factor* talking about sugar addiction, and she tracked me down. She was living in the Hamptons, and I worked with her on the phone on her sugar addiction. And each week, she'd go on *The Today Show*, and afterwards she'd tell Katie about this High Voltage person who she thought would be great for her.

"Prior to hooking up with Katie," she continued, "I worked as a life coach with the richest people on the planet. I always tell them the same thing: stay hydrated, work out, think positively, and do something good for others."

For $7,500, High Voltage took her clients away to a spa for a week of tough love. For a lower fee, she showed up three or four afternoons a week at Katie's apartment, where they did cardio and weight workouts.

"Katie is much more conscious of what she eats and the choices she makes," High Voltage said. "She has a lot of energy, and she uses it to empower herself. . . . Katie is much prettier than most people realize, and I see her with no makeup on. I can promise you that she has not had anything done, and I am a firm believer in plastic surgery. I've been known to take clients to the plastic surgeon. But Katie has no need for it."

The transformation of Katie Couric was dramatic. Her fat melted away, and a whole new woman emerged who had the fit and finish of an athlete. As *Allure*'s editor-in-chief Linda Wells remarked: Katie now had "the best legs in television."

Katie took every opportunity to show off those legs. Her colleagues on *The Today Show* began to joke about the new wide-angle camera shots of Katie in a leather jacket, short skirt, and stiletto heels.

"When she first started out," said a producer, "she was a horrible dresser. But she became more stylish, more New Yorkish. It was a conscious image change."

The physical changes were accompanied by a change in her demeanor. She became more of a diva. There was consternation in the *Today* wardrobe room because Katie, who was in her early forties, insisted on dressing as though she were ten or fifteen years younger.

The press started to get a whiff of some of the problems on *The Today Show* set. But according to Frank Radice, NBC's senior vice president of advertising and promotion, Katie's glam makeover did not—at least initially—hurt her with the viewing audience.

"You'd hear all those negative things in the press," he said, "but our research and focus groups didn't show any of that. My personal opinion is that she'd gone through a devastating thing, and she changed her look because she was breaking out. I don't think the public was saying there was any problem with that. The public got that Katie was trying to find her own life. She had to find out what her life was going to be without her husband, with this great success she had. And I'd send her e-mails saying how great she looked."

A Hollywood agent (not Alan Berger) had a short and snappy explanation for Katie's makeover: "Show me a woman in her forties who lost her husband, and who doesn't totally remake herself to become more attractive to the other sex," he said. "Katie was like an actress in her forties who had to change her act."

THAT CHANGE INCLUDED the purchase of a splendid new cooperative apartment on Park Avenue—what Katie called "my new beginning."

New Yorkers are normally blasé about the celebrities in their midst. For instance, few people knew, or cared, that Diane Sawyer camped out in a cozy penthouse duplex in an East Side hotel, or that Peter Jennings had a sprawling cooperative apartment in The Beresford on Central Park West, or that Morley Safer owned a townhouse in the east sixties. But when Katie Couric moved from her four-bedroom, three-bath apartment to a $3.6-million, twelve-room apartment with four bedrooms, five baths, and a library, it was treated like a major news event.*

By this time, Katie had become fodder for the gossips, and the smudgy line that had once separated her private life from her public life had all but disappeared. Newspapers and magazines chronicled her every move, and Katie—who was becoming more and more desperate to stave off the challenge from Diane Sawyer—was a willing accomplice in most of this coverage. Thus, just as she had given *Newsweek* the exclusive story about her new four-year, $28-million contract, she now gave *Good Housekeeping* a first look at her new Park Avenue apartment.

---

* Katie also sold her ten-acre weekend retreat in Virginia.

Katie was anxious not to come across as a hoity-toity celebrity, and she made sure that the editor of *Good Housekeeping* put a positive spin on the story. She claimed that her move to Park Avenue was not of her own choosing, and that she would have preferred to remain in her more modest West Side apartment "where she and Monahan had built a family together."

Katie also tried to play down the cost of the renovations and interior decorations to her new abode. For instance, the Steinway piano in the living room was there for its "therapeutic" value, she said. Her high-priced interior decorator and her personal publicist, who were present during the interview, looked on with straight faces.

During the interview, Katie excused herself to take a call from a U.S. general in Germany. When she returned, she launched into a series of anecdotes aimed at demonstrating how she had decorated her apartment with bargains.

"She shows off the comforter on [her daughter] Carrie's bed that she picked up while on assignment in Los Angeles at a 75-percent-off linen sale," reported *Good Housekeeping*. "Then she's off to the front hallway, where she's hung her proudest find—a series of pen-and-ink sketches of historic New York that she bought for $42 apiece in an antique shop.

"Of much more importance now is Couric's struggle to cope with her loss while celebrating her husband's legacy. 'I think Jay would have really loved this apartment,' she says. 'I think he would have been happy seeing all the things that he loved being used and enjoyed by us. I really miss him so much. But I also miss his input, because he just had that certain something that would have made everything look fabulous.' "

ON ONE LEVEL, Katie's decision to grant an interview to *Good Housekeeping* made perfect sense; she knew the magazine would handle her with kid gloves. But on another level, the decision was puzzling, since the article exposed Katie's lavish lifestyle and raised a potentially troubling question: Would Katie's millions of loyal female viewers be green eyed with jealousy when they saw photos of her luxurious new apartment?

The skeptics needn't have worried. The article turned out to be a public-relations masterstroke. It was the opening shot in a brilliant campaign aimed at establishing Katie as a far more sympathetic figure than Diane Sawyer. Where else but in a woman's shelter magazine could Katie let down her hair and talk about her family's grief and suffering over the death of Jay Monahan?

"Someone sent me a picture of Jay in his navy uniform, and Ellie [her eight-year-old] said, 'Can I have that for my room?'" Katie recalled. "And I said, 'Sure.' Jay looked really handsome—well, he looked handsome in all his photographs. But Ellie took the picture into her room. After a while she came into the kitchen, and she'd been crying. Sometimes, I forget how things affect her. It's not that I forget, really, but it just crops up at unexpected times. . . .

"[At age three, Carrie is] extremely precocious, so I try to use real-life situations to explore different areas with her," Katie continued. "The other day she said, 'All my Barbies are dead.' So I asked her what she thinks happens to dead Barbies. We had a whole conversation about whether they go to heaven and who else is in heaven."

It was in this same *Good Housekeeping* article that Katie announced she was making the fight against colon cancer—the disease that killed her husband—her personal crusade. She was launching a bold new campaign, called the National Colorectal Cancer Research Alliance, in memory of Jay.

"Get your butt to the doctor!" she said. "It could save your life. . . . I have visions of getting toilet paper manufacturers to write WIPE OUT COLON CANCER at the end of the toilet paper roll. I want to get people talking. Colon cancer is no laughing matter. But I think if you have a sense of humor, it may alleviate some of the anxiety."

If Katie's first signature career moment had come in 1996, when she interviewed Bob Dole and established her bona fides as a *serious* journalist, her second career moment certainly came in 1999, when she publicly bared her feelings about widowhood, and sealed her reputa-

tion as a *compassionate* journalist. From then on, whenever Katie interviewed a person suffering a personal tragedy, she appeared authentic.

This was no small feat. After all, how could Katie Couric, one of
the most famous, well-paid journalists in the world, still make ordinary people believe that she felt their pain?

Chapter Sixteen

Columbine

THE ANSWER TO THAT QUESTION CAME ON TUESDAY, APRIL 20, 1999, when Katie's beeper went off while she was attending a matinee performance on Broadway.

She called the NBC news desk and learned that two teenagers, Eric Harris and Dylan Klebold, had gone on a murderous rampage at Columbine High School near Denver, killing twelve students and a teacher in the deadliest school shooting in United States history. Within hours, Katie, along with her executive producer Jeff Zucker and a small army of *Today Show* cameramen, audio technicians, makeup artists, engineers, and assistants was on a plane headed for the site of the shooting in Littleton, Colorado.

On Thursday morning, as a steady snow fell on Clement Park in Littleton, Katie sat down under a tent and interviewed two people who had lost family members in the tragedy. One was a sixteen-year-old white boy named Craig Scott, whose sister had been shot dead. The other was Michael Shoels, a black father who had lost his son, Isaiah.

The interview ran, without commercial interruptions, for an amazing seventeen minutes, and it featured a goose-bump-producing moment when it looked as though Michael Shoels was going to have a breakdown on camera. Instinctively, Katie reached out and touched his arm in a gesture of consolation.

Sitting in a nearby satellite truck, Jeff Zucker ordered a cameraman to stay on a close-up shot of Katie's hand as it rested on Shoels's arm. Then, Zucker spoke into Katie's earpiece, prompting her to inform the TV audience that NBC was skipping its next scheduled station break so that the interview could continue uninterrupted.

Zucker was ecstatic.

"I realized from the outset," he said, "that we had something special going on—an honest, compassionate dialogue free of the all-too-typical setup questions and answers."

Later, Katie told Dusty Sanders, the broadcasting critic of the *Rocky Mountain News*, that her husband's death had made her more sensitive to personal tragedy like the one that had taken place at Columbine High School.

"I'm much more aware of the grief families endure following the loss of loved ones," she said. "Everyone deals with a loss differently. But I feel, at times, my responses during interviews help put individuals at ease. Perhaps wounded persons like Craig Scott and Michael Shoels realize this when they talk to me."

For the next several days, MSNBC, CNBC, and NBC's owned-and-operated affiliates played reruns of Katie's riveting interview. In New York, NBC PR man Frank Radice promoted the interview as a defining moment in Katie's career.

"That interview with the father of the boy who was killed in Columbine came right in the middle of all the negative talk in the press about Katie," he said. "And that was one of the most compelling interviews I had ever seen. It showed that she was the consummate pro."

LIKE MANY PUBLIC figures who are deeply invested in their image, Katie had never been satisfied with the coverage she received in the media.* She constantly prodded her public relations people to come

_____

* As part of her effort to control her image, Katie made photographers agree not to sell photos they had taken of her without her permission.

up with dramatic stories about her exploits that would appeal to a broad mass audience.

Frequently, these "untold stories" about Katie would turn up in the pages of the *Globe* and other supermarket tabloids. And this led some people to suspect that Katie and the tabloid editors had a secret you-scratch-my-back-and-I'll-scratch-yours understanding. Whether or not that was true, the *Globe* featured just such an untold story about Katie in its May 11, 1999, edition.

"Millions of viewers sat riveted during Katie Couric's heartbreaking [Columbine] interview," the *Globe* reported. "But what viewers didn't see was the emotional toll the 17-minute, gut-wrenching segment took on the *Today* show host. Afterward, Katie, her voice choked with anguish, pleaded with her co-host, Matt Lauer, to give her the strength to keep going.

" 'I'm losing it . . . do something,' a distraught Katie sobbed through her headphones [*sic*] in Littleton, Colo., to Lauer, who was listening 1,600 miles away at NBC's Manhattan studio.

" 'That poor father . . . that young man . . . This is tearing me apart. Talk to me, Matt. I don't know if I can get myself back together in time.'

"Katie took a deep breath, and with the courage of a veteran journalist, resumed her reporting from a makeshift studio in Clement Park, located next to the school."

SIX MONTHS AFTER Katie's Columbine triumph, Jeff Zucker suffered a second cancer scare, and surgeons removed 90 percent of his colon. Though he was absent from *The Today Show* for six weeks, he never let up on his office politicking. He was still locked in a mano-a-mano struggle with News President Andy Lack over who would be first in line to succeed Bob Wright as NBC's top executive.

The smart money was on Zucker. But, as always, he didn't take anything for granted. While on sick leave, he began to explore several opportunities *outside* NBC. And he made sure that those *inside*

NBC—especially Bob Wright, who didn't want to lose him—were made aware of what he was up to.

"Jeff had held the job of *Today Show* executive producer for almost ten years, which was a record, and a test of his absolute willpower," said an admiring NBC producer. "He was figuring out what he was going to do, and one option was to do something outside NBC, either by himself or with Katie."

Katie and Jeff Zucker were both represented by Alan Berger at International Creative Management (ICM).* However, at about this time, Berger left ICM to join Michael Ovitz's newly created Artists Management Group, and he brought Katie with him to Ovitz's new company.

In no time at all, Ovitz was on a plane to New York, where he proceeded to demonstrate his famed talent for juggling several negotiating balls at one time. He met *alone* with Zucker, who was trying to work out a deal with Bob Wright. He met *alone* with Katie, whose contract was coming up for renewal. He met with both of them *together*. And to make matters more complicated, he held meetings in which he represented Katie *against* Zucker in her contract negotiations with NBC.

At one point, Katie had hoped to be Tom Brokaw's successor. But the TV landscape had changed since then, and hard news was no longer the chief subject on her mind.

"Katie's great motivation," said someone intimately familiar with her thinking, "was where do I go from here? How is my career going to look looking backward? What *is* my career? And how can I turn that into something that is better for me and my children, something that translates into money?"

Before she could answer those questions, Bob Wright changed the rules of the game. Rather than lose Zucker to another network, he made him president of NBC Entertainment, replacing Garth Ancer.

---

* Berger also represented Larry King and Jay Leno, among many others.

The hapless Ancer had failed to carry out Wright's repeated demands to develop a successful reality show, a primetime genre that had recently catapulted ABC back into the ratings game and had made Fox a serious contender as a major network.

Jeff Zucker jumped at the chance to leave *The Today Show*. For one thing, Shelley Ross and *Good Morning America* were breathing down his neck, and he didn't want to be around if *GMA* reclaimed bragging rights as the top show in the morning. For another, his appointment as NBC entertainment czar meant that Zucker had lapped Andy Lack, and was now in the lead to succeed Bob Wright as the head of the Peacock Network.

On December 14, 1999, Katie showed up on *The Today Show* wearing a pair of glasses—a fashion faux pas that had been strictly forbidden by Jeff Zucker.

"So why wear them that day?" asked Verne Gay, the TV columnist for Long Island's *Newsday*. "Because Zucker would shortly announce that he would become president of NBC Entertainment. He would be Katie's boss no longer. So back to the glasses. A little inside joke? A fun and harmless act of rebellion? Or perhaps an angry gesture, as in, 'Hey, you're leaving me, pal, so I can wear my glasses if I want to. So there.' Probably not, but still, you have to wonder."

The subsequent NBC press release said that Zucker would give up his role as executive producer of *The Today Show* and move to the West Coast. But the announcement was notable as much for what it *didn't* say as for what it *did*. After ten years of being joined at the hip, Jeff Zucker and Katie Couric were being separated.

"Katie and Jeff were codependent," said a former high-ranking NBC executive. "They could complete each other's sentences. But she was limited by that relationship, and needed to get away from Jeff, because at a certain point she outgrew him.

"That was the upside," this person continued. "The downside was that Katie never managed to develop as great a relationship with the executive producers who followed Jeff. She never achieved the same level of comfort with his successors. And that left a vacuum of power, leadership, and maturity.

"Stars like Katie need to be managed. If, after Jeff left, she had had a great executive producer and front office to manage her destiny, Katie wouldn't have gotten into the kind of trouble that would mar her final years on *The Today Show*."

PART III

Diva

Chapter Seventeen

The Big Makeover

Despite her reputation as a fiercely self-reliant woman, Katie had never hesitated to make use of men who could advance her career—whether it was Guy Pepper in Atlanta, Bill Thompson in Miami, Tim Russert in Washington, or Jeff Zucker in New York. To be fair, those relationships were never a one-way street; the men used Katie—romantically or professionally—as much as she used them.

Of all those relationships, the one with Jeff Zucker was by far the most important. For nearly a decade, he had carefully built and nurtured Katie's image, turning her into the most valuable brand in television news. Like Oprah, Cher, and Madonna, everyone came to recognize Katie by her first name. There might be a lot of Mikes, as in Mike Wallace (Mike Myers, Mike Gallagher, Mike Tyson, and Mike Ovitz), and a lot of Barbaras, as in Barbara Walters (Barbara Bush, Barbara Boxer, Barbara Mandrell, and Barbra Streisand), but as far as America was concerned, there was only one Katie.

Jeff Zucker had guarded Katie's precious brand name with his life. Few people beyond *The Today Show*'s cast and crew were ever permitted to glimpse The Killer Katie that lurked beneath the Zucker-created persona of The Girl Next Door.

Now, however, with Zucker three thousand miles away in Los Angeles (and no one around to take his place), Katie was suddenly cut loose from her customary male moorings. Set adrift, she immediately began to experiment with her image.

Her motives for doing so were mixed. In part, she was relieved to be free of Zucker, who, like an old-time Hollywood mogul, had insisted that she play the same role over and over again. She was sick of being typecast; the statute of limitations on "perky" had run out, she declared. Partly, too, she was threatened by Diane Sawyer, who was gaining on her in the ratings. Katie wanted to give Diane a run for her money in the glamour department.

"I think for a long time, earlier in my career, there was a part of me that didn't want to be too attractive—not that I'm attractive now, but you know what I mean," Katie said. "But I think there was something deep in my psyche. Something to do with feminism, where I thought that since I wanted to be accepted for my brains, looks shouldn't matter. [Still,] it's nice to feel that you look pretty. And I'm no spring chicken. I don't think people will think I'm superficial or vapid for having fun with my appearance, because I think I've proven myself in other areas."

Whatever her reasons, Katie began a major makeover. In the spring of 2000, she appeared on *The Today Show* with a new highlighted and layered hairstyle by Laura Bonanni of the Louis Licari salon (cost: $555). She was wearing darker, heavier eye makeup, and her lips looked as though they had been plumped up with collagen injections. Thanks to her thrice-weekly workouts with High Voltage—and a rigorous diet that excluded flour, sugar, and salt—she had lost eight pounds, which, on her small frame, made a huge difference in how she looked.

"She is toned and tan and taking care of herself, projecting a new physical sexiness that, somewhat to her embarrassment, has attracted a legion of male TV fans in love with her legs," noted the magazine writer Joanna Powell.

One morning, Katie showed up on the set in a hot pink trench coat, four-inch stiletto heels, and gold hoop earrings. With each passing week, the hemline of her skirts rose higher and higher, as did the number of male viewers. When, on occasion, she wore pants instead of a skirt, men by the thousands phoned in to complain they had been denied a glimpse of her beautiful gams.

One website (www.tunc.biz/athina_simonidou.htm) ran a feature called "The Curious and Kinky Case of Katie Couric's Legs." "Every weekday morning about 7am, this site gets its first hit seeking Katie Couric's legs," the website reports. " 'Gimme my early morning leg fix, man. I need the sight of those smooth, oiled thighs. What a way to start the day!' The hits keep coming until about 10am. Then it goes quiet until people get home from work at 6pm, and the Katie Couric searches start all over again. We get more than 300,000 hits a month from folks wanting Katie Couric's legs."

Katie professed to be offended when the media focused on her legs and wardrobe, calling such stories "sexist." Why, she asked, didn't reporters write about *Charlie Gibson's* hair or his necktie? Of course, Katie knew the answer. Fairly or not, women on television were held to higher standards of personal appearance than men.

In fact, Katie loved the attention. In a move that recalled Diane Sawyer's vampy photo shoot for *Vanity Fair* more than a decade earlier, Katie posed for *Vogue* magazine in a Carolina Herrera black silk moiré dress with a long train, wearing a priceless Fred Leighton necklace.

Like Hillary Clinton, who seemed to change her hairstyle every time she woke up in the White House, Katie couldn't leave her hair alone. Why switch so often? she was asked by *USA Today*. To which Katie replied: "I just get bored. I'm like every woman in America."

In any case, she looked a whole lot better than when she debuted on *The Today Show* at age thirty-three in 1990.

"Back then," wrote Rebecca Traister in the online magazine Salon, "she looked like a high-octane, rabbity gymnast; with her gummy grin and lesbian-soccer-mom haircut, she could have been airlifted straight out of the bulk paper goods aisle at Wal-Mart."

As for her new glam look, Traister added, "America ate it up."

THOSE WHO WORKED with Katie couldn't help but notice that her makeover went well beyond hairdo and wardrobe. She also changed in less visible ways. Some of her colleagues thought she had become deeper and more introspective since the death of Jay Monahan. Other, less charitable observers said that she talked incessantly about herself and had crossed the line into certifiable narcissism.

In any case, there *was* something new about the self-absorbed way in which Katie discussed her life. She had been seeing a psychotherapist on a regular basis ever since her husband's illness, and perhaps as a result of all this introspection, her comments became more intimate and confessional.

"I don't need a man 24/7, but I get lonely," she confessed. "My parents, being of a different generation, probably feel it's [seeing a psychotherapist] extremely indulgent, in a way. I don't think they would cotton to the notion of talking about themselves for an hour with some professional. . . .

"I think I never fully dealt with my husband's death, because I kept going," she continued. "And I was so focused on my kids, making sure they were as healthy and whole as could be after going through an experience like this. But it's been helpful to me, because a lot of delayed grief issues . . ."

Without a daily reality check from Jeff Zucker, Katie slipped into the kind of self-centered world usually inhabited by Hollywood stars. She preferred the company of people who told her exactly what she wanted to hear—especially when they repeated that she alone was responsible for her success. That, of course, wasn't true, but Katie preferred to listen to the toadies and sycophants who encouraged her divalike behavior, and who applauded when she heaped scorn on anyone who displeased her.

"In the morning," one staffer told *The New Yorker*, "when the anchors go over the copy and make last-minute changes, Couric doesn't say, 'Hey, guys, think we can change this?' Instead, she says, 'This sucks!' Everyone hears it."

The only person who had ever had the courage to tell Katie that *she* sucked—Jeff Zucker—was gone. In his place was a gaggle of yesmen who didn't make a fuss even when Katie flouted the rules and played dirty tricks on her competition.

On one occasion, she went overtime, apparently on purpose, during an interview with an eighty-three-year-old Florida grandmother who had survived three days in her overturned car. The grandmother, Tillie Tooter, had promised to do back-to-back interviews with *Today* and *Good Morning America*, but Katie hogged the airtime, forcing *GMA* to go to a commercial break while waiting.

"I think viewers would be surprised to see this kind of mean-spiritedness from Katie Couric," *GMA* producer Shelley Ross told *People* magazine after the incident. "I think we can compete on loftier levels."

For a long time, the public refused to believe the gossipy tales portraying their perky morning talk-show host as a temperamental diva. The reason for their disbelief was not hard to find. Jay Monahan's death had transformed Katie into an enormously sympathetic public figure. While Jeff Zucker was still running *The Today Show*, he had wisely exploited this emotional bond between Katie and her audience.

However, there had always been a catch to Jeff's strategy: in order to sustain her image as the grieving widow and single mother, Katie also had to play the role of Virgin Queen of Morning Television. Even the slightest hint of an illicit love affair could have undermined her spotless reputation. But the longer Katie played that role, the less chance she had of finding a husband and a father for her two children. This was not a tradeoff she was willing to make indefinitely.

Thus, no sooner had Jeff Zucker left for California than Katie began dating a New York plastic surgeon by the name of Carroll Lesesne (pronounced luh-SANE). Everyone called him by his rakish nickname, Cap, which seemed to fit his reputation as a ladies' man.

"I was the first guy she went out with after Jay died," Cap Lesesne told the author of this book. "I had just gone through a nasty divorce, and an agent at ICM, who was one of my patients, set me up on a blind date with Katie. We talked on the phone for two hours before we went out. I had never seen her, because I didn't watch television, and she was shocked. She knew [the historian] Michael Beschloss, my classmate at Andover, from their days together at the University of Virginia, and she had Beschloss check me out."

Beschloss apparently gave Cap Lesesne a clean bill of health. But among savvy New York women, he was viewed as a risky choice for someone with Katie's high profile. True, Cap was handsome, well educated (Andover, Princeton, Duke University School of Medicine), and socially adroit. But he was also seen as something of a publicity seeker who dated famous women in order to get his name in the papers.

What could Katie possibly see in this guy?

The answer was simple enough. As with other men in Katie's life, Cap Lesesne had something she wanted. In his case, it was expertise in cosmetic surgery. Just before Katie and Cap were introduced, his name had appeared in several newspaper accounts in connection with Hillary Clinton. It was said that the first lady had secretly visited Doctor Lesesne to consult him on having a facelift.

"If Katie was looking for something from me," Cap said, "it was over that. She asked me about Mrs. Clinton, and I said, 'I'm not going to get into that.' In jest, she asked, 'What do you think of these forehead lines of mine? How do I look?'"

Was Katie thinking of having a facelift from the doctor who had reportedly performed plastic surgery on Hillary Clinton? If so, that subject didn't come up on their first date. They agreed to meet for a cup of coffee at a bistro off Madison Avenue. He arrived at the appointed time, six-thirty, but Katie never showed up.

"At 7:15, tired of wasting my time and a little miffed, I finally left," he recounted in his memoir, *Confessions of a Park Avenue Plastic Surgeon.* "Not three paces into my walk uptown, a black limousine pulled alongside me. The window rolled down. It was Katie. Nice timing. She apologized profusely for being late.

"'Are you hungry?' she asked, and I said I was. 'Forget coffee,' she said. 'Let's go to my favorite restaurant.'

"She got out and we walked to Coco Pazzo, on Seventy-fourth and Madison. As soon as we entered, everyone, it seemed, came over to greet her. She was New York royalty. I'd been out with notable women before, but never someone this recognizable. We were given a quiet table for two. Katie didn't bother to look at the menu. 'What are you having?' I asked.

" 'Nothing,' she said. 'I've eaten dinner with my children.' "

As Cap Lesesne recalled in the interview for this book, Katie talked a lot about her dead husband:

" 'Jay used to do this . . . Jay used to do that. . . .' I felt that I was the schmo who was the recipient of all her angst. It was clear that, even if she had had a lot of trouble with her husband, she was still very much attached to him."

On their second date, they discussed how much they had in common and how that might lead to a serious relationship.

"She had to be up for work at five; so did I," he wrote. "She didn't really drink; neither did I. Professionally, we seemed equally driven. The conversation was, as it apparently couldn't *but* be with her, delightful and fast-paced and constant. . . .

"My first impression of her, physically, was that she was extremely cute but a little shorter than my type," he continued. "And like any plastic surgeon—like any man—I started to scan her face for the quick readout. But none came. No 'bone structure this' or 'jaw line that.' My radar simply stayed off. And that's not meant to be a backhanded compliment."

By the summer, they were talking on the phone practically every day. What's more, Katie acted as though they were a committed couple, and that she didn't care who knew. For instance, she suggested that they have dinner at Elaine's, the famous Upper East Side saloon favored by writers, actors, journalists, and cops.

"Are you sure you want this?" Cap Lesesne asked Katie. "Once we set foot in Elaine's, word gets around."

"I don't care," Katie replied.

Predictably, someone tipped off the tabloids about the lovebirds, and the papers started running stories about Katie's new boyfriend. When Cap Lesesne called her to see how she felt about being outed, she told him not to worry. But he detected a note of concern in her voice.

"Is something wrong?" he asked.

"There may be other things to worry about."

"Like what?"

It turned out that the supermarket tabloid *Globe* was about to run a story reporting that Dr. Carroll Lesesne had been arrested, three years before, and spent the night in jail on charges that he had physically abused his wife. Though the charges against him had been dropped, the *Globe* splashed the headline on its front page: KATIE'S BOYFRIEND'S DARK SECRET PAST! A few days later, the *New York Post* followed with its own front-page screamer: KATIE'S BOYFRIEND SHOCKER.

Shortly after those stories appeared, Katie and Cap Lesesne met for a date. As he remembered it, Katie told him that she was in contract negotiations with NBC and couldn't afford to be involved in a sordid scandal.

"You've got enough baggage to get yourself to Puerto Rico," she told him.

He never saw her again.

ON THE REBOUND from Cap Lesesne, Katie began dating other men, including Steven Rudinsky, a Nabisco executive, and Stephen Hannock, a painter whose Turneresque landscapes were popular among celebrities including Sting. As a result of her serial dating, Katie's romantic life became the subject of widespread media scrutiny.

Television is a fiercely egalitarian medium, and those who make a living delivering the news on the tube cannot afford to give the impression that they think they're better than everybody else. Despite her glamorous new hairstyle and sexy wardrobe, Katie had avoided leaving that impression up to that point. But the chronicles of her flirtations with rich and famous men were different; they threatened to put her on the other side of the great divide that separated celebrities from ordinary folk.

In fact, Katie now faced the same she's-too-big-for-her-britches accusation that had undermined the career of *GMA* host Joan Lunden. But Katie was wise enough to recognize the problem in time and to come up with a creative solution. She devised a weeklong series of TV programs devoted to the subject of colon cancer.

During that week, Katie used words on *The Today Show*—"rectum," "colon," and "bowels"—that many people were still reluctant to use in their own homes. And in a dramatic climax to the series, *The Today Show* featured a live broadcast of Katie's colonoscopy—replete with scenes of her lying on her side in a rumpled cotton hospital gown and graphic images of her "pretty" (her word) colon.

By then, Katie had turned the prevention of colon cancer, the disease that had killed her husband, into her personal cause. She and Lilly Tartikoff, the widow of Brandon Tartikoff, the former president of NBC Entertainment, who had died of Hodgkin's disease, formed the National Colorectal Cancer Research Alliance. Katie got Congress to designate March as Colon Cancer Awareness Month. And she planned a black-tie gala to benefit the new Jay Monahan Center for Gastrointestinal Health at the New York Weill Cornell Medical Center.

"The most difficult part of Jay's illness," she explained, "was to see someone you love so much suffer and get gypped out of life. But another really agonizing aspect was how powerless I felt. I'm one of those people who likes to fix things and make everything okay. Even though I tried everything I could, save throwing on a lab coat and becoming a cancer researcher, which I couldn't be because I'm not nearly smart enough, I just couldn't do it. There was nothing I could do to make Jay better. And so assisting other people has been a great antidote for that feeling of helplessness."

Katie's willingness to expose her large intestine for a good cause produced important results. Across America, colonoscopy rates jumped by more than 20 percent—a phenomenon that saved countless lives and came to be known among cancer researchers as the "Katie Couric Effect." Of equal importance to Katie, her colonoscopy restored her image as "just plain folks," and replenished the reservoir of goodwill that people had about her.

Some of Katie's critics (in particular, those at ABC's *Good Morning America*) charged that she was exploiting Jay's death to further her career.

"If GE brings good things to life," they said, parodying GE's famous ad slogan, "then cancer brings good things to Katie."

Other, less cynical observers were appalled by this kind of grotesque humor.

"Television is such a bitchy business," said one. "There is so much money involved and so much stardom. Katie clearly wanted to honor Jay, no matter what their marriage was like."

It was left to Liz Smith, the syndicated gossip columnist, to come up with the most nuanced explanation.

"One thing I will say is that given that she's such a target, Katie Couric did a very clever thing by turning the fight against colorectal cancer into something that made her a more sympathetic figure," wrote Liz. "I'm sure she would have rather had the husband than have had the excuse, but she used that very well and lots of people just adore her for it. You have to admire how she turned a horrible thing into a good image and something that helps people."

Chapter Eighteen

The Greatest Aphrodisiac of All

I THINK IF IT HAD BEEN ME WHO DIED," SAID KATIE, "I WOULD WANT Jay to be with someone. My children fill me up so much, as do my friends and family. But I'm someone who liked being married and liked being in a relationship. It's so hard to replace someone whom you care about and who cared about you in that way. So I felt that I would start getting out and just try to socialize and have fun."

As might be expected, Katie's daughters, Ellie and Carrie, didn't exactly share their mother's idea of fun.

"Ellie asked me to promise that if I ever got remarried, I wouldn't have sex," Katie said. "And I assured her by saying, 'Don't worry, Ellie. Once people get married, that's when they stop having sex!' Just kidding—I'm just kidding about that! . . .

"Ellie cornered a guy I'd been seeing and told him that I was a compulsive gambler and that I had gambled away her college tuition," Katie continued. "It's so funny. She tries to think of any personality trait that I possess and then exaggerates it and spreads the word so as to dissuade any potential gentlemen callers."

To spare her children—and, not incidentally, to throw the paparazzi off her scent—Katie was careful not to have a parade of men traipsing in and out of her Park Avenue apartment. That, however, didn't seem to placate Ellie, who was now a precocious fourth grader.

"Ellie will always ask, 'Where are you going? What time will you be home?' Katie said. "I mean, it's a real role reversal. One time I said, 'Ellie, sometimes I feel like you're my mother.' And she said, 'Well, sometimes I feel like you're my daughter.'"

IN MAY 2000, Katie's agent, Alan Berger, and his wife, Phyllis, arranged a blind date for Katie with Tom Werner. Few men in Katie's age bracket (she was forty-three, he was fifty) were more eligible than this Hollywood mogul.

Just under six feet tall, Tom Werner had piercing blue eyes, a square jaw, and an unaffected manner that won him friends in the notoriously spiteful Hollywood community. He shunned the Armani power suits favored by many of his colleagues and dressed in khakis and button-down Oxford shirts. Moreover, unlike most Hollywood players, he was exceptionally well educated; he had attended Hotchkiss, one of the country's top prep schools, and Harvard, from which he graduated cum laude in English literature.

Back in the 1980s, Werner and his partner, Marcy Carsey, had opened a mom-and-pop TV production company in the Westwood section of Los Angeles above a 7-Eleven store. Their first try was a sit-com called *Oh Madeline*, starring Madeline Kahn, which lasted a full season—an auspicious start. Then, in the spring of 1984, they teamed up with Bill Cosby to create a sitcom about a solid upper-middle-class black family. Carsey-Werner's former employer, ABC, turned the show down flat, but NBC jumped at the chance to buy it. Eventually, syndication rights to *The Cosby Show* sold for more than $600 million. After that, the money flowed with hit after hit—*Grace Under Fire, Roseanne,* and *3rd Rock from the Sun.*

In fact, during their first decade in business together, Tom Werner and Marcy Carsey created so many TV hits that, in 1989, third-ranked CBS approached them with an offer to run the network's entertainment programming. Complex negotiations went on for months, but were finally ended with a statement from Carsey-Werner citing "time pressures."

The publicity from the CBS offer established Werner and his partner as stars in the Hollywood firmament. Then, Werner went a step
further and attained the dream of many rich men: he bought a part
ownership in the San Diego Padres baseball team and, later, in the
Boston Red Sox, which went on to win its first World Series since 1918.

A few weeks before his first date with Katie, Werner had legally separated from his wife of twenty-eight years. At about the same time, he
appeared as No. 46 on the *Los Angeles Business Journal's* list of the city's
50 Wealthiest People. *Forbes* estimated his net worth at $600 million.

WHEN TOM WERNER met Katie, he had only recently moved out of
the multimillion-dollar Brentwood estate he had shared with his wife,
Jill, and their daughter, Amanda, twelve. (The couple also had two
grown children: Edward, twenty-four, and Carolyn, twenty-one.)
Werner and his wife had been estranged for several years, and he was
on the lookout for a new commitment.

Werner had every reason to avoid press scrutiny of his bicoastal affair with Katie. After all, he was still legally married and in the midst
of a difficult divorce. Nevertheless, when reporters telephoned his
North Hollywood production office, seeking a comment on an upcoming tabloid story, a spokesman promptly returned the call and
generally offered more, rather than less, information on the couple's
private plans.

Some people suspected that Werner was behind this effort to court
the press. They recalled that he had successfully garnered a ton of
publicity by opening his Malibu mansion for the multimillion-dollar
"wedding of the decade"—the nuptials of golden couple Brad Pitt
and Jennifer Aniston.

"Having fireworks, half the stars in Hollywood, and the flashiest
wedding in years in your backyard is not the mark of a shy man who
avoids the limelight," said someone close to Werner.

But others suspected it was Werner's estranged wife who was tipping off the press.

"Quite frankly," said a tabloid editor, "I always believed it was a friend of Werner's wife, who worked inside his organization, who was tipping us off about his whereabouts and his romantic rendezvous with Katie. The information was just way too good. Not only did we know where Katie and Tom were going, we knew to the hour when they would be there."

In late July, the mystery source in Werner's office called the Boca Raton office of the *Star* with a tip that Tom and Katie were planning a tryst at the Four Seasons Hotel in New York City. The *Star*'s editor, Tony Frost, sent photographers to stake out both the Fifty-eighth and Fifty-seventh Street entrances of the hotel. And a veteran tabloid reporter was assigned to cover the story.

An hour after the phone tip—on a rainy, muggy Manhattan summer afternoon—the couple arrived in a cab at the Fifty-eighth Street entrance. Katie, who had just come from an interview with Laura Bush, the wife of presidential candidate George W. Bush, was pretty in pink; Werner was dressed in a black polo shirt and khaki Dockers. He and Katie (sans luggage) held hands and exchanged kisses as they walked past photographers and into the marbled corridor of the luxury hotel.

When heads turned in recognition of the television star, Katie smiled wanly. She looked acutely embarrassed as she and Tom ducked into a waiting elevator.

Just as the doors were about to slide shut, a hand intervened, and the *Star*'s reporter got into the elevator. When he produced a Canon Sure Shot camera, Katie jumped away from Tom to make sure that he was out of the frame of the picture. After the reporter took her picture, the lovers got out on the twenty-fifth floor and headed for room 2508. The reporter followed them down the corridor at a discreet distance and slipped his key card into No. 2506, the room next door.

While Katie was usually discreet, she appeared to throw caution to the wind during her brief afternoon rendezvous at the hotel. According to the tabloid reporter next door (who may very well have been embellishing his story), he couldn't help but hear the lovers through the hotel wall.

Katherine Ann Couric cheering on her high school classmates in Arlington, Virginia, 1975. Her blithe spirit masked a personality that was prone to feelings of embarrassment and humiliation.
James M. Kelly/Globe Photos Inc.

At the University of Virginia in the late 1970s. "Most of the kids just tried to get good grades and have a decent time," said one of Katie's classmates. "With her, everything was a political calculation."
Special Collections, University of Virginia Library

With her parents, Elinor and John Couric. If her mother was the engine that drove Katie's ambition, her father gave that ambition a clear direction, inspiring her to pursue a career in journalism.
Barry Talesnick/Retna Ltd.

Watergate stars Bob Woodward and Carl Bernstein at the *Washington Post*, 1973. Once journalists became glamorous celebrities, Katie decided, "If my face didn't stop a clock, I'd try television news." *Bettmann/CORBIS*

ABC Evening News co-anchor Barbara Walters interviews Yasir Arafat in Beirut, Lebanon, 1977. "Katie's goal," recalled a college boyfriend, "was to be the next Barbara Walters." *HK/Stf/Koundakjian/AP Photos*

NBC News Washington bureau chief Tim Russert. One meeting was all it took for Russert to size up Katie's enormous talent. He became the first boss who didn't underestimate her.
Steve Grayson/WireImage.com

"Great blonde hope" Deborah Norville tells David Letterman she's leaving *The Today Show* to have a baby. The likable and energetic Katie was everyone's favorite choice at NBC News to replace Norville. *AP Photos*

Jeff Zucker on the set of *The Today Show*, 1991. "I thought he was the cockiest guy I had ever met," Katie commented about the twenty-six-year-old Zucker, who was nicknamed after the teenaged doctor on the popular TV series *Doogie Howser, M.D.*
Fred R. Conrad/New York Times/Redux

Katie tears up while saying goodbye to cohost Bryant Gumbel on his last day on *The Today Show*, 1997. As much as Katie secretly wanted Bryant to go, she also feared his departure might destabilize the show. *Reuters/Str Old*

Good Morning America's Diane Sawyer. The confrontation between Katie and Diane would become one of the longest-running rivalries in television news. *Ron Galella, Ltd./WireImage.com*

Morning TV's ratings leaders Al Roker, Katie, Matt Lauer, and Ann Curry. "Being a morning anchor is the hardest job on TV," said an expert. "It requires Katie to wear a multitude of hats—hard news, human interest, celebrity-interview, and household features." *Chester Higgins Jr./New York Times/Redux*

Mixing it up with Ross Perot on *The Today Show*. A relentless inquisitor, Katie established her chops as a hard-news journalist—as tough as the toughest male interviewers around. *Jim Estrin/New York Times/Redux*

The Donald and The Katie appear together on *Today*'s Halloween special, 2004. In the world of infotainment, where showbiz values trumped hard news, female stars like Katie were the dominant force.
David Atlas/Retna Ltd.

Channeling Marilyn Monroe on *Today*'s annual Halloween special, 2005. "She's the everything gal," wrote the *Washington Post*'s Tom Shales. "She's an apple a day. She's real, she's natural, she's totally at home on the air."
Albert Ferreira/Reuters/Landov

Katie's fitness guru, High Voltage, flexing her muscles, 1998. Katie's physical transformation was dramatic, leading *Allure*'s editor Linda Wells to remark that "Katie has the best legs in television."
Jim Cooper/AP Photos

Sitting in for Jay Leno on *The Tonight Show*, 2003. Carpenters cut away the front of Jay's desk to expose Katie's legs while she interviewed *American Idol* judge Simon Cowell.
Neal Preston/Retna Ltd.

Arm-in-arm with Jay Monahan. The mounting demands of Katie's career posed a serious dilemma for Jay, making it nearly impossible to maintain his own identity in a city where he was known as "Mr. Katie Couric."
Robin Platzer/Time Life Pictures/Getty Images

With Jay and Ellie in New York City, 1996. "Whenever we'd eat out, people would always come up to Katie," said Ellie's nanny, Nancy Poznek. "Jay would lean over to me and whisper: 'Ego, ego, ego.'"
John Barrett/Globe Photos, Inc.

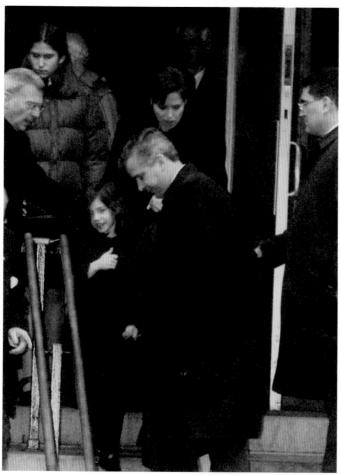

Katie and Ellie at Jay's funeral in
St. Ignatius Loyola Church, 1998.
"He did not go gently into that
good night," Katie eulogized.
"He fought until the bitter end."
Globe Photos, Inc.

The grieving widow wearing
Jay's wedding ring on her
necklace. She told viewers,
"Words will never describe how
devastating this loss has been
for me and my daughters and
for all of Jay's family as well."
Walter McBride/Retna Ltd.

Park Avenue plastic surgeon Dr. Carroll "Cap" Lesesne. After a tabloid ran the headline KATIE'S BOYFRIEND'S DARK SECRET, Katie told him: "You've got enough baggage to get yourself to Puerto Rico."
Stephen Lovekin/WireImage.com

With Hollywood mogul Tom Werner in Beverly Hills, 2002. Katie always chose men to help advance her career and few were in a better position than Werner to lend a hand when her contract came up for renewal.
Frazer Harrison/Getty Images

Boy Toy Brooks Perlin. The seventeen-year age difference between Katie, fifty, and Perlin, thirty-three, was even greater than the fifteen-year gap between Demi Moore and Ashton Kutcher.
asiphoto. com

With Washington businessman Jimmy Reyes. Katie made no secret of the fact that she wanted to get married, but Reyes—the divorced father of two—wasn't exactly the marrying kind. *LDP Images*

With jazz trumpeter Chris Botti at a New York Knicks game, 2005. "Their relationship was very public," said a close friend, "and Chris thinks Katie used him to make Tom Werner jealous." *James Devaney/WireImage.com*

Entering the Metropolitan Museum's Costume Institute gala, 2005. At the top of her game, Katie became a juicy target for NBC's competitors, prompting a TV critic to declare, "And now begins the battle for Katie Couric."
Erik C. Pendzich/Rex USA

Waving farewell on her last day on *The Today Show*, 2006. Until she had a binding agreement with CBS's Leslie Moonves, Katie was in a state of almost continuous nervous agitation, yelling at the crew and getting into spats with the cast. *Richard Drew/AP Photos*

After fifteen years on *Today*, Katie kisses NBC's Jeff Zucker goodbye, 2006. "Jeff has gotten through the 'I'm pissed' stage," said a friend, "and moved into the 'I'll deal with it' stage."
Richard Drew/AP Images

Dan Rather in 2006. Though many at CBS were happy that Rather was forced to relinquish the anchor chair, they were horrified by Moonves's plans to "commercialize" the news.
Lester Cohen/WireImage.com

Viacom's cranky chairman Sumner Redstone with Tom Freston at the MTV Awards. In the race between Moonves and Freston to succeed Redstone, Moonves turned out to be the more adroit corporate player.
Jim Smeal/WireImage.com

CBS president Moonves with his prize at the Museum of Television & Radio gala, 2006. A programming genius, Moonves saw Katie as the ideal modern broadcast journalist—someone who appealed to the heart as well as the brain.
David Livingston/Getty Images

Rick Kaplan, executive producer of the *CBS Evening News*. In hiring a TV warhorse like Kaplan, Moonves was looking for someone who could extract better results from Katie.
Paul Hawthorne/Getty Image

Katie in the eye of the storm. She found it impossible to reconcile her ambition to be a serious broadcast journalist with her personality as a cute, girlish performer. *Mario Anzuoni/Reuters*

A few hours later, the couple strolled out of the hotel arm in arm. They acted as though they were oblivious to the phalanx of photographers who had assembled from all over Manhattan after word swept through the paparazzi underground network that Katie was holed up in the hotel.

Two and a half months after their afternoon at the Four Seasons, on October 16, 2000, Werner took the decisive step of filing for divorce, citing irreconcilable differences, and requesting that the court award him joint custody of their twelve-year-old daughter and not give his wife any spousal support.* To many of his friends, it looked as though he was setting the stage to marry Katie Couric.

KATIE HAD ALWAYS chosen men who could help advance her career, and few men were in a better position than Tom Werner to lend a hand when Katie's NBC contract came up for renewal.

"Katie and Tom spent a great deal of time discussing possible deals they could do together, from an Oprah-like talk show, to a late-night program to compete with *The Tonight Show*," said a source who was familiar with their conversations. "They even talked about a sitcom in which Katie would essentially play herself, or a character very much like herself.

"Werner was talking deals where Katie would be an owner of the show, no longer an employee of a network," this source continued. "It was a heady formula that gave Katie a power buzz unlike anything she had ever experienced before. Tom talked about how much fun it was to discuss Katie's career. It was the biggest turn-on. Knowing that Tom Werner wasn't full of hot air, and that he really could make it happen, was an aphrodisiac for Katie."

---

* It would take years to sort out the community property and other issues between the couple.

Chapter Nineteen

"The Charm Ran Out"

For the first time since the death of her husband and the departure of Jeff Zucker for California, Katie did not feel alone. Now she had Tom Werner looking out for her welfare, and thanks to his unsurpassed network of powerful friends in the Los Angeles entertainment industry, she was being courted like a queen.

But once again, at a moment that should have been filled with confidence and hope, fate dealt her a terrible blow. On Wednesday, July 19, 2000, she received a phone call from her sister Emily.

"Knowing how much I worry about our parents," Katie recalled, "[Emily's] first words were, 'Don't worry—it's not Mom or Dad.'"

Then Emily broke the devastating news.

"Yesterday," she said, "I learned that I had cancer of the pancreas, and that the cancer had spread."

At the time, Emily was a popular Virginia state senator and was running on the Democratic Party ticket for lieutenant governor. She was not only expected to win, but many political observers thought she had a good chance of eventually becoming the Old Dominion's first woman governor.

After Emily's hair began to fall out as a result of her chemotherapy treatments, many people thought she would retire from public life. But she kept her seat in the Virginia legislature and became the co-chair of the state Democratic Party. Her gallant struggle against cancer went on for fifteen months, and inevitably there came a time when she had no choice but to withdraw from the lieutenant governor's race.

She and Katie stayed in daily phone contact, discussing the latest advances in cancer therapies. And Emily, who had published several books on the legal profession, continued to write. *The Virginia Quarterly Review* posthumously published her last piece, titled "Seasons":

When the leaves come and go on the sycamore tree, changing color, falling to the ground, and starting fresh as new buds, they remind me of the passing seasons—and the passing time. . . . Of all the seasons, winter time is the most intriguing, when I can look out my window and study the tree's mottled bark and gaze with fascination at the rows of burly round fruit hanging from its spindly limbs.

But also in the winter I get a better look at the traffic on the street and passers-by on the walk. . . . In every person, I see the seasons of humanity, the passing of my own life, in slow but steady stages. . . .

It's frightening to see them—all the different ages—moving by so quickly: Sometimes I want to close my blinds and shut them out. Instead I try to look at the sycamore tree and its changing seasons, and to see nothing more beyond.

KATIE WAS HOSTING a segment on *The Today Show* when the terrorists struck the World Trade Center towers and the Pentagon on the morning of September 11, 2001.

Her first thought was for the safety of her parents, whose house, like the Pentagon, was in Arlington, Virginia. (Her children were out of harm's way; they attended a private school in Manhattan that was located several miles north of the World Trade Center.) Though Katie was desperate to alert her parents to the danger, she couldn't leave her anchor chair because NBC News had stopped airing commercials and had gone to uninterrupted coverage.

"I had a stage manager call my parents and tell them to go into the basement," she recalled.

Several minutes later, she learned that an American Airlines plane bound for Los Angeles had been commandeered by another group of terrorists and gone down in a field in western Pennsylvania. She began to panic. Katie feared that Tom Werner was a passenger on that plane.

The night before, at her urging, Werner had delayed his scheduled departure from New York City. Instead, he left the next morning, September 11, on an American Airlines flight for Los Angeles.

To some, Katie's anxiety over the safety of her parents and Tom Werner might have seemed excessive. After all, her parents' Arlington home was miles away from the Pentagon. And the odds were long that Tom Werner had booked out of dozens the one flight that ended up crashing in the Pennsylvania woods.

Nonetheless, from childhood on, Katie had been haunted by such irrational fears. She had grown up in a family that was preoccupied with loss—the loss of wealth, social status, and religious identity. Her childhood sense of impending doom was only aggravated in her adult years by the death of her husband and the cancer that had metastasized in her sister's body.

Katie was not at all like the blithe spirit she portrayed on *The Today Show*. Deep down, she always feared the worst: that her ratings would tank, and she would lose her job; that the money she had prudently put aside for a rainy day would disappear, leaving her penniless; that yet another of her loved ones would fall ill and die.

And so, at the first opportunity on 9/11, Katie ducked off camera and burst into tears. After she had composed herself, she asked to speak with Peter Greenberg, *The Today Show*'s travel editor.

"You've got to find Tom," she implored Greenberg.

Greenberg hurried upstairs to his office and frantically began calling his sources at the airlines. He soon located Tom Werner, who was stranded in Kansas City. His plane—like all aircraft that day—had been grounded. Werner planned to rent a car and drive all the way to L.A.

"I found him," Greenberg told Katie when he came down to the newsroom. "Tom's safe."

*   *   *

SIX WEEKS LATER—on the afternoon of Sunday, October 21, 2001—
Katie stood before a congregation of mourners at St. Paul's Memorial
Church in Charlottesville, Virginia. She was there to deliver the eu-
logy for Emily, who had succumbed to cancer at the age of fifty-four.

Katie looked out over the crowd. A number of celebrities were in
the audience, including Matt Lauer, singer Mary Chapin Carpenter,
and actress Sissy Spacek. The front pews were occupied by family:
Emily's husband, Dr. George Beller; her children from her first marriage, Ray and Jeffrey Wadlow; her stepchildren, Michael, Amy, and
Leslie Beller; her sister Clara Couric Batchelor and her brother, John,
and their families. Katie's children, Ellie, ten, and Carrie, five, were
seated near Tom Werner, who by now had become practically a member of the family. Katie's mother and father were prostrate with grief.

The news of Emily's cancer had come in the wake of yet another
medical blow to the family.

One day, Katie had noticed that her father's hand was shaking.

"What's wrong with your hand, Daddy?" she asked.

"Oh, I'm just nervous," John Couric said.

But it turned out to be more than nerves. Her father had Parkin-
son's disease.

"I sort of naïvely thought that having a high-profile job on television would protect me from bad things," Katie said. "I had lived a
charmed life, and thought it would continue indefinitely. But the
charm ran out."

Chapter Twenty

The $65 Million Woman

FOR YEARS, *THE TODAY SHOW* HAD BEEN HAILED AS THE MOST financially successful program on television. With profits in excess of $250 million a year, it accounted for half of NBC's total profits, and contributed more to NBC's bottom line than *Friends*, the number-one primetime sitcom. However, after September 11, 2001, the show's ratings went into a sudden decline, and as Christmas approached, its lead over ABC's *Good Morning America* shrank to 600,000 viewers—half of what it had been before 9/11.

As panic set in at NBC, the atmosphere over at ABC turned to one of jubilation. There, much of the credit for closing the gap between the two morning shows went to Shelley Ross, *GMA*'s hard-charging executive producer. But the lion's share rightly belonged to *GMA*'s hosts, Diane Sawyer and Charlie Gibson, whose appeal had significantly expanded in the post-9/11 era, because they conveyed a greater sense of authority than Katie and Matt Lauer.

"Diane and Charlie just felt more secure covering 9/11 and its aftermath," said a producer who worked with them. "Katie and Matt might be warmer, but Diane and Charlie had more political heft. *They* were the voices of experience. And remember, it was *Good Morning America*, not *The Today Show*, that won a Peabody award for its 9/11 coverage."

People who toiled in the volatile world of television immediately grasped the enormous implications in this shift in viewing habits. Hollywood publicists—those powerful gatekeepers to the stars— started to view *Today* and *GMA* as roughly equal in value and began booking their clients accordingly. Thus, for the first time in years, *GMA* landed several bigger "gets" than its opposition at NBC. Even more important, the leveling of the playing field between the two shows translated into fewer advertising dollars for NBC and more for ABC.

Executives at General Electric, the parent company of NBC, looked around Studio 1A for someone to blame. But there was no convenient scapegoat in sight. Jeff Zucker had hightailed it out of New York just before the fall in ratings and was now safely ensconced in Los Angeles. His replacement as executive producer of *The Today Show*, Jonathan Wald, was too new to be held responsible for the waning viewership. At the time of Jonathan Wald's arrival, NBC president Bob Wright was still struggling to staunch the hemorrhage in ratings, though he had figured out a way to make up for the show's declining profits. He simply expanded the show to three hours, thus adding $70 million to its annual revenues.

But that did not address Wright's bigger problem: how was he going to keep Katie Couric on the NBC reservation when her contract expired in May 2002—just one short year away?

It was an open secret on *The Today Show* set that Katie was unhappy with the way things were going. And she often took out her frustrations on Jonathan Wald. Many of his suggestions were met with Katie's harsh rejoinder: "Well, that's not the way *Jeff* did it."

"It simply wasn't a great fit between Katie and Wald," said someone who worked on the show. "She was never satisfied with the way he did things."

As the time approached for serious contract negotiations, agent Alan Berger seized the opportunity to exploit his client's unhappiness. Through selective leaks to favored reporters, he and his partner Michael Ovitz let it be known that Katie was restless at NBC and was interested in exploring "other challenges."

A host of suitors immediately lined up to make her offers. Gerald Levin, the chief executive of AOL Time Warner, whose Telepictures Productions company produced the *Rosie O'Donnell Show*, laid out a media smorgasbord from which Katie was free to pick and choose. It included an Internet venture, a column in *Time* magazine, a show on CNN, and the chance to take over the time period occupied by the *Rosie O'Donnell Show*, whose host had announced she was retiring.

Don Hewitt, the creator and executive producer of CBS's *60 Minutes*, came calling on Katie with a fistful of dollars in one hand and a fistful of flattery in the other.

"Certain people have an indefinable something," said Hewitt. "It's what made a Walter Cronkite a Walter Cronkite. It's not easily defined. It just is. It's a mystique."

Katie had always dreamed of working on *60 Minutes*. But now she wasn't so sure.

"I grew up watching that show, and I admire it so much," she said. "I really respect that no-nonsense approach to telling a story. [But] I don't think I could do that job until my kids are much, much older—like married, with children of their own!—because the travel is so excessive.

"I had to think long and hard about whether doing one piece every couple of weeks [for *60 Minutes*] and working in that kind of ensemble would have been ego gratifying enough," she continued. "It's something that I worry about—becoming addicted [to the daily routine of *The Today Show*]. The exposure is intoxicating. I'm very intoxicated.... Hi, I'm Katie and I'm addicted to daytime."

The public courtship of Katie Couric had all the earmarks of an elaborate Michael Ovitz seduction. But then, in the summer of 2001, Alan Berger and Ovitz had a falling-out, and Berger angled for Ovitz's old talent agency, Creative Artists. He took his star client Katie Couric with him.

Still, the offers kept coming—from Sony, DreamWorks, Fox, Viacom, and Disney. "Everyone and their mother had a meeting with Katie and Alan," said one studio executive.

*   *   *

ALTHOUGH TOM WERNER didn't participate in those meetings, he played a key role as Katie's consigliere. He helped her sort through the many offers and weigh their pluses and minuses. For instance, Katie was initially attracted by the notion of owning her own syndicated talk show. But after Tom Werner pointed out that the failure rate of such shows was 90 percent—and that those few shows that succeeded did so by going the tawdry tabloid route—she lost interest.

A better model for Katie, Werner argued, was Barbara Walters's deal at ABC. Barbara was the highest-paid person, male or female, in the network news business. She had her own production company, which owned her primetime specials. And she and ABC were each half owners of the daytime moneymaking machine called *The View*. Estimates of Barbara's annual earnings ran as high as $20 million, which, if true, put her in the same rarefied category as the Hollywood superstars she interviewed on her Oscar-night specials.

Werner was aware that Katie had long dreamed of becoming the next Barbara Walters. Well, he said, wasn't it time to make that dream come true?

FEARING THE DISASTER that would befall NBC if it allowed Katie Couric, its biggest news star, to slip through the network's fingers, Bob Wright turned for help to his most trusted lieutenant, Jeff Zucker. He asked Zucker to step in and talk some sense into his old friend.

The trouble was, Katie and Jeff were no longer as close as they had been when he was still the executive producer of *The Today Show*. Then, Jeff and Katie had been partners whose fates were intimately intertwined. Now, as head of NBC Entertainment (and soon to be named president of the entire network, including its news division), Jeff was a member of the NBC front office. Put simply, he and Katie sat on opposite sides of the negotiating table.

Not that they had become adversaries. On the contrary, they still considered themselves friends. They talked on the phone frequently and shared the latest office gossip. But Katie could never bring herself to forgive Jeff for abandoning her when he went off to California for a bigger and better job.

As one of Katie's early bosses had once put it, "Katie keeps the hurts."

Of course, Jeff Zucker dared not let on that his influence with Katie had waned. That would have exposed a weakness—a fatal mistake for someone climbing the slippery pole of corporate politics. Instead, Zucker—who, like most producers, believed that you could never flatter a TV star too much—called upon Frank Radice, the network's chief flatterer and in-house promotion chief, to do the sweet-talking for him.

"Jeff asked me to prepare a tape, kind of like VH1's *Behind the Music*, except in this case it was Behind Katie Couric," Radice said. "He wanted to show her how much we cared for her. It became a huge effort on the part of the company. It included interviews with people like Sam Donaldson and Reese Schonfeld, her first boss, who recounted her story. It turned into *This Is Your Life*. And we sent this tape to her house to watch."

Said Zucker: "We've made it clear that whatever she wants to do is certainly possible at NBC in ways that it's not possible almost anywhere else. . . . Whether it's early morning, prime time, afternoon, whatever she wants to do is her oyster."

THE WEEK BEFORE Christmas—shortly after 7 P.M. on December 18, to be exact—Katie finished taping an interview in New Jersey and ducked into a waiting limousine for the ride back to Manhattan. While her interview was in progress, Alan Berger had phoned with an urgent message. Now Katie, who rarely had a moment to herself, settled back in the seat, flipped open her cell phone, and dialed her agent's number.

"What's going on?" she asked.

"Katie," said Berger, "we have a deal with NBC!"

NBC was trying to keep the contents of the deal under wraps so that the news division's other "big foots" (major on-air personalities who regularly trampled on lesser talents) would not immediately demand an upward adjustment in *their* salaries, too.

Anchors invariably earned a lot more money than their bosses. Of the three major network evening news anchors, Dan Rather was both the longest running and the lowest paid, at $6 million a year. Tom Brokaw came next, with a salary of $10 million (about the same as Diane Sawyer's). Peter Jennings had the sweetest contract; it stipulated that no one at ABC News could make more than he did. When Barbara Walters signed a contract for $12 million a year (which did not cover her side deals with ABC on *The View* and her specials), Jennings got to match her dollar for dollar.*

At $7 million a year, Katie had already surpassed Dan Rather as well as the top-paid talent on *60 Minutes*—Ed Bradley, who made $4.6 million, and Mike Wallace, who was paid $4.5 million. Katie was widely expected to do even better this time around, perhaps even matching the $10 million that NBC paid Tom Brokaw, the face of the network.

As it turned out, Katie exceeded everyone's wildest expectations. NBC agreed to pay her the astonishing sum of $65 million over the next four and a half years. That translated to nearly $15 million a year, or $3 million more than Barbara Walters and Peter Jennings each made. Apparently, either Katie or her agent leaked the story of her huge windfall, and the press instantly crowned her the highest-paid journalist in the history of television news.

"She wanted the numbers out," a source at NBC told *The New Yorker*. "She was proud. She enjoyed the moment. She felt somewhat validated by it."

---

* Stratospheric salaries were a recent phenomenon. At the height of his popularity, "America's Most Trusted Man," Walter Cronkite, earned $900,000 a year—a piddling sum by today's outlandish TV salary standards.

Chapter Twenty-one

The Queen of Sheba

WHEN A WOMAN MAKES THE KIND OF MONEY KATIE COURIC IS making," noted Liz Smith, "she's going to be hit with a tomato any-time she steps out."

It didn't do Katie any good to argue that the jealousy and resent-ment incited by her eight-figure annual salary reflected her critics' ig-norance of the economics of network news. Like Hollywood stars who were paid to open movies and professional athletes who were paid to fill stadiums, TV news personalities were paid to attract viewers.

Long gone were the days when the Founding Fathers of the three networks—William Paley at CBS, David Sarnoff at NBC, and Leonard Goldenson at ABC—swore allegiance to the ideals of news as a public service. The old guard had been replaced by a far less fastidious breed of men—Sumner Redstone (CBS), Jack Welch (NBC), and Michael Eisner (ABC). Though these corporate chieftains paid lip service to old-fashioned journalistic virtues, they were more interested in their stock price.

"The corporatization of news means that news is seen only in the service of the corporate interest," Dan Rather told the author of this book. "The primary purpose of TV news is no longer to promote democracy by assuring an informed public. Instead, the purpose of TV news is to deliver stockholder value, and to help the corporation in its regulatory and tax needs in Washington. Sumner Redstone doesn't want his news division doing investigative stories of the very people he is lobbying in Washington for favors."

THOUGH KATIE DENIED that it was she who had leaked the details of her contract, that hardly seemed to matter. What mattered was that the news of her exorbitant salary shocked everyone, including, most important, her fans.

"At some point, you can't earn that much money and convince people that you're one of them," Andrew Tyndall, whose *Tyndall Report* monitored network TV news, told the author of this book. "When she signed that $65-million contract, her image veered off. That was too much."

Forbes.com agreed. "Industry sources assert that her yearlong and very public contract negotiations with NBC have tarnished her all-American image, making her look greedy," the business website reported. "Sources also bemoan her new, less wholesome persona, which includes glamorous, sophisticated and sometimes even vampy hair, makeup and clothes on the set."

"What happens to the appeal of America's morning sweetheart when she's suddenly incredibly, publicly rich?" Elizabeth Kastor asked in the May issue of *Good Housekeeping*. "Will she still be Katie to the viewers at home, or will she join the sports stars and other celebrities whose astronomical paychecks grate a bit on the goodwill of their fans?"

Shelley Ross, the executive producer of *Good Morning America*, thought she knew the answer to that question. When ABC did opposition research on Katie, Shelley said, it discovered that the "new" Katie was turning off many longtime *Today Show* viewers.

Katie had always had a high Q score (a measurement of a personality's likability), and she was still one of the most popular figures on television, but at the same time she had also become one of the most *un*popular. She was emerging as a divisive figure whose negative Q scores were beginning to catch up with her positive scores.

"Katie beat Diane Sawyer, the host of *GMA*, in popularity," wrote

Bill Carter in *Desperate Networks*, "but she now was also beating Sawyer . . . in terms of negatives. Couric had an even higher negative score than Dan Rather.

"Zucker had seen the numbers," Carter continued, "and had sat down with Katie in February, gently advising her to tone down some of the touches that viewers apparently objected to: her frosted hair, her glamorous clothes, her public superstar salary."

"Viewers were conflicted over her big salary, her new glam look, her being too blond, and showing too much leg," Shelley Ross said. "You can't be both The Girl Next Door and the Queen of Sheba."

OF COURSE, THE more money Katie made, the more pressure she was under to deliver the goods.

"As a result," said a *Today Show* producer, "Katie constantly conveyed to the people who worked with her that she was dissatisfied with them. Whatever [executive producer] Jonathan [Wald] did was never enough. She wanted more and more."

During his eighteen-month run on the show, Wald was never able to win Katie's allegiance and support.

"No situation is perfect, and this one wasn't," Wald told the *New York Times*. "We are a family, and it would not be prudent for me to discuss disagreements in public. There's always tension of some sort. A gentleman doesn't talk about that."

Those tensions came to a head in the spring of 2002, when nine coal miners became trapped underground for seventy-seven hours in a flooded mine shaft in Somerset County, Pennsylvania. It was a story ready-made for television: dramatically lighted nighttime rescue shots, weeping family members, and remorseful mine operators and public officials. Katie went ballistic when the rescued miners turned up for an interview on *Good Morning America*.

You didn't get to be Katie Couric by being a good loser, and predictably enough, Katie demanded that someone take the fall for the loss of the live interview with the surviving miners. Within a matter of weeks, Jonathan Wald was gone from his job.

* * *

To FILL HIS PLACE, NBC announced it had raided the competition and was hiring Tom Touchet, the senior broadcast producer of *Good Morning America* under Shelley Ross. Secret negotiations between NBC and Touchet had been going on for months, during which time he was asked to write several memos explaining how he would halt the *GMA* juggernaut and restore *The Today Show* to its morning dominance.

By the time Bob Wright was ready to conclude a deal with Touchet, it was the dog days of August, and Katie was on her annual two-week summer vacation in the Long Island resort town of East Hampton, about 110 miles east of New York City. The network sent Touchet in a limousine to meet with Katie, but when he arrived at her rented house, she wasn't there. The maid informed him that Katie had driven her boyfriend, Tom Werner, to the airport.

While he waited, Touchet played with Katie's daughters, Ellie and Carrie, and chased after the family cairn terrier, Maisey, when she ran away and got lost in the woods. Finally, the dog was found, and Katie returned from the airport, still dressed in tennis whites. She and Touchet moved to a picnic bench on the back porch to discuss his memos, which she clearly had not read.

Katie was not much of a reader; she got most of her information by listening, which in part explained why she had developed her skills as a good interviewer. She grilled Touchet on his memos, and when she thought he was trying to duck a question, she didn't let go until he answered it. After a couple of hours of this incessant interrogation, she seemed satisfied.

Now, Touchet had a chance to pose a question of his own. One of the issues addressed in his memos was the need to define the future roles of the talent on *The Today Show*.

"What is it you want to do next?" he asked Katie. "What is it that *you* want to do?"

To his surprise, the question seemed to throw Katie off balance, and she stumbled over an answer. The fact was, Katie had no idea what she wanted to do next.

*   *   *

PART OF KATIE's problem had to do with the changing relationship between her and her cohost, Matt Lauer. In the past, Katie had conducted the majority of *Today*'s heavyweight interviews; now, Matt was getting at least 50 percent of them. While he was growing in stature, landing bigger and bigger interviews, she appeared to be running in place. The role reversal bothered Katie a lot, and she and Matt fought over everything.

Her relationship with Ann Curry, the show's attractive news-reader, wasn't any better. Katie did everything in her power to make Ann's life miserable, going so far as to restrict her assignments, so that Ann wouldn't outshine her.

Katie also took out her frustrations on the cast and crew. One person described *The Today Show* as "a weird high school where no one had graduated." Some of the "short-timers" on the show had been there for ten years; several producers had celebrated their twentieth anniversary. The show's veterans felt they deserved more respect than they were getting from Katie, and they retaliated by sniping at her behind her back.

Their favorite joke was to compare Matt and Katie to Felix Unger and Oscar Madison in the *Odd Couple*. Matt was Felix, the diligent one; he called his producers each afternoon to see if there had been any changes in the lineup for the following morning and he came to work fully prepared. Katie was Oscar; she got into the habit of rolling into work as late as 6:45 A.M. and crammed for the show in the fifteen minutes before it went on the air.

Sometimes, her sloppy preparation work was reflected in her interviews. She would get to the right question, but it would take her too long, which meant she would eat into Matt's airtime. That, too, became a point of contention between them.

In her competition with Matt for the big gets, Katie was at a disadvantage in one important respect. The Republican administration of George W. Bush considered her to be too liberal for its taste and refused to talk to her. As a result, during the 2004 presidential election campaign, Matt got the lion's share of the Bush staff interviews.

That situation changed after Tom Touchet went to Washington and promised White House Press Secretary Dan Bartlett that Katie would treat the president the same way as she treated his Democratic opponent, John Kerry. That is to say, she would be equally tough on both men.

"PEOPLE LIKE KATIE—people who truly want to be famous—possess this odd gene," remarked one of her producers. "This gene makes you seek the adoration of people who don't know you—*total* strangers. But this gene also makes you not care about seeking the love of the people who *do* know you—your intimate friends and colleagues.

"I saw those aspects in Katie's personality," he continued. "She was a very complex person who was playing an uncomplicated person on television."

As time went on, Katie trusted fewer and fewer people. Among those trusted few were her parents. When she called her father and mother—sometimes during *and* after each show—she frequently forgot to turn off her microphone, and her producers could listen in on the conversation. Katie, they recalled, constantly sought her parents' approval, but more often than not, she failed to get it. Her father and mother were better at telling her what she had done wrong than what she had done right.

When she went on road trips for *The Today Show*, she often took along Tom Werner. He was careful to say very little in front of others. In fact, he seemed to operate in a zone of virtual silence.

"I recall being in a Miami hotel room, just Katie, her daughters, and Tom Werner," said a *Today* staffer. "Tom said maybe three sentences the whole evening."

Though Tom was one of the strongest influences in her life, Katie tried to play down his involvement in her career.

"How do I describe him?" she joked. "My boy toy? He doesn't want to be described as a 'brainiac' anymore. He said, 'Please call me ruggedly handsome.' "

Next to her parents and Tom Werner, Katie's closest confidantes were women she had befriended years ago in her early days at CNN. This group included Lisa Gregorisch-Dempsey, the managing editor of *Extra*; Wendy Walker Whitworth, Larry King's producer; and Tammy Fuller, an NBC producer in Miami.

Katie's friends felt that she had become the victim of antifeminist attacks, and in a misguided effort to protect her, they often refused to speak with reporters. Their silence only hurt Katie, since it meant that the only information about Katie came from those who did not particularly like her or, worse, wished her ill.

The emergence of this negative portrait did not do Katie full justice. During moments of relaxation, she could be hilariously funny and charmingly outrageous. For instance, while *The Today Show*'s hairdresser, Laura Bonanni, worked on Katie before a show, Katie would often launch into a sidesplitting, raunchy recitation on her love life.

"She had what I call a 'sorority mouth,'" said a staffer who was a fly on the wall during many of Katie's intimate monologues. "She'd talk about her lovemaking, everything up to and including the blowjobs. And she'd say things like, 'I can't believe that he and I fooled around for two hours. The sex was great!'"

ONCE A MONTH, Jeff Zucker would fly in from L.A., and ask Laura Bonanni to cut his hair—or what was left of it. On those days, when Zucker and Katie crossed paths, they barely acknowledged each other's presence.

"Jeff and Katie had the weirdest working relationship I'd ever seen," said a producer. "On the one hand, they were incredibly cold. And yet, they were like a divorced couple. She had so much resentment that he had left her behind. And he knew that he couldn't talk to her anymore.

"Here was this incredibly powerful man and woman, and they were only talking to each other through other people," he continued. "Never directly to each other. When she was acting out, people would ask Jeff, 'Please, will you step in and talk to her,' and Jeff would say to Tom Touchet, 'Tom, you tell her that I say ...'

"On the one question Katie wanted answered—*what's next for me?*—Jeff couldn't come up with a response. He wanted her to stay on *The Today Show* forever. Why should he want her to leave? After all, the show was grossing hundreds of millions a year. Why change something that's not broken?

"Meanwhile, Bob Wright was asking Jeff, 'What's going on at *The Today Show?*' and Jeff'd tell him, 'Bob, I'm going to make sure that Katie's going to stay.' And Tom Touchet, who was in on these meetings between Bob and Jeff, would say, 'She's gone. She's over this place.'

"Jeff didn't want to hear that, and he'd say, 'Katie's not going anywhere.' And Tom would say, 'I respectfully disagree. She's been over this job since I got here. She rarely returns calls. She doesn't even listen to her voice messages. She hardly ever sends in story ideas. The only thing she consistently watches on TV is *60 Minutes*. *60 Minutes* is the only thing she cares about. She has her sights set on *60 Minutes*. If you want to keep her here at NBC, you've got to give her a *60 Minutes*–type forum.'"

"Tom doesn't think Katie's the future of the show, but I do," Zucker told Wright. "We need someone who believes, as I do, that Katie is the future."

It wasn't long after this that Touchet was given his walking papers.

"By this time," said a *Today Show* source, "Katie's reputation had taken such a beating that people automatically blamed her for Tom Touchet's firing. They said that in order to cover an important national story, Tom had ordered the cameras to cut away from Katie, and that had made her furious. They said that when Matt Lauer threw a going-away party for Tom Touchet, everybody was invited except Katie. But these people weren't being fair. Katie didn't initiate Tom's firing. It was Jeff Zucker's doing. Of course, Katie had to sign off on it, too."

Chapter Twenty-two

The End of the Affair

I REMEMBER MY SISTER [EMILY] TELLING ME NOT TO EVER PUSH Tom to move to New York, that he would resent it."

This was Katie Couric talking about her romance with Hollywood mogul Tom Werner. Over the past couple of years, Katie had spent occasional weekends with Tom in Los Angeles, where he was treated like a prince of the city. Other times, she flew to Boston for an afternoon with him, when he was tending to his new baseball franchise, the Boston Red Sox. But mostly, she counted on Tom's coming to New York City, *her* stomping grounds, where they managed to grab a few hours alone at the Four Seasons Hotel.

"One of the reasons that I think he's so wonderful," Katie said, "is that he's very engaged in the things he does, and passionate about what he does for a living. I would never want to put him in a situation where he felt like that side of him was neglected."

In the spring of 2002, Katie suggested that she and Tom try an experiment: if they were really serious about getting married, wasn't it time they tried to blend their two families? They had not attempted to do that until now, largely because Tom's divorce hadn't come through yet. To give the experiment a fair chance of succeeding, they decided to spend the upcoming Easter school vacation at a child-friendly resort in Hawaii.

Once again, someone in Tom's office tipped off the tabloids, and when Katie and her daughters, Ellie, eleven, and Carrie, seven, boarded a Hawaii-bound United Airlines flight at JFK Airport, a reporter followed them onto the plane.

He looked around and didn't see Katie. Like several other highly paid TV news personalities who had scratched and clawed their way to the top of their profession (Barbara Walters, Peter Jennings, and Mike Wallace), Katie was a notorious penny-pincher. To save money, she had booked airplane seats in coach with the expectation that when airline ticket agents recognized her, they would give her a free upgrade. But this time around, there were no available seats, and when the tabloid reporter settled into *his* first-class seat, he discovered that Katie and her kids were crammed into the back of the plane in coach.

At LAX airport, Katie and her children met up with Tom Werner and his fifteen-year-old daughter, Amanda. Tom's private jet had mechanical problems, so the two families (plus the tabloid reporter) flew first class to the Big Island in Hawaii and checked into luxurious bungalows of the Mauna Lani Bay Hotel on the Kohala Coast.

While the girls fed the wild turtles, took hula lessons, and learned Hawaiian weaving, Katie and Tom walked on the white-sand beach, splashed in the surf, and rubbed sunblock on each other. The tabloid coverage of the family getaway—plus subsequent photos of Katie wearing an old ring—prompted speculation that she and Tom were engaged to be married.

They weren't. In fact, things didn't turn out as well as they had expected during their week in Hawaii. The girls made it clear they were less than thrilled at the prospect of accepting Katie and Tom as stepparents. As for the adults, they discovered that a week in the company of three unhappy children did not have the same charm as a few passionate hours alone in a hotel room.

What's more, Tom took the opportunity to speak up about something that had been troubling him for quite some time. He was miffed that Katie was listening to her agent, Alan Berger, rather than to him when it came to her career.

Tom had wanted to create a whole new Hollywood-based career

for Katie so that she would move her family to Los Angeles and be near him. But Alan Berger had argued just as forcefully that Katie should accept NBC's $65 million package and stay at *The Today Show* in New York.

It became clear to Tom that, for all the advice he had given Katie and the plans he had made for her, she trusted someone else more than she trusted him. Even more important from his perspective, she had put *her* career ahead of *their* future together.

In early June, Tom called Katie at her Park Avenue apartment to tell her that it was all over between them.

"Tom could barely conceal his anger," said a source who was familiar with the conversation. "The harder he tried, the more it sounded as though he was ending a business relationship, and Katie was obviously very hurt. But he really couldn't put it any other way.

"She had hurt him, and he was striking back," this person said. "It was very emotional and very painful. He had allowed himself to dream about their future together, and as far as he was concerned, she had shattered the dream."

THEIR SEPARATION DIDN'T last very long. But even after Katie and Tom got back together, she found it hard to forget the unkind things he had said or the insensitive way he had treated her. The experience of being dumped by Tom Werner was a jolt to Katie's ego and triggered all her old insecurities.

When she was in such a disturbed state of mind, Katie invariably fell back on her mother's advice: *"Let them know you're here!"* And so, for the May sweeps in 2003, she came up with an idea for a publicity stunt aimed at expanding the power and reach of her brand name. She suggested to NBC that she and *Tonight Show* host Jay Leno trade places for one day.

Some traditionalists in the NBC News division expressed their concern that Katie was further blurring the lines between journalism and entertainment. But their voices were drowned out by the ratings-obsessed executives who ran the network.

The idea appealed to Katie on a number of levels, not the least of which was that her appearance on *The Tonight Show* would take place in Los Angeles under the nose of Tom Werner. As for Jay Leno, he thought the idea of switching jobs—and coasts—was a gas.

"Well," said Jay, "it's sweeps, so I know I'm doing a thing [on *The Today Show*] on 'Strip Searches in Catholic Girls' Schools—Are They Necessary?' and 'Housewife Hookers—Are They in Your Neighborhood and Is Your Husband at Risk?'"

For her appearance on *The Tonight Show* on May 12, 2003, Katie wore a low-cut black halter dress and sandals.

"*The Today Show* is basically a news show, as you know, so you have to dress appropriately," she said during her *Tonight Show* monologue. "I try to dress in a very businesslike fashion, but tonight I thought this would be a chance for me to wear something a little more fun, a littler sexier, so—what do you think?"

The live studio audience went wild. . . .

". . . And for all you people from L.A., who have never seen them before," she added, pointing toward her breasts, "these are actually real."

. . . more yells and whistles from the audience.

In its review of the show, the New York *Daily News* reported that, instead of using Jay Leno's regular solid desk, "workers cut away the front of her desk to expose her legs while she interviewed *American Idol* judge Simon Cowell and *Austin Powers* star Mike Myers."

"The staff of *The Tonight Show* were so great," Katie said after learning she had boosted the show's ratings by 42 percent. "Those writers—that is a tough job. . . . [T]o be funny night after night after night, and I think they got my sensibility right away. They sort of tailor-made some jokes for me. And, you know, my parents weren't too pleased with my performance. My dad told me, you know, stick with your day job. But I thought that I could be a little teeny bit more daring in that venue."

TOM WERNER's DIVORCE from his wife, Jill, finally came through on September 23, 2004. The details of the financial settlement were sealed by the court. But Jill, who had been married to Tom for nearly thirty years, presumably walked away with a healthy chunk of her husband's $600 million fortune.

Though Tom took a financial beating, news of the divorce came as a great relief to Katie, who had waited patiently four long years for Tom to be free. Any day now, she told friends, she expected Tom to present her with an engagement ring, and to set a firm date for their wedding.

"Katie and Tom are likely to exchange vows in L.A. after the [2004] May sweeps are over," said a friend who discussed the subject with Katie. "The wedding location will probably be at the four-million-dollar home Tom purchased a few years ago."

Eager to please Tom, who was a Jew, Katie revealed for the first time in public that her mother was Jewish.

"Someone tell Adam Sandler to add another name to his funny Chanukah song about stars who are even a drop kosher," wrote FOXNews.com gossip guru Roger Friedman. "Even though Katie was raised an Episcopalian, I'm sure Sandler will rhyme 'Couric' with 'tsouris' (that's 'trouble' in Yiddish)."

But Katie's acknowledgment that she was half-Jewish turned out to be wasted on Tom. For now that he was free to remarry, he wasn't at all sure he was ready for a new commitment.

During several heated arguments between Katie and Tom, he hemmed and hawed on the subject of marriage, and Katie interpreted his lack of enthusiasm as yet another instance of male abandonment—first Jay Monahan, then Jeff Zucker, and now Tom Werner.

This, of course, was not the first time she and Tom had reached an impasse in their relationship. The last time, following their family vacation in Hawaii two years before, Tom and Katie had clashed over the direction of her career. That was still a sticking point.

Finally, Tom got so fed up that he sent Katie a long e-mail.

"Katie's life fell apart when she turned on her computer one morning and read an e-mail from Tom," said a close source. "It was a long message, which described how Tom did not feel he could continue his relationship with her. . . . But Katie was upset that Tom didn't have the nerve to break up with her in person—or even over the phone. It

was embarrassing and humiliating for her—and she's never fully recovered from what he did."

DURING THE FEBRUARY 2004 sweeps, *Good Morning America* beat *The
Today Show* in six of the top-ten markets, including New York and
Los Angeles. And in April, *GMA* tied *Today* in the overnight ratings
in *all* of the top-ten markets.

"Our competition has copied everything—every innovation," complained Jeff Zucker, who had recently returned to New York to take
up his new post as president of all three major divisions of NBC—
Entertainment, News, and Cable. "That's what happens in television."
The Today Show, Zucker added, was "probably not as newsy as it was,
or I think it should be. It was too soft."

Zucker tried to lay the blame at the feet of the show's departing executive producer, Tom Touchet. But the print media preferred to single out someone with a higher profile. They settled on Katie.

"For years," wrote Rebecca Traister in the online magazine Salon,
"journalists have tread on cat's paws around Couric's Big Money Deal
and the issues it raised about journalism vs. celebrity. . . . The scent of
blood has overcome the respectful media: Unable to resist, they have
ripped off their widow's weeds and are cheerfully pumping Couric
full of lead."

"She's being treated in the same way a well-paid athlete would be
treated, or a big movie star," said Andrew Tyndall. "When she got
that raise, she crossed the line from journalist to personality. The
treatment she's getting now has nothing to do with her *ability* as a
journalist but with her [financial] *value* as a journalist. Part of being in
that income bracket is that people gossip about you."

WHAT PEOPLE CHIEFLY talked about was Katie's forehead.

In February, *Women's Wear Daily* ran an item, based on questionable
sources, alleging that Katie had undergone an Endotine brow lift, a
cosmetic-surgery procedure that raises the lined skin over a patient's

forehead by pulling it up with hooks buried in the scalp. Katie was so upset by the brow-lift story that she asked her old friend Wendy Walker Whitworth, Larry King's producer, to book her for an entire hour on *Larry King Live*. During the interview, Katie swore that she hadn't had a brow lift, and Larry King accepted her denial. However, he failed to follow up by asking her if she had had Botox treatments, which seemed to be the most likely explanation for the sudden disappearance of the deep lines on Katie's forehead and the crow's feet around her eyes.

Another subject of gossip concerned Katie's new boyfriend, a renowned jazz trumpeter by the name of Chris Botti. The handsome, forty-two-year-old Botti had met Katie when he performed with Sting on *The Today Show* in 2003, but they didn't start dating until a few weeks after her four-year affair with Tom Werner had ended.

Though an NBC rep claimed that Katie and Chris were only good friends, Katie acted as though the relationship was more serious than that. She talked constantly about Botti ("It's Chris this and Chris that," said a source on *The Today Show*), listened to his jazz tapes, and planned her summer vacation around his tour dates.

"She's amazing!" Botti said on *The Tony Danza Show*. "She's brilliant and beautiful and really, really fun!"

The most intriguing piece of gossip about Katie, however, had nothing to do with her appearance or her love life. Rather, it focused on reports coming out of Black Rock, the Eero Saarinen–designed CBS headquarters building, that the network's chairman, Leslie Moonves, was secretly wooing Katie with an offer to replace Dan Rather as the anchor of the *Evening News*.

Katie wouldn't be the first woman to anchor a major network news program. That distinction belonged to Barbara Walters, who *co*-anchored *The ABC Evening News* with Harry Reasoner from 1976 to 1978. Connie Chung followed in Barbara Walters's footsteps when she was made Dan Rather's *co*-anchor, an experiment that lasted from 1993 to 1995, and proved to be no more successful than the ill-fated Walters-Reasoner pairing.

But Moonves *was* offering Katie something entirely new: the chance to become the first *solo* woman network anchor.

This constituted a tipping point in the history of broadcast journalism—and not simply because Katie was a woman. The choice of Katie represented a rupture in a half-century-old broadcast tradition. Until now, anchor chairs were reserved for journalists who had distinguished themselves covering domestic politics and foreign wars, and who were far more knowledgeable than their audience about history, culture, and current events.

Katie was no intellectual slouch, but from her earliest days at CNN, she had been as much an entertainer as a journalist. True, she had done hundreds of interviews, but her big-league reporting experience was limited. Judged by her talent, temperament, and track record, she did not belong in the august company of past and present CBS anchors—a line of succession that stretched from Douglas Edwards (1948–1962) to Walter Cronkite (1962–1981) to Dan Rather (1981–2005).

But as it turned out, that was precisely what attracted Leslie Moonves to Katie. He wasn't interested in perpetuating journalistic tradition. On the contrary, he was determined to create a new kind of anchor, one who mimicked the audience in terms of age, attributes, and interests. By offering Katie Couric the anchor chair of his network's flagship news program, Leslie Moonves was signaling his determination to turn the world of broadcast journalism upside down.

PART IV

Anchorwoman

Chapter Twenty-three

Miracle Worker

ONCE EVERY GENERATION OR SO, A PROGRAMMING GENIUS COMES along with an uncanny instinct for what millions of people want to watch on television. During the 1970s, that person was Fred Silverman. In recognition of his record-breaking string of hits—*All in the Family, The Mary Tyler Moore Show, Charlie's Angels,* and *Starsky & Hutch*—*Time* magazine put him on its cover in 1977 and dubbed him "The Man with the Golden Gut."

Nearly twenty years later, Leslie Moonves laid claim to that title. As president of Warner Bros. Television in the 1990s, Moonves displayed a remarkable talent for picking one hit show after another—*Friends, ER,* and *Lois & Clark.* After he left Warner TV in 1995 to become the czar of CBS, Moonves repeated his success with such phenomenally popular shows as *Survivor* and *CSI: Crime Scene Investigation.*

As he approached the 2004–2005 TV season—a decade into his tenure at CBS—the fifty-five-year-old Moonves had accomplished a feat that no one had thought possible. He had smashed NBC's long-standing dominance of Thursday nights with its "Must-see TV" lineup. And he had taken his "geezer network," whose aging viewers were the target audience for Depends adult diapers, and led it to first place not only in overall viewers but also in the eighteen-to-forty-nine-year-old demos so highly valued by advertisers.

Even Moonves's competitors paid homage to his achievement.

"What he's done in ten years," said one NBC executive, "is as worthy of major applause as anything anybody has done in the past quarter century."

SUCH LAVISH PRAISE can swell a man's head and produce feelings of hubris—the excessive pride that leads to a downfall. And by 2004, those hubristic vibes were coming from Les Moonves, a diminutive ex–Hollywood actor whose fleshy, tough-guy features were proof of the old saying that, after a certain age, every man is responsible for his face.

While some of his colleagues at CBS saw Moonves as a man of deeply held convictions, others saw a boss who was a bully and control freak. Moonves appeared to possess the fatal flaw found in many self-made men—the mistaken belief that their achievement in one particular area of life means they possess the answers to everything.

"I understand why creative people like dark," Moonves said, "but American audiences don't like dark. They like story. They do not respond to nervous breakdowns and unhappy episodes that lead nowhere. They like their characters to be part of the action. They like strength, not weakness, a chance to work out any dilemma. This is a country built on optimism."

Moonves made this statement to Lynn Hirschberg, a writer for *The New York Times Magazine*, in September 2005, six years after the debut of HBO's *The Sopranos*, one of the *darkest* and most *successful* TV series in history. However, people who worked for Moonves were so intimidated by him that they were frequently afraid to tell him when he was wrong. Those who argued with Moonves risked becoming his enemy and the target of his volcanic anger.

For years, his chief adversary had been Jeff Zucker at NBC, the network that had dominated primetime till now. Ironically, Moonves had once tried to hire Zucker as the president of the CBS news division. But that was several years before, and nowadays Moonves enjoyed poking fun at his NBC rival as a clueless programmer who was in way over his head.

"The thing that Jeff does well is play for next week," Moonves told the *New York Times*'s Bill Carter. "He's like the old Washington Redskins, the Over the Hill Gang. Play for next week, not next year."

Moonves was a showman in the tradition of CBS founder William S. Paley. For the network's annual "upfront" presentation of its primetime schedule to advertisers, Moonves always booked glamorous Carnegie Hall. And this year, in a spoof of the movie *Million Dollar Baby*, he dressed up as a boxer and pretended to knock out an actor playing Donald Trump, the host of *The Apprentice*, the biggest hit in Jeff Zucker's primetime lineup.

"You know," Moonves told the audience, "this is my tenth time playing Carnegie Hall. I believe that is a new record for a Jew without an instrument."

IF MOONVES WAS tough on Jeff Zucker, that was nothing compared to how he treated CBS anchorman Dan Rather, whom he belittled as a country bumpkin. On election night 2004, he cringed when Rather launched into one of his classic cornball performances: "Bush is sweeping through the South like a tornado through a trailer park. His lead is now shakier than cafeteria Jell-O. Turn the lights down, the party just got wilder. . . ."

The thing that bothered Moonves most, however, was not Rather's Texas mannerisms. Nor was it his reputation for being a dyed-in-the-wool political liberal and corporate loose cannon.* What really bugged Moonves was that the *CBS Evening News with Dan Rather* had been mired in third place behind NBC's Tom Brokaw and ABC's Peter Jennings for seven out of the past ten years.

Moonves hated losing. And now that he had made CBS the undisputed champ in primetime entertainment, he was confident he could work the same miracle with CBS News.

---

* In September 1987, Rather walked off the set and let the CBS network "go black" for six minutes of dead airtime when executives allowed a tennis match to eat into his *Evening News* time slot.

"To [Moonves]," wrote Alan Weisman in *Lone Star,* a biography of Dan Rather, "there really was no distinction between news and entertainment—it was all 'content,' subject to the same programming and marketing laws."

IN THE TWENTY-FIVE years since CNN and cable news came on the scene, the audience for the three networks' evening-news broadcasts had been cut in half—from 54 million viewers to 27 million. And each year brought more bad news about audience erosion.

Moonves blamed the broadcasters, not the audience, for this loss of television's lifeblood. He was fed up with sanctimonious journalists who idealized a golden age of broadcast news that existed (in his view) only in their imagination. He didn't want the "Voice of God" delivering the news anymore. He told reporters that, if it were up to him, he'd "bomb the whole [CBS News] building." And if all that wasn't enough to send shivers up the spines of the CBS purists, Moonves half kiddingly praised a British TV show in which a naked woman read the news.

"Of course," he told the *New York Times,* "[instead of naked news readers] you could have two boring people sitting behind a desk. Our newscast needs to be somewhere in between."

But when Moonves looked around the CBS newsroom for a possible successor to Rather, the available talent left him decidedly *under-*whelmed. The leading candidate, White House correspondent John Roberts, a Dan Rather look-alike who subbed for Rather on weekends, was the favorite of News president Andrew Heyward. But Moonves's vote was the only one that really counted in the News division, and to his Hollywood sensibilities, John Roberts didn't have star power.

MOONVES HAD LONG regarded Katie Couric as the ideal modern broadcast journalist—someone who appealed to the heart as well as to the brain. And by the fall of 2004, he had all but made up his mind that she was his leading candidate to succeed Dan Rather.

Moonves viewed Katie as a "twofer." By stealing her away from his old adversary Jeff Zucker, he would strengthen *CBS Evening News* and, at the same time, deal a body blow to NBC's *Today Show*.

This was the kind of bold, strategic thinking that appealed to the hyper-competitive Moonves. But there was a personal dimension to his thinking as well. Anything that hurt *The Today Show* could help boost CBS's third-place *Early Show* and the career of its attractive co-host, Julie Chen. It just so happened that Moonves was crazy about Julie Chen and, despite their twenty-one-year age difference, was about to make her his second wife.

However, there was a hitch. According to a legal doctrine called tortious interference, which makes it unlawful to meddle in the business affairs of others, Moonves was not allowed to engage in direct negotiations with Katie as long as she was under contract with NBC. Her contract didn't expire until May 2006. But unbeknownst to NBC, Moonves had been holding "informal" (and therefore presumably legal) talks with Katie for the past couple of years.

"We drank many bottles of expensive wine on the sofa of my apartment," said Moonves, revealing how he had managed to conduct his long courtship of Katie Couric out of public sight. "Don't worry. My wife was in the next room."

Contract or no contract, Katie was eager to talk. In fact, as soon as she learned that she was on Moonves's short list to succeed Dan Rather, she ditched her latest heartthrob, jazz trumpeter Chris Botti, and rekindled her relationship with Tom Werner, who was an old Moonves acquaintance. Werner encouraged the CBS chief to meet with Katie for those friendly glasses of wine.

"Tom [Werner] made some well-placed calls to CBS and Les Moonves, hinting that Katie would make herself available for the job if the offer was right," said someone close to Werner. "As an esteemed rainmaker, Tom started a buzz in the CBS executive circles. Most of all, putting his imprimatur on the idea gave it a certain patina it wouldn't otherwise have had, and certainly helped move the courtship of Katie along."

As might be expected, Chris Botti did not appreciate the way he was unceremoniously dumped to make room for the better-connected Tom Werner.

"Chris feels like he was used by Katie," a close friend told the *New York Post*'s Page Six. "Their relationship was very public, and he thinks she used him to make Tom jealous. . . . Chris thinks he was just a pawn. He is heartbroken."

BEFORE MOONVES COULD move ahead with his plan to hire Katie, he had to deal with Dan Rather. For years, Rather had exercised a stranglehold on the news division. His power traced back to the early 1980s when the then-president of News, Van Gordon Sauter, gave Rather control over hiring and firing, and every other aspect of the news operation.

Inevitably, Rather and Moonves had tangled on numerous occasions.

"I had some uncomfortable moments with Les," Rather told the author of this book. "One of the most notable times was when the impeachment of Bill Clinton was under way—only the second president in history to be impeached—and Les made the decision, while the vote was being taken, to stick with an NFL football game. I didn't agree with him on that.

"Then, the first day of the Iraq war two—the current war in Iraq—Les elected to go with basketball rather than war coverage.

"The third thing we had a difference of opinion about was when he made a statement that Ed Murrow has been dead for forty years, and if he, Les, had his way, he'd blow up the whole CBS News. I thought that was wrong, not merely as a matter of taste, but because one of the things what CBS had to offer the audience in added value was the best of the Ed Murrow tradition."

Rather's contract ran for another two years, but it specified that he occupied the solo anchor chair "by mutual consent," which meant that he served at the pleasure of Les Moonves. If he were removed from the anchor chair for any reason, his contract stipulated that he would go directly to *60 Minutes*.

*   *   *

MEANWHILE, TALKS BETWEEN Moonves and Katie continued to drag on. At one point, Moonves confided to his Viacom partner, Tom Freston, that he feared Katie had slipped through his fingers and that he would have to settle for someone else.

"In addition to Katie, CBS had compiled a list of ten or more anchor candidates," said Robert Wussler, a former president of CBS News. "The News division had combed the TV universe, because there were people around Moonves who said he should consider other candidates. And Moonves said, 'Okay, make me a list, but I still want Katie.'"

At one point during his pursuit of Katie, Moonves's famous self-confidence seemed to desert him.

"Moonves calculated that the one thing he could not offer Couric was the bond she had with Zucker," wrote the *New York Times*'s Bill Carter. "He wondered if she would ever be able to walk down the hall to tell Jeff she was leaving."

However, there were several things Moonves *could* offer Katie that Zucker couldn't. One of them was an evening news anchor job. That position wasn't available at NBC, because Zucker had already promised it to Brian Williams in anticipation of Tom Brokaw's retirement.

RATHER HAD HEARD the drumbeat of rumors about Katie Couric, and he called his agent, Richard Leibner, to suggest they meet in a restaurant to discuss the situation.

"We've got to start thinking about the future," Rather told Leibner over dinner, according to someone familiar with their conversation. "I'm seventy-two years old. It's a young person's game. I'm living on borrowed time."

"Are you ready to make a move?" Leibner asked.

"I enjoy what I'm doing," Rather replied. "Maybe I love it too much."

Shortly after that dinner, Leibner had a talk with Moonves and Andrew Heyward, the News president, about Rather's contract.

"Guys," Leibner said, "what are you thinking? Dan's happy. He's not eager to leave. But it's got to happen sometime. So let's talk about what's next and a new contract."

Over the summer, Leibner and Moonves worked out the language of a new deal for Rather. He would relinquish the anchor chair in the second half of 2005 and join the *60 Minutes* repertory company. There, he would receive 68 percent of his former annual anchor salary (or about $4 million) for the first year and a half, and after that, his salary would be reduced on a sliding scale until his contract ran out in 2010.

AND THAT'S WHERE things stood when, in September 2004, Rather committed the greatest blunder of his career. He fronted a sloppily sourced broadcast on *60 Minutes II* that lambasted President George W. Bush for receiving special treatment during his National Guard service.

In rushing the show onto the air, Rather's longtime producer, Mary Mapes, had failed to check her facts as thoroughly as she should have, and Andrew Heyward green-lighted the flawed piece after personally screening it. And before you could say "vast right-wing conspiracy," the Internet was buzzing with conservative blogs challenging Mapes to prove that the questionable documents used on the show were authentic.

She couldn't. In fact, the documents turned out to be bogus.

The once-proud CBS News division was humiliated and the atmosphere turned poisonous. Under instructions from Heyward and Moonves, Gil Schwartz, the CBS communications chief, told Rather he had to defend the report. But Rather had made many enemies at CBS, and they seized the opportunity to get their revenge. Walter Cronkite, who had been banned by Rather from appearing on CBS News programs for more than twenty years, publicly called upon his successor to resign. In Washington, Bob Schieffer, the host of the Sunday political talkfest *Face the Nation*, and a man who despised Rather almost as much as Cronkite did, urged CBS to appoint an outside independent panel to investigate the scandal.

Eventually, CBS appointed such a panel, which came to the conclusion that the *60 Minutes II* story had been driven by "a myopic zeal."

Translated, this meant that Dan Rather's liberal bias had clouded his journalistic judgment. Inside CBS, the panel's report was seen as an effort to blacken Rather's reputation and whitewash the responsible executives—Heyward and Moonves. With that, Rather issued an on-air apology, leaving his reputation in shambles.

THE SCANDAL PRECIPITATED a period of chaos at CBS, and brought Sumner Redstone, the cranky eighty-one-year-old chairman of Viacom—CBS's parent company—into the picture.

At a Viacom board meeting, a furious Redstone blamed Rather for jeopardizing his company's fortunes. As a result of the *60 Minutes II* program, Bush administration officials had reportedly told Redstone that he could forget about the big corporate tax breaks his lobbyists had been seeking. Redstone didn't like to be told where to get off, especially when it impacted negatively on the one thing he really cared about—Viacom's stock price.

"I want anyone associated with that guy [Rather] to go!" Redstone hollered. "They all have to go!"*

Until now, Moonves had been running neck and neck with Tom Freston, the president of Viacom's cable operations and Paramount movie studio, in a race to succeed Redstone as the chairman of the company. Inevitably, there was speculation that the Dan Rather scandal had tipped the scales decisively against Moonves and in Freston's favor.

But Moonves was an adroit corporate player who had been careful to hedge his bets. He and his new wife, Julie Chen, had gone out of their way to court Redstone and *his* young wife, Paula. And their ingratiating attention had paid off. Moonves felt confident that he had the support of his mercurial Viacom boss.

Thus, where others saw only looming disaster for Moonves, he saw opportunity. Here, at last, was the perfect storm that he had been

---

* Mary Mapes was promptly fired, several other producers were forced to resign, and CBS News president Andrew Heyward was allowed to hang on for nine months, until he was fully vested in his pension. Moonves also canceled *60 Minutes II.*

waiting for—a storm that would sweep away the Old Order with Dan Rather and usher in a new one with Katie Couric.

"Until the Rather thing, Andrew Heyward had been allowed to run the News division as its titular head with a minimum of interference from Moonves," said a TV agent. "After the Rather thing, Heyward collapsed in a sweat and tried to please Moonves at all costs. The Dan Rather episode brought Les Moonves into the News division with both feet."

ABOUT A MONTH later—on the morning after George W. Bush was reelected president—Rather's agent, Richard Leibner, was summoned to News president Andrew Heyward's office, where he found Les Moonves impatiently awaiting him.

"Dan's got to go," said Moonves. "And the sooner the better."

"Look," Leibner said, "we need to do this in a classy way. The twenty-fourth anniversary of Dan in the anchor chair comes up on March nine. That would be a good time."

"I think I can make that happen," said Moonves, implying that he needed to run the idea by Sumner Redstone, who was pressuring Moonves to do whatever it took to get rid of Rather. "And by the way," Moonves continued, "the deal we were discussing this past summer regarding Rather's reduced salary on *60 Minutes* is no longer on the table. Give me a year, and we'll resume pretty much along the lines we worked out."

"Would you put that on paper?" Leibner asked.

"No," Moonves replied. "Not on paper."

MOONVES'S ONE-MAN RULE at CBS meant that he didn't have to take into account the opinion of others. Thus, in the fall of 2005, when he offered Sean McManus, who was already president of CBS Sports, the added title of president of CBS News, Moonves did not bother to tell McManus that he intended to make Katie Couric the face of CBS News. He only informed McManus of his plans on the day McManus was hired.

That same day, Moonves and McManus met with Shelley Ross, the talented executive producer of *Good Morning America*. They were considering Shelley for the job of McManus's second-in-command, and Shelley, whose days were numbered at *GMA*, was interested in the job.

"Katie is our Plan A," Sean McManus told her.

"I'm curious," said Shelley. "Why did you make a run for Katie rather than Matt Lauer? All my opposition research shows that when Katie takes time off from *The Today Show*, the needle doesn't move. But it does when Matt's off the show. Her negatives have gone up because she makes too much money, is too blonde, and shows too much leg."

"Katie's available, Matt's not," Sean said. "But we still don't know if we're getting Katie."

"Then what's your Plan B?" Shelley asked.

"We don't have a Plan B," Sean replied.

THE CBS EVENING NEWS wasn't the only thing Moonves was promising Katie.

"Mike Wallace is into his deep eighties and won't be around *60 Minutes* much longer," Moonves told Katie, according to a reliable CBS source. "I'll make you a star of *60 Minutes*, replacing Mike."*

When Katie was a girl, her father had told her that the number-one job in all of journalism was Walter Cronkite's anchor slot on the *CBS Evening News*, and that a close second was a correspondent's job on *60 Minutes*. Now, as Katie approached her forty-eighth birthday, Les Moonves was offering her the chance to make her father's dream for her come true.

"I'll put together a promotion campaign for Katie the likes of which TV has never seen," a CBS source quoted Moonves as saying. "I'll build the entire CBS News organization around her. *Katie* will be the star rather than the *news*.

"And down the road," he continued, "once Katie has run her string

---

* Mike Wallace's retirement from *60 Minutes* was announced six months later.

as the managing editor of the *CBS Evening News*, we'll develop a syndicated show for her and make her the next Oprah."

Clearly, Moonves was a true believer in Katie's matchless star power. Thanks to her versatility, he could amortize her salary over many different platforms—the *CBS Evening News*, *60 Minutes*, the Super Bowl pregame show, guest appearances on the CBS *Early Show*, primetime news specials, the CBS radio network, and a personal diary on cbs.com.

With that in mind, Moonves began whispering numbers with a lot of zeros after them into the ears of Katie's business representatives—agent Alan Berger and attorney Craig Jacobson. According to one reliable TV industry source, Moonves offered Katie $100 million over a period of five years, or $20 million a year. Other sources put the figure at $75 million for five years, or $15 million a year. The lower of these two figures came to be accepted by most TV reporters as accurate, though none of them seemed to factor into the equation incentive provisions, syndication-sales fees, and extra compensation for Katie's work on *60 Minutes*.

"I talked with Katie about Moonves and his offer," said a former NBC News executive who spoke with the author of this book on condition of anonymity. "She felt she had run her course at *The Today Show*. Jeff Zucker offered her some nice stuff—a long transition out of *The Today Show* to do various things in primetime. My understanding is Jeff really upped NBC's financial offer to match Moonves's. I heard the figure of twenty million a year. Jeff even offered her Fridays and summers off, just like Johnny Carson. Jeff didn't want to see his archenemy Moonves getting Katie."

"I'm trying to figure out what I want to do," said Katie, sounding as though she was torn between her loyalty to Jeff Zucker (to whom she was barely speaking) and the anchor spot waiting for her at CBS. "I'm trying to make a thoughtful decision while being in the middle of this media spotlight, which I am trying to ignore."

In the fall of 2005, Katie met with her agent and lawyer for dinner at a Manhattan restaurant.

"[Alan] Berger had come prepared, though in a low-tech fashion," the *New York Times* reported. "He had a yellow legal pad with a line drawn approximately down the middle in ink. On each side he and [Craig] Jacobson had written a list, the pros and cons. The list was long on each side. It reportedly included a multimillion-dollar promise by Moonves to launch a raid on other networks to hire major news talent. But even then, one item on the pro side stood out. The anchor position was a job that Katie Couric wanted to do and thought she could do."

QUITE A FEW of Dan Rather's colleagues were happy to see him go. They welcomed Rather's interim replacement, Bob Schieffer, as one of their own, and came to appreciate Schieffer for his decision to show-case correspondents (rather than himself) on the *Evening News*. They were ecstatic when the homespun Schieffer put into words the jour-nalistic credo by which they lived:

> People don't turn on the news to be entertained. They turn on the news because they think they need to. They think you're going to tell them something they need, information that they need to make the decisions that any good citizen has to make.

But the same news purists who embraced Schieffer were horrified when they discovered that Moonves intended to make good on his promise to revolutionize the news. Moonves had ordered Andrew Heyward to put together trial heats of a revamped *Evening News*. For the time being, Moonves went along with John Roberts in the anchor chair. But after Heyward had produced three such dry runs, Moonves was still dissatisfied.

"No, no, no," he told Heyward. "That's not different enough. I want a total break with the past. Go back to the drawing boards."

"I thought some of that was pretty good, Les," Heyward said. "What is it you didn't like? What is it you want?"

"I don't know what I want," Moonves said. "But I'll know it when I see it."

Through leaks to the press, CBS staffers let Moonves know that they opposed his plan to "commercialize" the news.

"News is commerce, too," an indignant Moonves responded. "The news people are all being paid lots of money. So it's a little hypocritical to claim that I [am] turning news—a sacred tradition—into commerce. . . . Well, you know what, guys? When your agent calls, he's not being shy about asking for money. He views this as commerce."

To tamp down the revolt brewing in the newsroom, Moonves sought out Mike Wallace, the veteran CBS journalist, and asked for his understanding.

"He told me that he was sensitive to the charge that he didn't care about news, and that he resented the charge, and wanted to prove that he did care," said Wallace. "And, of course, the lady he went after [Katie Couric] came out of the News division of NBC.

"Moonves made some stupid comments, like wanting to blow up the CBS News building," Wallace continued. "But he's not a bad guy by any means. He's a talented guy and savvy, and he's sensitive to the fact that people are skeptical about him and how he's trying to take over the News division, which wasn't permitted in the days of Mr. Paley. But today's CBS is a tough one to run. Moonves has got to make money. He's got to be the genius who makes it all work."

Chapter Twenty-four

Damaged Goods

Some at CBS were concerned that in his single-minded effort to shake up the *Evening News*, Moonves had failed to take into account one of Katie's most glaring shortcomings—her unabashed bias in favor of liberal causes. These people argued that by appointing Katie to replace Dan Rather (who had been a favorite target of conservatives ever since Watergate), Moonves was simply substituting one transparent liberal for another.

Katie had often expressed her sympathy with the left and her distaste for the right. For instance, she had once called Ronald Reagan an "airhead," and had denounced the Reagan administration for promoting "greed" and "ignoring" the poor—all without offering any proof for her assertions. What's more, she had conducted a number of interviews that were featured on conservative websites as conspicuous examples of her left-wing leanings. Some examples:

• When she had Whoopi Goldberg on *The Today Show*, the comedian alluded to an occasion when she and Katie had "marched together" in an abortion-rights demonstration. "Nooo," Katie interrupted, giggling. "I'm not allowed to do that [take sides on social issues]." To which Whoopi replied: "Oh, no, that's right. We have *not* marched together. It was somebody who *looked* like you."

- During an interview with Hillary Rodham Clinton, Katie said (referring to Hillary in the third person): "Why do you think Hillary Clinton elicits such powerful emotions? . . . Don't you think there's an awful lot of projection that goes on in terms of how people view her, placing their own confused states or their role in society or [beliefs about] how powerful women should be, and it's sort of projected upon her as an individual?"*

- With Oliver North, Katie said: "Some people are very concerned about talk shows, radio talks shows in general, of course. Most of them around the country have a decidedly conservative bent. The rap that some people give them is that they reflect the views of a very vocal minority, the extremists in this country, and don't really reflect the true nature of political debate in the United States. And, as a matter of fact, they tend to be quite divisive and sort of have a bad, a negative impact on the country."

- Interviewing former Texas governor Ann Richards, Katie said: "Let's talk a little bit more about the right wing . . . a climate that some say has been established by religious zealots or Christian conservatives."

But as far as Moonves was concerned, Katie's politics didn't enter into the equation. To him, hiring Katie Couric made all the sense in the world. Women news anchors had long outnumbered men in local TV newsrooms. They appealed to women viewers, who controlled 80 percent of household purchases. If Katie Couric could transfer that kind of *local* success with women to the *network*, the increased profits would pump life into Viacom's sagging stock price—and put Moonves on the fast track to replace Sumner Redstone when the old man finally stepped down.

Of course, there was a vast difference between local and network news. On many local stations, newscasts were on the air for two to three hours each afternoon, leaving plenty of time for so-called an-

---

* When Katie received an award from the group Women in Communications, she was given the opportunity to choose anyone she wanted to present it to her. She picked Hillary Rodham Clinton.

chor "tell stories"—narratives that carried an emotional punch and were often told best by women. By contrast, the thirty-minute evening news shows on CBS, NBC, and ABC were interrupted by so many commercials that they devoted only eighteen to twenty-two minutes to the news. And the network anchors were seen on screen for an average of only four or five minutes.*

With more and more people—especially *young* people—shunning newspapers and television and getting their news on the Internet, some experts viewed the evening news anchors as "dinosaurs." Moonves agreed that the Internet was changing the rules of the game, and that, in the future, online users—not "omniscient" anchors—would decide which stories they wanted to watch. But he parted company with those who were inclined to write obituaries for the evening newscasts.

What counted, Moonves believed, was that the networks still minted money on their nightly newscasts; together, they earned $600 million a year in ad revenue. However, CBS accounted for only one-quarter (about $150 million) of total network advertising. By revolutionizing the way the news was packaged and delivered, Moonves projected that CBS could squeeze at least another $50 million a year out of that thirty-minute time frame.

Thus to Moonves, the day was coming when CBS News would no longer be in the business simply of imparting information. It would be in the business of using warm, womanly emotions to court valued demographic niches.

IN THE END, Katie's decision to go to CBS was influenced by factors that were largely beyond her control.

To begin with, she was pushing fifty—an age that put her out of sync with the younger audience sought by *The Today Show*. She didn't

---

* Back in the fall of 1963, when CBS broadcast its first half-hour evening news program, there were four minutes of commercials and twenty-six minutes of news. Today, the three major evening news shows average twelve minutes of commercials and only eighteen minutes of news.

want to become the Miniver Cheevy of morning television. After years of slugging it out with Diane Sawyer, she was losing her enthusiasm for the fray. She was often heard complaining to her hair and makeup people about her grueling, crack-of-dawn schedule.

"I can't believe that I'm still doing this!" she would say.

With Katie's reign as the queen of morning television apparently drawing to a close, *Good Morning America* launched an all-out assault on *The Today Show*. *GMA* began running sneak previews of two of ABC's wildly popular primetime shows, *Desperate Housewives* and *Lost*. This move paid off big time. On one particular Monday, Diane Sawyer and Charlie Gibson beat Katie and Matt Lauer by 800,000 viewers.

There was growing concern inside NBC that Katie had become "damaged goods." The publicity about her $65-million *Today Show* contract (which should never have been made public), her leg-baring short skirts (which should have been vetoed by her producer), her celebrity friends (which should have been downplayed), her divalike behavior (which should have been reined in), her made-for-tabloid romances (which should have been kept under wraps)—all this undermined her Girl Next Door image and damaged her Q scores. One telling sign that Katie had lost some of her mojo: NBC decided to send *Nightly News* anchor Brian Williams, instead of Katie, to host the Winter Olympics.

In April 2005, as Katie's Q ratings fell lower than even those of Dan Rather, Alessandra Stanley, the TV critic of the *New York Times*, dropped a bombshell. Lately, Stanley wrote, Katie's "image has grown downright scary: America's girl next door has morphed into the mercurial diva down the hall. At the first sound of her peremptory voice and clickety stiletto heels, people dart behind doors and douse the lights. . . . *Today* has turned her popularity into a Marxist style cult of personality. The camera fixates on Ms. Couric's legs during interviews, she performs innumerable skits and stunts, and her clowning is given center stage even during news events."

Scenting blood in the water, the sharks at *The National Enquirer* moved in for the kill.

"Insiders say that Katie's sweet public persona is in stark contrast to how she acts when the cameras are off," the *Enquirer* wrote. " 'She sends assistants running to the ladies' room in tears,' a spy at NBC's Studio 1A told *The National Enquirer* . . . 'She expects everyone—even the interns—to get her what she wants as soon as she says "I need . . ." According to Katie, everyone is an imbecile and nobody deserves to work with her.' "

When AOL invited its subscribers to comment on Katie's diminishing appeal, there was an avalanche of responses.

"I don't want to see someone with bare legs and open-toe shoes giving me the news," one AOL user typically complained. "Why can't she look professional?"

In a lengthy analysis of Katie's "Cruella syndrome," Salon.com contributor Rebecca Traister tried to cut her some slack, but only made matters worse: "Couric is . . . a successful and wildly wealthy woman who is still a cultural anomaly; her job is to be one of us—it's how she's been sold," wrote Traister. "Of course, she's tough and ambitious—you don't just bubble your sweet little way up through the ranks of a national news organization. But the perk makes her palatable, disguises her as unthreatening. The more she can frost her steely insides with a spun-sugar exterior, the more she can convince us that she is one of us, the more successful she becomes, the more she becomes an anomaly."

Katie insisted that she paid no attention to such negative coverage.

"I didn't read it," she said of Alessandra Stanley's piece in the *Times*. "I just knew it was going to be snarky and nasty."

But Frank Radice, head of advertising and promotion at NBC, told a different story: "Katie and I talked about that Alessandra Stanley piece a lot," Radice said. "There were people within NBC who were sending vitriolic notes to the press. Katie has heart and soul, too, and when people say bad things about her, it bothers her. When you're in the public eye, you need protection. Even though she's a superstar, she's still human."

YET ANOTHER OUTSIDE factor that influenced Katie's decision was the unexpected changing of the guard at the evening-news shows. Suddenly, all three anchors who had dominated the nightly news for nearly twenty years were gone: Tom Brokaw stepped down in favor of Brian Williams at NBC; Dan Rather was replaced temporarily at CBS by Bob Schieffer; and Peter Jennings, who died from lung cancer the previous August, was succeeded at ABC by co-anchors who were twenty years his junior—Elizabeth Vargas, forty-three, and Bob Woodruff, forty-four.

If she took the CBS anchor job, Katie wasn't sure she could overcome Brian Williams's commanding lead in the ratings, but she felt confident she could beat Elizabeth Vargas and Bob Woodruff, who, despite their relative youth, came across on camera as oddly stiff and old-fashioned. If Katie could add as little as a half a ratings' point, she'd more than pay for herself in added revenues, and become a hero by making CBS the number-two network in news.

"People don't want to see robo-anchors regurgitating whatever is on the teleprompter in front of them," she said. "They want people to be natural, people who feel things, who react to things."

If those words sounded strangely familiar, that was because they echoed the sentiments of Les Moonves. In fact, Katie (with her ambition to be taken seriously as a journalist) and Moonves (with his excessive pride and arrogance) had discovered that they were a perfect match.

At least, that's how Jeff Zucker interpreted Katie's behavior. As far as he was concerned, Katie was already out the NBC door in mind and spirit, if not yet in body.

"Jeff has already gotten through the 'I'm pissed' stage," said one of his friends, "and moved into the 'I'll deal with it' stage."

Indeed, Zucker felt he couldn't waste any time. He had to start looking for the next Katie Couric.

Chapter Twenty-five

Wooing Meredith

IN THE FALL OF 2005, WHILE KATIE WAS CHATTING WITH LES
Moonves over a glass of wine, Meredith Vieira received a call from
Jeff Zucker. He wanted to know if Meredith—host of *The View* and
Who Wants to Be a Millionaire?—could see him right away.

"My schedule makes it difficult," she told Zucker, "because I go
right from *The View* to the *Millionaire*."

"Well, can I give you a ride?" he asked.

"The *Millionaire*'s just around the corner from *The View*," she said.

"Well," Zucker replied, "I'll drive slow."

When Meredith climbed into Zucker's SUV, he rolled up the
tinted windows and introduced her to his driver, Mike. Then he
turned to her and said:

"I don't want to beat around the bush. You and I have been down
this road before. There may be changes at *Today*, and you'd be terrific."

"I though you'd want to skew younger," said Meredith, who was
about to turn fifty-two.

"I want experience," Zucker replied.

Meredith rolled her eyes.

"At least you could say I'm young," she joked.

Minutes later, the SUV pulled up in front of the *Millionaire* studio,
at Central Park West and Sixty-sixth Street (*The View* was shot at

West End Avenue and Sixty-sixth Street), and Meredith got out. Her agent, Michael Glantz, was waiting for her.

"What happened?" asked Glantz, who knew she had been talking with Zucker.

"There's interest," she told him.

FIVE YEARS BEFORE, Meredith Vieira had had a similar conversation with Les Moonves and the then–CBS News president, Andrew Heyward. They wanted to bring her back to the CBS *Early Show*, which she had briefly cohosted in the early 1990s when it was still called the *CBS Morning News*.

At the time she met with Moonves and Heyward, Meredith was still enjoying her gig on *The View*, the Barbara Walters–created kaffeeklatsch. Her three children were young, and her husband, Richard Cohen, who had suffered from multiple sclerosis since the age of twenty-five, was recovering from a recent bout with colon cancer.

"Back then, the timing wasn't right," Meredith recalled. "And I didn't have confidence in that [CBS] broadcast. But by now, I was a little itchy with *The View*. So I met with Jeff Zucker a second time, in my agent's office, and I really liked him."

After Zucker left, Meredith turned to her agent and said, "No matter what happens, I think Jeff's a great guy. You know, I feel excited."

As CHRISTMAS APPROACHED, stories began appearing in the press about Katie's plans to leave *The Today Show*. In most of those stories, Meredith Vieira's name was mentioned prominently as a likely replacement.

Katie had ambivalent feelings about Meredith. Years before, Meredith had quit *60 Minutes* because the incessant travel for interviews forced her to be away from home many weeks of the year. As a result, Meredith had acquired a reputation in her profession as being a woman who put family before career—just the kind of reputation that Katie herself had sought, with mixed results, to achieve.

On the other hand, Meredith had never attained Katie's level of television stardom, and she made only a fraction of Katie's salary. Katie didn't think much of Meredith's ability to draw and hold an audience on *The View*.

"You know," Katie told *Forbes*'s James Brady in an unguarded moment, "their [*The View*'s] numbers aren't that good. They get talked about and they promote very well, but don't have the ratings. Who watches it?"

Katie was aware that Meredith had replaced her as the most important person in Jeff Zucker's life. As Katie saw it, Jeff seemed downright eager to get rid of her. He was talking about releasing Katie early from her contract, so that she could negotiate with CBS's Les Moonves and he could get on with a smooth transition on *The Today Show*.

Of course, Katie's feelings in these matters were no longer Jeff Zucker's chief concern. He had something more important to worry about—namely, saving *The Today Show* from collapse post-Katie. And so, when Michael Glantz, Meredith's agent, called Jeff and told him that Meredith was interested in pursuing their conversations further, Jeff was delighted.

"Well," he said, "let's have her meet Matt."

As it turned out, Meredith was up against four contenders from inside NBC. But in the eyes of Jeff Zucker, each of these candidates had a serious weakness. Campbell Brown was considered to be not warm enough for the morning audience; Natalie Morales didn't have enough hard-news experience; Alexis Glick looked too young; and Ann Curry didn't come across as strong enough.

With no obvious in-house candidate, Matt Lauer had come up with the idea of approaching Meredith Vieira, and he had sold the idea to Jeff Zucker.

Meredith did not know that she was Matt's first choice when they met in December. Nor was she aware of how desperate Matt was to replace Katie, who no longer had her heart in the job. In fact, Matt had privately told several executives at NBC that he would quit his job if they signed up Katie for another four years.

"It was a blind date that absolutely worked out," Meredith recalled of her meeting with Matt. "I told Matt, 'I'm not looking to travel a lot. I don't have that craziness. I don't have that old drive and hysteria for the big gets.'"

"Why are you telling me that?" Matt asked.

"Because you asked me what concerns I had about joining the show. And I wanted you to know that I'm not as aggressive as that. Also, as I told Jeff, if he's looking for someone to go to events at night and show the *Today* flag, he's got the wrong girl. I go home to my family. That's who I am."

IN JANUARY 2006—just as Meredith's negotiations with NBC and Katie's negotiations with CBS were shifting into high gear—a roadside bomb exploded thousands of miles away in Iraq, upsetting the plans of all three television networks. The bomb gravely injured Bob Woodruff, one half of the new ABC anchor team. The next day, Elizabeth Vargas, the other half, dropped a bomb of her own: she told ABC News president David Westin that she was pregnant.

When Diane Sawyer received word that Bob Woodruff had suffered a massive head wound, she rushed over to ABC's *World News Tonight* studio, carrying an anchor-ready black dress. Diane had gone after the anchor chair once before, after Peter Jennings's death, and her interest in the job only intensified after she heard that CBS's Leslie Moonves might make Katie Couric the first solo woman anchor.*

David Westin asked Diane and Charlie Gibson to become alternating substitutes for Woodruff on *World News Tonight.* That created a kind of journalistic bakeoff between Diane and Charlie. But an unanswered question hovered over ABC News: Did Diane Sawyer really want the job enough to fight Charlie Gibson for it?

"Yes and no," Diane said.

"Westin was again in a tough spot," wrote *New York Magazine.* "Not only did he have Gibson eyeing the door [if he didn't get the

---

* In May 2006, Vargas announced she was going on maternity leave.

job], but he had repeatedly told Vargas she would still be a co-anchor of *World News Tonight* after her maternity leave, and she was expecting that promise to be kept. But more important, he had yet to fully discern the desires of ABC News' resident sphinx Diane Sawyer, in large part because she herself couldn't make up her mind."

Nor could Westin. In fact, he was in a desperate quandary. If he gave the anchor job to Diane Sawyer and, as a result, Charlie Gibson quit, that would leave *GMA*—ABC News division's cash cow—without a major star.

"In my opinion, Westin should have given it to Diane anyway," said a TV agent, reflecting the views of many in the industry. "Westin still had Charlie Gibson under contract. He should have kept Charlie in the morning and brought Meredith—an ABC person—over to replace Diane. If he had done that, he would have scored a brilliant trifecta—depriving Zucker of a strong candidate for *The Today Show*, creating Diane as the first solo woman news anchor on ABC, and making Moonves's investment in Katie look late and ridiculous."

But things didn't turn out that way. Instead, Westin played it safe and, in May 2006, he tapped the sixty-two-year-old Charlie Gibson as the permanent anchor—and Diane Sawyer's lifelong dream of becoming a nightly news anchor went up in smoke. This broke the talent logjam and left Jeff Zucker free to continue his pursuit of Meredith Vieira.

"Jeff got incredibly lucky that he could get Meredith Vieira," said a former NBC News executive. "ABC fucked that one up."

FOR ALL THE Sturm und Drang at ABC, the media's chief focus was on Katie.

"I actually had it easy when those changes were happening, because so much of the spotlight was on Katie," Meredith later remarked. "She was going to the *Evening News*, and there had never been a woman to be the solo anchor of an evening newscast. So I felt like . . . everyone was gunning for her in a way. I felt very bad the way a lot of media reacted to Katie. And I could to some degree slip in, not that there wasn't a lot of pressure. How's she gonna do filling the shoes of Katie Couric? But I didn't feel I think the same kind of pressure that Katie did."

While the press was speculating about Katie's future, Meredith felt it was time to have a talk with Barbara Walters.

"Barbara was okay about it," Meredith said. "She reminded me about the hours and the grind of a morning show. Afterwards, she said to me, 'You didn't ask for my opinion, but if you had, I'd have said, "Take it." ' "

"If ABC had come back with something to counter the NBC offer—not necessarily money, but some kind of indication that they wanted to keep me—I would have had second thoughts," Meredith continued. "I liked filling in on *Good Morning America* or doing specials. I wanted to be *wanted*. But [David Westin's] attitude was 'We love you, but we don't have anything for you.' "

"BECAUSE OF MY HUSBAND, Richard's, condition, I think I have become more understanding of others," Meredith said. "My children are now seventeen, fifteen, and thirteen. Everything in our lives is a family decision. When I told the children about *The Today Show*, they wanted to know, 'What's in it for us?' And I told them, 'You can go to the Olympics, the political conventions, and concerts.' My son, Gab, wants to be a sportscaster or writer, and I told him, 'You can be there on the set of *The Today Show* and see how it's put together.'

"From the beginning," she continued, "Richard always thought I should do it. Certain opportunities come along in life, and you've got to do it. So you find a way. Of course, it's always scary to change. I had to overcome fear of change.

"*The Today Show* is a hybrid; one moment you're giving the news, the next you've got a monkey in your lap. But Jeff Zucker and Jim Bell said they wanted someone who could come in and make a smooth transition. They liked me. They felt that my personality would work, and that I had credibility after twenty years in journalism."

*   *   *

SHORTLY AFTER MEREDITH was named Katie's successor, the two women had a chance to talk on the phone.

"Katie called me after the announcement," Meredith said, "and we laughed about how everyone is asking us the same thing: 'The pressure, the pressure, how are you going to handle the pressure?'"

Chapter Twenty-six

"A Celebration of Moi"

By now, stories were appearing everywhere about Katie's likely defection to CBS. But she still didn't have a binding agreement with Leslie Moonves, and the uncertainty of living in contractual limbo seemed to be driving her crazy. She yelled at her crew during commercial breaks and got into so many spats with other members of the cast that her agent, Alan Berger, flew in from the West Coast to act like a hall monitor on the set of *The Today Show*.

It was at this time, when Katie was in a state of almost continuous nervous agitation, that Les Moonves had his first real glimpse of the vulnerable side of her personality—the fearful, childlike woman who hid behind Katie's carefree facade.

Moonves didn't seem overly troubled by what he saw. His years at Warner Bros. Television had taught him how to care for the egos of temperamental stars. He was especially adept at making himself available to such difficult personalities. Thus, even as the CBS lawyers were hammering out the final details on Katie's contract, Moonves emerged as Katie's chief guide and counselor—the latest in the long line of strong male figures that included Guy Pepper, Bill Thompson, Tim Russert, Jeff Zucker, and Tom Werner.

* * *

MOONVES UNDERSTOOD THAT Katie had reached a breaking point at NBC; there was nothing Jeff Zucker could offer her except more money and, down the line, a copycat Oprah-like talk show. In sharp contrast to the limited options in Zucker's bag of tricks, Moonves was offering Katie a whole new lease on life—a more humane working schedule (no more five-thirty in the morning wakeups), extra time with her daughters (who were entering their teen years), and the chance to re-create a network news division (and make her father proud).

Even at this late date, however, not everyone at CBS shared Moonves's faith in Katie. In fact, internal CBS research showed that a large portion of the television audience still had trouble getting their news from a woman.

"Nervous executives at CBS have been examining tapes of Couric from August 2001—and nitpicking her performance—when she substituted for a vacationing Tom Brokaw," Matt Drudge wrote in the Drudge Report. " 'Politely put, it's just not there,' warned a top CBS suit who spoke on condition of anonymity. 'Look, why do you think NBC passed her over for Brian Williams? They can say she was worth more to them in the mornings, but I really think it came down to how she came off in the [anchor] chair.' "

Such talk didn't cut much ice with Moonves. He did not subscribe to the school of thought that said success in news depended on journalistic gravitas. He was a creature of Hollywood, a man who had unlimited faith in star power and who measured things in terms of dollars and cents.

On April 2, *Television Week* broke the news that a deal between Katie Couric and CBS was completed "in principle." Two months later, with the ink barely dry on the contract, Moonves appeared at an investors' conference in Santa Monica.

"Katie probably paid for herself in the first week of our upfront [sales to advertisers]," Moonves boasted. "We brought in about fifteen million dollars more for the . . . *Evening News* in the first week. . . . She will be one of the best bargains. I've already made my money back. There aren't too many Katies."

Katie wasn't quite as ebullient.

"If I said I wasn't trepidatious at all—there's a good SAT word—I would be lying," she said. "Every time you make a big change that gets a lot of attention, it's a bit—what shall I say—anxiety producing. I may lay a big fat egg. I just hope this is fun. I said to the people at CBS, 'This better be fun.' "

"It was really a very difficult decision for a lot of reasons," Katie told *The Today Show* audience in April, when she announced her move to CBS. "First of all, because of the connection I feel with you," she continued.

> I know I don't know the vast majority of you personally, and it may sound kind of corny, but I really feel as if we've become friends through the years. And you've been with me during a lot of good times and some very difficult times as well. And, hopefully, I've been there for you. I can't tell you how grateful I am for the support you all have given me. And I so appreciate that you've included me in your morning routine.

"She seemed like her old self last week, starting with the teary, gracious announcement that she was—gasp—taking the new job," reported *Newsweek*. "That night, she reportedly called [Bob] Schieffer at home to thank him for being so supportive. During a photo shoot for *Newsweek*, she also received a congratulatory call from [Meredith] Vieira, and the two chatted and laughed like old friends. Couric also got a call from Hillary Clinton and a note from Nancy Reagan—how many people hear from those two in the same week?"

Everyone in television land was eager to see how Jeff Zucker would handle the loss of his biggest news star. Never one to let a ratings' opportunity pass him by, Zucker pulled out all the stops for Katie's farewell broadcast on *Today*.

"Obviously," Zucker told Howard Kurtz, the *Washington Post*'s media reporter, "it's a little awkward when someone is going to work for the competition. But there's no acrimony here, and a great deal of fondness for Katie. The fact is, she's been an incredibly important part of *Today* and NBC. . . . I think even she is sometimes embarrassed by the amount of attention that she and similar people get in these positions."

Indeed, Katie described her three-hour marathon send-off on *The Today Show* on May 31, 2006, as a "celebration of moi, ad nauseam." It included clips of her first day on *The Today Show* in 1991, her ambush interview with former President George H. W. Bush, and her live coverage of 9/11. Zucker pushed good taste to its limits when he gathered a group of colon-cancer survivors and brought them on stage wearing T-shirts that read THANK YOU, KATIE on the front and YOU SAVED MY LIFE on the back.

There were worshipful tributes from Katie's cast mates. Matt Lauer saluted Katie's "unsurpassed grace, wit, and charm," and called her the "perfect combination of Edward R. Murrow and Lucille Ball"—a description that would surely have left both Murrow and Ball scratching their heads.

"We all love you, Katie," said Ann Curry, who had tangled with Katie on numerous occasions. "You know you've affected our lives not just professionally but personally. I'm a different person because I know you, because you've made me better. You've made me love you, and don't be a stranger because if you do, I'll come calling. I mean really!"

To which Katie replied: "You're starting to freak me out, Ann!"

Chapter Twenty-seven

Great Expectations

THE ERA OF PRETENTIOUS ANCHORING IS OVER," KATIE DECLARED IN the summer of 2006 as she prepared to take over the *CBS Evening News*.

To mark this break with the past, Les Moonves ordered construction crews to tear down Dan Rather's old set in the "fishbowl"—as the CBS newsroom was called—and put up a new one for Katie. But instead of designing a set that reflected an unpretentious broadcast, Moonves proceeded to build a colossal, illuminated anchor desk with as many digital bells and whistles as the Astro Vision screen in Times Square.

While construction on this multimillion-dollar set was in progress, the newsroom operation was moved to the CBS cafeteria. And it was there, from a makeshift studio, that interim anchor Bob Schieffer conducted his remaining broadcasts, and continued to confound Moonves by attracting viewers with his "old-fashioned," voice-of-God style of delivery.*

---

*Bob Schieffer increased the viewership of the *Evening News* by more than 300,000 during his year-and-a-half reign.

*   *   *

IN THE FOUR MONTHS between Katie's tearful farewell on *The Today Show* and her much-ballyhooed debut on the *CBS Evening News*, she was involved in every aspect of the show's makeover. Yet her decisions—like Moonves's—seemed to reflect a curious ambivalence about the shape of the future newscast.

To take one example: her "look producer," Bob Peterson, asked Oscar-winning composer James Horner to write new theme music for the show. Katie said she wanted something that would evoke "Americana" and "waving fields of wheat." But instead, she chose a showy fanfare that conjured up old Hollywood movies of Cleopatra's entry into ancient Rome.

Another example: Katie eagerly welcomed Walter Cronkite's offer to lend his gravelly baritone to the newscast's voice-over introduction— even though the ghostly acoustical presence of the ninety-year-old Cronkite hardly represented a break with the past.

Katie brought with her from NBC half a dozen producers, a personal assistant, and a secretary. These people had been part of NBC's first-place news team, and from the day they arrived, they didn't let the old-timers at last-place CBS forget it. The inevitable clash of cultures caused confusion and resentment on all sides.

As part of Katie's plan to emphasize health-related stories, she replaced veteran medical correspondent Elizabeth Kaledin with Jonathan LaPook, the doctor who had arranged Katie's famous on-camera colonoscopy. With his halo of white hair and mush-mouthed delivery, LaPook seemed out of place in front of a television camera.

Katie also okayed several new segments for her broadcast, including one called "Free Speech." A visual Op-Ed page that allowed outsiders to bloviate each night for 90 seconds, it wasted precious time that should have been devoted to more substantive matters.

*   *   *

SHE WAS IMPATIENT to get on with things.

"It's been an out-of-body experience to watch these major news events unfold in my pajamas," she joked with reporters during a conference call. Then, turning more serious, she added, "The downside of all the attention is to suggest I'm going to single-handedly save anything. I'm just going to try to be a contributor with a great group of people who are already in place."

Actually, the group in place at CBS wasn't so great. As Katie discovered to her dismay, years of cost cutting and scandal had badly tarnished the Tiffany Network. Of the major networks, CBS had the fewest bureaus, the fewest correspondents, and the smallest contingent of writers, editors, and producers. Its equipment was old and decrepit, and the CBS broadcast facility on West Fifty-seventh Street was in a state of woeful disrepair.

"Moonves promised Katie that he would build CBS News around her," said a veteran CBS reporter. "But what he didn't tell her was that CBS News had been hollowed out. It had become more of a news-*packaging* operation than a news-*acquiring* operation."

With several notable exceptions, the ranks of CBS News were staffed with dead wood—aging, insular, self-important journalists who still got high on the fumes of CBS's past glories.

"There are a lot of old-timers there," said Jonathan Klein, president of CNN/U.S. and a former CBS executive. "There's a great history and great pride in what they used to be, a great yearning to return to their heyday and in this world there is no certainty of that."

"It's a big organization," said Sean McManus, the CBS News president. "I'm sure there are people who were very comfortable with the way it was done. The fact was, it needed to be energized. It needed to be confirmed to everyone that being number three was not acceptable."

OF MORE IMMEDIATE concern to Katie was the choice of her new executive producer. Like the manager of a baseball team, the executive producer, or EP, chose the daily batting order (of stories) and called the plays (how to play those stories). Katie's EP, Rome Hartman, was a popular figure who had come from *60 Minutes*, where he had distinguished himself producing segments for Lesley Stahl, among others. But it soon became apparent to Katie that Hartman was the wrong choice for a crisp, fast-paced evening news show.

Then, too, Katie was unsure about the credentials of news president Sean McManus, the son of legendary sportscaster Jim McKay. McManus was widely credited with bringing CBS Sports back to life. But even his most ardent supporters wondered about the breadth of his vision when it came to news. To make up for his inexperience in news, McManus hired as his deputy a veteran producer named Paul Friedman, who had worked as Peter Jennings's EP on *World News Tonight*.

"Katie grew up at NBC, and it was hard for her to go to a new network like CBS, where you have to learn the systems and figure out who you can trust to give you an honest answer," said an NBC executive who knew Katie well. "That takes time. Wherever you are, you have to have a supporting group around you. She went to CBS as the managing editor, and found it hard to find a balance. She's got to be a role model—the boss—but she needs the support of a strong partner who can tell her 'No.'"

Perhaps most troubling of all, Katie had been led to believe by Moonves that Sean McManus would be given the budget to capitalize on her famous name. She expected McManus to attract new talent and turn CBS News into a murderers' row of star broadcast journalists. But that didn't happen. Instead, McManus made a rather awkward bid to hire George Stephanopoulos, host of ABC's Sunday talk show, as a replacement for the aging Bob Schieffer on CBS's *Face the Nation*.

Predictably enough, Schieffer emitted a loud yelp of protest, which was heard all the way to Viacom's corporate headquarters. Was this any way to reward the loyalty of someone who had held down the fort until Katie's arrival? The answer came back from on high—*No!*—and McManus was told to drop his plans to hire Stephanopoulos.

* * *

IN THE MEANTIME, Moonves made good on at least one of his promises to Katie. He launched a $13 million publicity blitz that promoted her as though she was the star of a forthcoming Hollywood blockbuster.

Her face was plastered on hundreds of New York City buses. She turned up on the cover of several magazines, including *Parade,* where she was featured wearing jeans, a man-tailored shirt, and no shoes. Her face (shot through a gauzy, soft-focus lens) was seen by millions of people all over America in promos that ran during commercial breaks on CBS's most popular primetime shows.

The entire CBS organization seemed to be carried away by its expectations for Katie. In such an intoxicating atmosphere, major screwups were probably inevitable. CBS's in-house magazine illustrated a glowing piece on Katie with a digitally altered image that shaved several pounds off her five-foot-two-inch frame. Tampering with photos is a journalistic no-no, and Katie went ballistic, tearing into Gil Schwartz, the head of the CBS publicity department.

"She read him the riot act," said a CBS source.

"Everything is fine between Katie and Gil now," said Katie's personal PR man, Matthew Hiltzik. "She was upset, and now she's not."

KATIE HAD HIRED Hiltzik back in November 2005, using the excuse that she needed someone with Hiltzik's PR background to handle her philanthropic work. But that didn't make sense to those who knew Hiltzik. A slightly built man who spoke in a near-whisper, Hiltzik was, in fact, one of the roughest and toughest PR men in America. His clients included Miramax's Harvey Weinstein (no slouch in the diva department) and Hillary Rodham Clinton, for whom Hiltzik devised the listening tour that successfully kicked off Hillary's first Senate campaign.

As Hiltzik saw it, Katie had a serious image problem. Many people, in and out of her profession, viewed her as a broadcast lightweight. What made matters worse, Katie found it hard to respond to such criticism.

"Maybe it's my size," she told Jacquelyn Mitchard, who interviewed her for *Parade.* "Maybe it's my looks. Maybe it's my gender. Maybe it's just . . ."

"She doesn't use the word 'jealousy,'" Mitchard wrote, "but it hangs, unspoken, in the air."

To counter the impression that Katie didn't have the chops for the nightly news, Hiltzik created a fifteen-page briefing book that laid out Katie's qualifications to be a news anchor. It noted that she had interviewed dozens of heads of state, world leaders, American politicians, and business tycoons, and it cited stories that had run in the media about Katie's achievements.

Hiltzik also sent Katie on a Hillary-esque listening tour, with stops in San Diego, San Francisco, Dallas–Fort Worth, Denver, and Tampa.

"In Minneapolis," noted *Good Housekeeping*'s Jenny Allen, "she took time out to pose with the city's statue of Mary Tyler Moore and, Mary-like, toss her baseball cap into the air."

"If you believe the version of events from CBS," wrote Jon Friedman in MarketWatch, a widely read Dow Jones website, "the listening tour is an opportunity for Couric to see what we ordinary folk think about the news, the country and the government. But let's get real for a moment. It's really nothing more than a piece of media manipulation designed to see what we think about . . . Katie."

For all the razzle-dazzle of the listening tour, however, Hiltzik's most interesting work for Katie was conducted behind the scenes and out of sight of the public.

IN THE EARLY summer of 2006, Hiltzik was approached by David Pecker, the president of American Media, Inc. (AMI) and publisher of such supermarket tabloids as *Star, The National Enquirer,* and *Globe.* Pecker asked Hiltzik if he would be interested in becoming AMI's public relations representative.

Seeing an opportunity to help Katie, Hiltzik said that he was definitely interested in the job. But there was one condition: He would only take the assignment if Pecker promised that the tabloids would be "fair" to Hiltzik's other clients, especially Katie Couric.

Pecker agreed. From now on, he told his editors, all stories about Katie would have to be run by Hiltzik for his personal approval *before* publication. The editors were to work with Hiltzik to resolve any is-sues he might have.

Along with Oprah, Kathie Lee Gifford, and Kelly Ripa, Katie was frequently portrayed in the tabloids as "breaking down," "collapsing," "exploding," or, at the very least, "in tears." Normally, the tabs had a policy of sending publicists so-called comment letters, which briefly described contentious points in stories and headlines. But thanks to his extraordinary deal, Hiltzik had ratcheted up that disclosure policy several notches.

"Stories about Katie and Matt Lauer had traditionally sold papers for us," said one tabloid editor. "Now that she was the first female network news anchor, she could become an even bigger seller. But by cutting the deal with Pecker, Hiltzik clearly hoped to head off the tabs at the pass."

The Hiltzik-arranged truce between Katie and the tabloids didn't last very long. It began to unravel in August, after the Gallup Organiza-tion disclosed that Katie had come in as number eleven in its popularity poll of TV personalities. Katie trailed behind Diane Sawyer, Charles Gibson, Brian Williams, and even the recently disgraced Dan Rather.

The Gallup poll represented an embarrassing blow to Katie on the eve of her *Evening News* debut, and Tony Frost, a hard-bitten veteran of the Fleet Street newspaper wars in Britain, ordered his tabloid re-porters to jump on the story.

Frost wasn't overly concerned about Hiltzik's reaction. For by this time, Pecker had decided that Hiltzik wasn't doing AMI much good. However, after the *Globe* story was written, Frost assigned a senior edi-tor to call Hiltzik and read him the headline—KATIE BREAKS DOWN—and the topics that were covered in the piece, including references to the fact that Katie was "in tears" and was devastated by the news.

According to the senior editor, Hiltzik flew into a rage, shouting obscenities over the phone, and saying he would see to it that the arti-cle would never be published.

"I cannot go on like this!" Hiltzik reportedly said.

Then he slammed down the receiver.

In the end, Frost had no trouble convincing Pecker to run with the story. It contained a prominent statement from a Katie "spokesman" (presumably Hiltzik) denying that her "life is a mess," or that she had "collapsed in tears." Indeed, the spokesman was quoted as saying that Katie "is in a very good place in her life."

Nonetheless, it appeared that Hiltzik had overplayed his hand.

"Hiltzik tried to make apologies for his outburst, but it was too late," said the senior editor. "With his temper tantrum, he gave away the fact that he had promised Katie more than he could deliver. At the end of September, our agreement with Hiltzik expired, and our coverage of Katie returned to normal."

LIKE MANY CELEBRITIES, Katie had an ambivalent relationship with the media. On the one hand, she was annoyed by their constant invasion of her privacy. On the other, to get attention and keep up her ratings, she encouraged the tabloid feeding frenzy with incessant talk about her dead husband, her children, and her life as a single mom on the dating scene.

"Asked if she's in a romantic relationship," reported *The National Enquirer,* "[Katie] didn't deny that she has a special guy, coyly replying: 'I have a fun, happy social life. I will just say that I have been having a good time and am really happy.'"

Katie was now involved with a tall, handsome Washington, D.C., businessman by the name of Jimmy Reyes, who was six years her junior. Little was known about Reyes other than the fact that his immensely wealthy family owned a sprawling real estate and food-and-drink distribution business.

Gossip columnists in New York and Washington identified Reyes as a big supporter of President George W. Bush. They suggested that his Republican connections might have had something to do with his appeal to Katie, who was looking for a way to soften her reputation as a liberal Democrat. But on closer inspection, it turned out that Reyes's political contributions to Republicans were quite modest, and no one at the Bush White House had ever met him.

"Jimmy is not a political guy to the degree his parents and brothers are," said a family friend. "He just looks after his business interest and lets it go at that. He has never attended political parties, schmoozed with politicians, and sought out White House invitations like his father. Jimmy would rather go to a rock concert of a classic rock act like Elton John. That's what he enjoys."

The relationship with Katie had Reyes's friends scratching their heads. Katie made no secret of the fact that she wanted to get married, but Reyes—the divorced father of two—wasn't exactly the marrying kind. Shortly after his own divorce, the billionaire bachelor became engaged to a young woman, only to get cold feet at the last moment and call off the wedding. A few months later, he was seriously dating the vivacious conservative commentator Laura Ingraham. By April of 2005, the couple was engaged. But soon afterward, when Ingraham announced she was fighting breast cancer, he broke off that relationship, too.

The callous double dumping of two fiancées inspired *New York Daily News* columnist Lloyd Grove to dub Reyes the "runaway groom."

"Jimmy hates entanglements and loves his freedom," said a friend. "Katie is in danger of making the classic mistake women make in relationships: she thinks she is going to be able to change him and make him the marrying kind. The odds are Jimmy is more set in his ways now that he has been on his own for almost five years."

Asked why Katie, with her multimillion-dollar salary, would be attracted to Reyes, a person acquainted with both of them said:

"Katie is like many women who get rich. It just gives them the appetite for more and, at the same time, makes them fear losing what they have. Katie's future in television news is only as good as the next Nielsen rating, and she knows it. With two young girls to raise, and a pretty lavish Park Avenue–house-in-the-country lifestyle, her savings could be depleted pretty quickly.

"Katie has mused to me about running for politics one day, or writing a novel," this friend continued. "A marriage to Jimmy Reyes would end her money worries forever, and free her to indulge her whims in early retirement."

An even more likely explanation was that Katie simply enjoyed being around happy-go-lucky Reyes, especially at a juncture of her life when she was under so much pressure at CBS. Jimmy Reyes liked to laugh and have a good time. So did Katie. Jimmy loved rock music. So did Katie. Jimmy was a jock. So was Katie. Jimmy was a fraternity boy at heart. And so (despite her gender) was Katie.

Katie Golightly

H<small>I, EVERYONE</small>!"

Katie's girlish informality on her opening-night broadcast stunned many of the older, more traditional viewers who usually watched *The CBS Evening News*. And they weren't alone in their reaction. On September 5, 2006, more than 13.5 million people (many of them borrowed from NBC and ABC) sampled Katie's debut—an astonishing number that appeared to certify Leslie Moonves's claim to be The Man with the Golden Gut.

Judging by the initial Nielsen ratings, Moonves's $100 million gamble on Katie was paying off. She not only beat NBC's Brian Williams and ABC's Charlie Gibson on week one, but she repeated that feat in week two—marking the first time since July 1998 that *The CBS Evening News* had won back-to-back weeks.

"I am very pleased with what happened with Katie," said Moonves. "I learned early on in the television business you never make predictions. We've been in last place in the news for well over a decade, and now we're competitive. That's all I can ask for."

T<small>HE EUPHORIA THAT</small> swept through the corridors of CBS didn't last very long, for it quickly became apparent that something wasn't sitting right with viewers at home.

To begin with, Katie seemed uncomfortable reading the news from the teleprompter. For someone who was justly famous for her off-the-cuff style, she had an unnatural way of speaking from the anchor chair. She emphasized too many words in each sentence, making it appear as though she was giving a public recitation, rather than chatting one-to-one with each member of her audience.

More troubling, Katie didn't even *look* like Katie. Her makeup was slathered on too thickly, and her forehead didn't move when she spoke. Her severely arched eyebrows gave her an angry expression. And this look only seemed to get worse with each passing night.

"What's with the eyebrows?" one of her bosses asked her.

"What do you mean?" Katie replied, feigning ignorance of the rumor that she was having Botox treatments.

"Come on," said her boss, "I'll show you a tape to compare last night with tonight."

Then there was the matter of her clothes.

"We hired a wardrobe person," said a CBS News executive, "and Katie agreed to spend time shopping and paying for new clothes. We told her, 'Stick to simple, dark business suits.' But she would wear them three or four days a week, and then say, 'Fuck it,' and turn up in something awful.

"The reason her blouses and jackets don't fit is that she's vain," he continued. "She always buys clothes that are one size too small. And when people point to her clothes, she says, 'Well, Charlie Gibson looks shabby. So why do they pick on me? Because I'm a woman? It's so unfair!'"

UNFAIR OR NOT, Katie became the object of extraordinary media scrutiny. And the fault-finding wasn't confined to her appearance. Her skills as a journalist were also called into question.

Her first outing on *60 Minutes*—an interview with Condoleezza Rice—was a case in point. Instead of engaging Rice in a serious discussion of foreign policy, Katie seemed to morph into a juvenile reporter from a school newspaper. She asked Rice such girly questions as:

"[H]ow does one go about asking the secretary of state out for a date?" And she wondered out loud whether "the U.S. is a bully, imposing its values on the world."

"What's wrong with assistance so that people can have their full and complete right to the very liberties and freedoms that we enjoy?" Rice asked.

"To quote my daughter," replied Katie, reverting to teen slang, 'Who made us the boss of them?'"

Remarked *Variety* TV critic Brian Lowry: "As for Couric, the trajectory of her personality-driven leap to CBS has proven strangely predictable: enormous initial curiosity followed by the dawning realization that there's not much 'there' there—a point starkly underscored by her 'How does one go about asking the secretary of state out for a date?' interview with Condoleezza Rice on *60 Minutes*."

It was at about this time that Katie's friends began to notice a strange disconnect between her grown-up responsibilities as the face of CBS News and her adolescent behavior off camera.

Less than a month after her CBS debut, she attended a cancer fund-raiser in Manhattan where she was introduced to a tall, good-looking young man by the name of Brooks Perlin. Unlike the self-made types Katie had been attracted to in the past—Jay Monahan, Tom Werner, and Chris Botti—Perlin came from a family of privilege. And at thirty-three years of age, he was, biologically speaking, young enough to be forty-nine-year-old Katie's son.

Perlin grew up in the tony suburban community of Darien, Connecticut. After graduating from Hotchkiss (the same elite boarding school attended by Tom Werner), he went to Williams College. There, he was known as a jock who liked to parade around—à la John F. Kennedy Jr.—without his shirt on.

Though Katie found herself drawn to the young and energetic Perlin, their nearly seventeen-year age difference gave her pause. But when Perlin called for a date, Katie couldn't resist saying yes.

"They seem comfortable with each other," said one of her friends.

"She's a very young fifty. She's playful. She's cute. She's down-to-earth. And he's mature. They seem happy."

"It's a great match," said another friend of Katie's. "They both are honest and up front. They make one another really happy."

Somehow, they managed to elude the paparazzi and keep their love affair secret for several months. They skied in Sun Valley and sunbathed on the beaches of Mexico. And when they were in New York, they often spent the nights at each other's apartment.

"Her behavior was a puzzle," said someone who was familiar with Katie's relationship with Perlin. "An anchor is supposed to be synonymous with wisdom. Going out with a man who is seventeen years your junior may be a sexual turn-on, but it's not the height of wisdom. Keep in mind that she is grist for the tabloid mill, and that she'd inevitably be caught. Seen that way, her behavior can only be described as self-destructive. And you can be sure that if Les Moonves knew about it, he'd have thrown a conniption fit.

"It's my guess that Katie didn't really understand why she was flaunting this relationship with a younger man, and how, in an unconscious way, that might have been connected to her discomfort in the role of a serious news anchor," this person continued. "She would have told you that she had fallen in love. That she and Perlin were so compatible. A Demi Moore–Ashton Kutcher kind of thing.* But it sure looked like she was acting out in a very serious way."

By October, Executive Producer Rome Hartman and his immediate boss, Sean McManus, had become deeply troubled by the collapse in Katie's ratings. Despite the network's huge investment in Katie, she and *The CBS Evening News* were back where they started—in third place.

According to scuttlebutt from the CBS fishbowl, Rome Hartman was afraid to criticize Katie to her face, whereas Sean McManus came down hard on her, telling her exactly what he thought was wrong with each show.

---

* The age difference between Demi Moore and Ashton Kutcher is fifteen years.

But Katie did not want to listen.

"Katie is like Peter Jennings," said a CBS executive. "She's always saying, 'I know what's good for me. My way is the best way.' It's her vanity. And it comes through in many different ways. She has her assistants do things that other on-air personalities do for themselves. She's got this divalike behavior. Her secretary is a bitch. She's got her PR guy, Matthew Hiltzik, copied on all memos at CBS that have to do with her."

As Katie stumbled from one dismal broadcast to another, she began to blame Sean McManus for her troubles. She took to calling him "Sports Boy" behind his back, and went over his head to complain to Les Moonves.

"This is the worst organized place in television," she was quoted as saying. "There's nobody here. There's no talent. Andrew Heyward [the former president of News] let things go down the drain."

She didn't get along with her staff. In early October, she summoned the CBS News investigative unit to a meeting and chewed them out.

"Your [investigative] stuff isn't strong enough, it's not compelling enough," she shouted at the head of the unit in front of his entire staff.

Another time, a technical glitch left her standing without a script—or anything to say—for several minutes at the end of a show. As soon as the red light on top of the camera went off, she yelled: "Get me McManus! Get me Moonves!"

"Just a minute," one of the executives in the fishbowl said. "Katie, the reason you make fifteen million a year is to carry off these little glitches like a pro."

"In the newsroom . . . are crammed three groups, compared by one dramatic industry type as the Sunnis, Shiites and Kurds of network news," Rebecca Dana wrote in the *New York Observer*. "There is the old CBS crowd of Mr. Rather's era; the new CBS crowd of Mr. Hartman's; and the privileged clutch of producers who came to the network with Ms. Couric, the NBC crew. They aren't exactly warring factions, nor are they a seamless melting pot."

Indeed, "the NBC crew" failed to bond with "the old CBS crowd" of floor directors, cameramen, and graphics people. And Katie's attitude toward the staff only made matters worse. When she wasn't chastising people, she was spending time alone in her office above the fishbowl, which effectively removed her from day-to-day operations. The NBC imports let it be known in many subtle—and not-so-subtle—ways exactly what they thought about the ancien regime at CBS: *not much*. As far as the NBC people were concerned, the CBS people were total losers who didn't know what the hell they were doing.

"If you're going to be the managing editor of the *Evening News*," said one CBS veteran, "you're expected to get in early and stay late. That's the only way you can mold the program and provide leadership. But Katie didn't come in early and she didn't come down from her aerie until late in the day. Then she tried to throw her weight around.

"Everyone in the operation keys off the anchor," he continued. "They are sensitive to your mood. They have to see you covering stories, circulating around, saying 'hellos,' 'how's your son'—that sort of thing. They want to believe you are the *best* reporter in the whole world, because only the *best* deserves to be the anchor."

The loudest moans came from CBS correspondents, who complained that the *Evening News* was becoming a star turn for Katie, and, as a result, they were getting less and less airtime.

"I look at it as a good thing for the correspondents," Katie said. "Now, instead of having to rush to get pieces on the air every night, they get an extra day or two to work on them."

Among those who dismissed Katie's explanation as disingenuous was the network's young, glamorous chief foreign correspondent Lara Logan. With her streaked blonde hair, well-filled-out sweaters, and on-camera derring-do, Logan came across as a rising star—one of the few reasons to tune in to *The CBS Evening News*.

Like many of the CBS women, Logan was concerned that fewer and fewer stories were being assigned to female reporters; in fact, according to one estimate, women received 40 percent fewer assignments under Katie than they had under Bob Schieffer.

On one occasion, when Logan reported on house-to-house street fighting near the Green Zone in Baghdad, her footage was deemed too raw to be aired on the *Evening News*. Upset, Logan retaliated by sending an e-mail to friends, asking for their help.

"I would be very grateful if any of you have a chance to watch this story and pass the link on to as many people as you know possible," she wrote. "It should be seen. And people should know about this."

The implication was clear: Katie Couric, the managing editor of the *Evening News*, was not doing her job.

KATIE'S WEAKNESS AS an anchor was on abundant display during CBS's election-night coverage in November. While Brian Williams over at NBC and Charlie Gibson at ABC handled the tricky assignment with their usual panache, Katie had to rely on the expertise of Bob Schieffer to get her through the night. And she didn't do much better two months later when it came to her coverage of President Bush's State of the Union Address.

"While Couric read from prepared historical information about past State of the Union Addresses, Schieffer did the up-to-date political analysis," Tom Shales wrote in the *Washington Post*. "In fact, he seemed to get even more screen time than Couric in the minutes leading up to the speech."

"[H]er lack of serious reporting experience severely handicaps her on hard news," commented Al Neuharth, founder of *USA Today*.

Even Katie's celebrated interviewing instincts seemed to desert her. She devoted half of one show—a full nine minutes—to a fireside interview with Karen James, the widow of a climber who had lost his life on Mount Hood. It turned out to be a *Today Show*–style tearjerker that deserved no more than forty-five seconds on an evening news program.

"Nobody at CBS had the balls to tell Katie, 'There's nothing here,'" said a person familiar with the internal debate at the network over the Mount Hood widow interview. "But Katie got so caught up in trying to prevent *The Today Show* from getting Karen James first that she lost all perspective."

BY THE BEGINNING of the new year, the top brass at CBS were trying to shift the blame for Katie's failure to someone else. News President Sean

McManus pointed an accusing finger at a convenient target—the news media. He charged that they had sabotaged Katie with their "absurd set of expectations for her." When someone pointed out to him that it wasn't the members of the media who had raised those expectations— that it had been Les Moonves and his hype—McManus was unable to come up with a convincing response.

As one of the major architects of CBS's failed revolution in news, McManus knew that his job was on the line. After his blame-the-media excuse fell flat, he tried a more politically correct explanation. Katie's problems, he said, were due to rampant sexism.

"I think it is a fact there are probably people, both men and women, who are perhaps uncomfortable having a woman anchor the news," he said. "The way [Katie] is scrutinized, I think sometimes unfairly, quite frankly, I think a lot of that has to do with gender."

Katie herself played the "chick" card in her CBS blog. Writing about a White House briefing for network anchors, she noted:

> As I was looking at my colleagues around the room—Charlie Gibson, George Stephanopoulos, Brian Williams, Tim Russert, Bob Schieffer, Wolf Blitzer, and Brit Hume—I couldn't help but notice, despite how far we've come, that I was still the only woman there. Well, there was some female support staff near the door. But of the people at the table, the "principals" in the meeting, I was the only one wearing a skirt. Everyone was gracious, though the jocular atmosphere was palpable.

As the critical February "sweeps" period approached, Katie's public mask—the affable, spontaneous, loosey-goosey Katie—seemed to melt away, revealing the frightened, confused, angry Katie underneath. Why, she demanded to know, were people criticizing her for being her natural self? After all, wasn't that why Les Moonves had hired her in the first place?

Weren't her amusing asides during the *Evening News* exactly what Les asked for? She didn't hear Les object when Dr. Jonathan LaPook, discussing a vaccine to prevent cervical cancer, spoke candidly about the dangers of teenage sex, and Katie (the mother of two adolescent daughters) ad-libbed with the crack "You've just ruined my day."

Did Moonves complain when, on another occasion, Katie introduced a story about Arnold Schwarzenegger by imitating Ah-nuld's funny way of talking? That was her shtick. That was what she was known for.

And didn't Moonves find it amusing when Katie handed a pair of pink slippers to correspondent Steve Hartman after he did a feature on a Texas sheriff who forced his prisoners to wear pink?

"I think I'm pretty judicious about [using off-the-cuff remarks]," she said. "I think that, probably, it may be off-putting at times to some people who are used to a very, very buttoned-up newscast that doesn't have much leeway for an occasional glimpse of personality, but you know, I try. I've always had the 'less is more' philosophy, believe it or not, but there are times when I think it's personally fine. If people feel discomfort, maybe they should consider a suppository!"

HER CRITICS PORTRAYED her as someone who lacked the gravitas to be an anchor. And judged by her choice of a tadpole boyfriend, her use of tasteless language ("Bite me" was another one of her favorite expressions), and her bizarre behavior, Katie seemed determined to prove her critics right.

In January, she and her friends decided to celebrate her fiftieth birthday with a big blowout at Tiffany. They organized a themed party patterned after Holly Golightly, the fey call girl played by Audrey Hepburn in the 1961 movie *Breakfast at Tiffany's.*

At this critical juncture of her career, Katie's choice of Holly Golightly seemed particularly revealing. For like Holly, Katie couldn't seem to make up her mind whether she wanted to be a mature and responsible woman or a cute girl. For the Tiffany party, she donned Holly's black cocktail dress, long black gloves, and a tiara, and invited two hundred friends for cocktails, dinner, and dancing.

"It was the first time we'd ever done anything like this," said Fernanda Kellogg, the head of public relations at Tiffany & Co. "The aspect about the birthday that caught our attention was that all the gifts were going to colon cancer research in honor of Katie's husband, Jay Monahan. . . . It was quite lavish, the spirit was lavish. We have an entertaining space for customers on the fifth floor, and the space was transformed for the evening with blue tableclothes, votives, and Tiffany settings."

Katie greeted each of her guests at the door and handed tiaras to the women as they entered. The store remained open for business so that people could purchase items of jewelry during the party, with the proceeds going to charity.

"There were drinks made of vodka and a blue dye to match the color of Tiffany blue," said someone who was at the party. "Tony Bennett and Bette Midler performed. Dinner began at about eleven-thirty. They served a lot of American comfort food—meatloaf and ribs. And dancing went on until one-thirty in the morning. Katie didn't want it to end."

Chapter Twenty-nine

No Way Out

DURING THE FOUR "SWEEPS" PERIODS OF THE YEAR—NOVEMBER, February, May, and July—the networks rolled out their best programs in an effort to boost ratings. The February sweeps took place in the dead of winter, when people were indoors watching television, which explained why February was packed with so many major events, such as the Super Bowl, the Grammys, the Winter Olympics, and the Academy Awards. Everyone in television considered the month a must-win.

In her fifteen years at *The Today Show*, Katie had always come out on top in the sweeps. But the February 2007 results, announced by Nielsen Media Research at the beginning of March, revealed a very different story. In her first six months, Katie had (a) failed to increase the number of viewers who watched *CBS Evening News;* (b) failed to hold on to the gains she had made in her first few months; and (c) lost nearly 10 percent of the viewers she had inherited from Bob Schieffer.

It was the weakest performance Katie had ever turned in, and the critics were waiting in the wings to pounce.

"It's impossible for me to make any sort of evaluation at all about [Katie], BECAUSE I CAN'T BELIEVE HOW BAD HER MAKEUP IS," Nora Ephron blogged in capital letters on the Huffington Post.

"I wonder if anyone at CBS has concluded that the time has come to move Couric back to where she belonged all along: early-morning television," said Dow Jones media columnist Jon Friedman. "I suspect that CBS could find a place for Katie on the couch, yukking it up with Harry [Smith], Hannah [Storm] and Julie [Chen]."

The CBS Evening News, wrote *South Florida Sun-Sentinel* columnist Tom Jicha, "has become so soft that if someone slammed a door in your home, the screen would collapse like a soufflé."

And so it went. . . .

One minute, Katie was accused of being too soft on Karen James, the Mount Hood widow; the next, she was criticized for being too hard on Democratic presidential hopeful John Edwards and his cancer-stricken wife, Elizabeth.

"Couric . . . told John Edwards that some people might judge him 'callous' for campaigning through what might be his wife's last months," blogged Barbara Ehrenreich in the Huffington Post. "Is Couric forgetting that she was working as a $7-million-a-year NBC anchor while her own husband was dying of colon cancer?"

"Some people," said Katie, "are rooting for me to fail."

For once, the critics agreed with her. The media coverage of Katie did indeed seem to contain a large element of schadenfreude, the perverse enjoyment some people derive from the misfortune of others. On CNN's Sunday edition of *Reliable Sources*, host Howard Kurtz and Gail Shister, the television columnist for the *Philadelphia Inquirer*, tried to dissect this schadenfreude about Katie:

Kurtz: [Katie] recently told *Esquire* that the critics are after her and some people are rooting for her to fail. What do you make of that?

Shister: I think some people are rooting for her to fail, and I don't think it's because she's a woman; it's because, part of it is the money that she's making—estimated $15 million a year—and there's a lot of resentment about that.

Kurtz: The jealousy factor.

Shister: Yes, the jealousy factor.

* * *

There was no shortage of jealous people at CBS News. They set up an office pool and bet on how long it would take Les Moonves to chop off the head of Rome Hartman, the executive producer of the *Evening News*. Those who bet on the second week in March won.

To replace the soft-news Hartman as EP, Sean McManus tapped a hard-news guy, fifty-nine-year-old Rick Kaplan. A TV warhorse, Kaplan had begun his career at CBS in the early 1970s, working as a producer for Walter Cronkite. Since then, he had wandered the networks, serving as executive producer for some of the biggest news stars in the business, including Peter Jennings, Ted Koppel, and Diane Sawyer.

A six-foot-seven bear of a man whose nickname was Baby Hughie, Kaplan had a reputation for throwing fits—and, at least on one occasion, for threatening to throw someone out the window. His temper tantrums had frequently gotten him in trouble; he had been fired from his last two jobs, as head of CNN and MSNBC. For the past couple of years, Kaplan had been living in a kind of forced exile at Harvard's Kennedy School of Government.

His friends insisted that he had mellowed at Harvard.

"Rick was on the beach, couldn't get a job for two years in broadcasting, and that tends to give you a perspective on life," said a close associate. "Rick is more mature. He's got a broader point of view. He's a more tolerant person."

But Moonves and McManus weren't looking for mature and mellow; they were looking for energy and excitement—and for someone who could extract better results from Katie Couric.

"Beneath his gruff exterior, Rick really cares about news," said a CBS correspondent who had worked with him. "He's a newsperson to the core. His challenge will be to convince Katie that he's here to save her, and that she's got to help him. Even if they disagree, she's got to trust him and go along with whatever he says."

People at CBS were shocked to learn that Katie hadn't been informed about Kaplan's hiring until the day before it was announced.

What was the point of having the title of managing editor, they asked, if you couldn't choose your own executive producer?

In fact, Kaplan's arrival signaled a major shift in power at CBS News. By making Katie the managing editor of the *Evening News*, Les Moonves had allowed her to launch a virtual coup within his own company. Now, realizing that he had made a big mistake, he launched what amounted to a counter-coup, withdrawing power from Katie and giving it to the triumvirate of Sean McManus, McManus's deputy Paul Friedman, and Rick Kaplan.

Any lingering doubt about who was calling the shots on a day-to-day basis was cleared up in short order by the hard-charging Kaplan. His first big breaking story concerned the scandalous conditions at Walter Reed Army Medical Center, where many veterans of the Iraq war received treatment for serious wounds. President Bush was thrown on the defensive by the shocking details of neglect and malpractice, and he appointed former Senator Robert Dole to head a commission of investigation.

"I'm going to interview Dole," Katie announced one day in her usual I-know-best fashion.

"You're *not* going to interview Dole," Kaplan said. "The Dole commission hasn't done anything yet. You want to interview one of the generals who was fired from Walter Reed."

As ordered, Katie interviewed the general.

She also dropped her breezy "Hi, everyone" nightly opener. Now, under the new Kaplan regime, she greeted her audience with the slightly more proper "Hello, everyone."

"THERE IS A SUREFIRE way of knowing when your stock is slipping at a network," said a TV correspondent who was still delivering the news on camera after forty-five years in the business. "All you have to do is observe the behavior of the man who's driving you around in the company car. He knows everything. If he doesn't make you sign his voucher, that means you're an important person and still on top. If you have to sign it, you're in trouble."

By April, the signs were everywhere that Katie was having to sign the voucher.

- Over at ABC, Charlie Gibson, who, like Katie, had made the jump from morning to nightly television, succeeded in knocking NBC's Brian Williams from his longtime perch as number-one in the ratings. In a dig at Katie, the press started referring to the white, male, sixtyish Gibson as "the anti-Couric."
- When AOL conducted a poll asking its users, "Was switching to CBS a good move for Couric?" 82 percent responded "No." Similarly, 78 percent answered "No" when asked, "Was choosing Couric a good move for CBS?"
- On April 16, *TelevisionWeek* published its annual list of "The 10 Most Powerful People in TV News." Conspicuously missing was the name of Katie Couric.*
- Also in April, someone blew the cover on Katie's six-month-old love affair with her boy toy, Brooks Perlin. The *New York Post* reported: "Couric has often been spotted getting out of her limousine and heading to Perlin's East Side apartment near Sutton Place." The embarrassment this caused Katie (and her daughters) was nothing compared to the damage it inflicted on her reputation as a serious journalist. After all, how could a woman involved in such foolish behavior hope to replace Walter Cronkite as the most trusted person in America?

THERE WERE OTHER signs of Katie's diminished power.

"Remember CBS' news anchor Katie Couric?" *Broadcasting & Cable*'s J. Max Robins wrote after the May "upfronts." "The network

---

* *TelevisionWeek*'s unscientific list: 1. Roger Ailes, chairman and CEO of Fox News; 2. Steve Capus, president of NBC News; 3. Charles Gibson, anchor, *ABC's World News;* 4. David Westin, president of ABC News; 5. Tim Russert, moderator of *Meet the Press;* 6. Keith Olbermann, host of MSNBC's *Countdown with Keith Olbermann;* 7. Sean McManus, president of CBS News; 8. Jon Klein, president of CNN/U.S.; 9. N. S. Bienstock, talent agency; 10. Jon Stewart, anchor of Comedy Central's *The Daily Show.*

was a little hazy on the name last week. Save a passing reference to *60 Minutes,* Couric received the persona non grata treatment at Wednesday's upfront at Carnegie Hall. Last year, Couric bounded on stage to thunderous applause, greeted as the one anointed to resurrect *CBS Evening News.* But everybody at the hallowed Hall knows how that turned out. Ratings are down significantly from the first flush after Couric took the helm, and even if the quality of the newscast is improved, the show seems mired in an endless downward spiral."

Everyone at CBS News could sense that Katie was no longer in a position to reward her friends or punish her enemies. She had nothing to say, for instance, about the hiring of Jeff Greenfield as the show's new political analyst. She watched as one of her favorite NBC imports, a producer, was forced off the show. She was vulnerable, an easy target, and people began taking shots.

"From the moment [Katie] walked in here, she held herself above everybody else," a CBS staffer told the *Philadelphia Inquirer*'s Gail Shister in an article that shook the TV industry. "We had to live up to her standards. . . . CBS has never dealt in this realm of celebrity."

Shister noted that CBS had become a sieve of negative leaks about Katie: "seven correspondents, producers and executives at CBS and other networks" were interviewed for her story. There was "a growing feeling" at CBS, Shister wrote, that hiring Katie was "an expensive, unfixable mistake." Then, Shister dropped a bombshell: Katie might stay in her job only through the 2008 election.

Who were these people saying such negative things about Katie? According to FOXNews.com's Roger Friedman, the chief detractor was none other than Bob Schieffer.

"Indeed," wrote Friedman, "one of Couric's frequently mentioned enemies is Bob Schieffer, the lovable, durable veteran journalist who filled in as anchor of *The CBS Evening News* between Dan Rather's departure and Couric's arrival. But sources say that Schieffer has been unhappy lately, mainly because his airtime, which was prominent when Couric first started, has dwindled in recent weeks."

Schieffer denied that he had anything to do with the negative talk about Katie. But that didn't stop FOXNews.com's Friedman from naming a second Katie critic—*60 Minutes'* Lesley Stahl.

A highly reliable source, who spoke to the author on condition of anonymity, said that Stahl told her: "CBS News is in a terrible state of disarray and disillusionment, Katie won't take advice about anything. She's very high handed. She's taken young correspondents off the air. The majority of people at *60 Minutes* dislike her intensely, because she's not up to the kind of work they do, and tends to do pull-at-your-heartstrings type of stories."

Faced with something close to a revolt, Rick Kaplan called an emergency meeting. Everyone on *The CBS Evening News* staff—from Katie on down—attended.

"Does anyone have questions?" Kaplan asked toward the end of the meeting.

"Yes," said a female producer. "How long are we going to take this crap against CBS?"

THE ANSWER WAS not long in coming.

CBS organized a PR campaign aimed at countering the negative leaks coming out of the network. The goal was to convince members of the print media—especially those who had trashed Katie during her first pathetic months on the *Evening News*—that they needed to take a second look. The show had been totally revamped, Rick Kaplan told reporters, and its sober tone, emphasis on hard news, and production values were now as good or better than the competition's at ABC and NBC.

By springtime, the PR campaign seemed to be producing results in more positive coverage of Katie.

"The massacre at Virginia Tech gave Katie Couric her biggest test yet as *The CBS Evening News* anchor—and she did fairly well," wrote David Bianculli of the *New York Daily News*. "During her days in Blacksburg [Virginia], anchoring *The CBS Evening News* twice and a *48 Hours* special, she contributed her greatest strength: the compassionate interview."

In order to win the trust of wary reporters, Kaplan and McManus spoke with a combination of candor, humility, and self-confidence.

"I'm really not focused on the numbers right now," McManus told Phil Rosenthal, the media columnist of the *Chicago Tribune*. "I fixated over them for a while. They are what they are. I do believe that over a period of years they will get better, and I remind myself, and I remind people when they ask me, that it was in Tom Brokaw's 14th season that he became No. 1."

Perhaps CBS's biggest PR gamble came in May, on the eve of the networks' annual "upfront" presentation of its primetime schedule to advertisers. The network arranged for Bill Carter, the TV reporter of the *New York Times*, to interview everyone at CBS News—Moonves, McManus, Friedman, Kaplan, and Katie.

The ensuing article was no whitewash.

"In the latest week's ratings," Carter began, " 'CBS Evening News' had its worst performance since the Nielsen company installed its 'people meter' ratings system 20 years ago."

But the *Times* article did give Les Moonves and Sean McManus a chance to address the most damaging rumors about Katie.

"Am I surprised by the attention?" said Moonves. "No. Am I surprised by the vitriol? Yes."

"It's a flat-out lie that there has been any consideration, any meeting or any discussion about replacing Katie," McManus said.

"This," declared Moonves, "is a long-term commitment."*

LESLIE MOONVES's open-ended commitment to Katie had to be taken with a grain of salt.

In the past, Moonves had made pronouncements that turned out to be wrong. Not the least of his miscalculations had been his decision to

---

* Not long after the *Times*'s piece appeared, the results of the May sweeps were announced. For the first time in eleven years, ABC's *World News* came in first, attracting 7.95 million viewers. NBC's *Nightly News* was second, with 7.30 million viewers. And CBS's *Evening News* was third, with 6.09 million viewers—its lowest May sweeps ratings since Nielsen began storing data electronically in 1991.

move Katie away from hard news and toward feel-good news just as the public's interest in the Iraq war and the presidential campaign was on the rise.

"These are very serious times," Rick Kaplan said. "People need serious information. It's a more complicated world. There's a need for clarity and credibility. . . . It's up to us to present news of the day in a way that viewers can assimilate, understand, and be satisfied by."

Another miscalculation by Moonves was his misplaced faith in the long-term viability of the traditional nightly newscast.

"People are just not gathering around the TV set right after dinner at home anymore," said Paul Levinson, professor and chair of the communications and media studies department at Fordham University. "Not only will the evening newscasts not grow, they will continue to dwindle, playing to an ever-aging audience. I predict total viewership on all three networks' evening newscasts will be below 10 million [from the current 22 million] by 2010, and even that will continue to diminish."

Some members of the advertising community were openly skeptical about the durability of Moonves's commitment to Katie.

"At some point, they are going to have to cut the bleeding," said Brad Adgate, director of research for Horizon Media, a New York advertising agency. "I don't know if there is some magic ratings number, but maybe after she's been on the job for a year, they'll have to do something."

Others thought that Moonves was stuck with Katie, at least for the time being.

"I don't believe Les is looking for someone to replace Katie right now," said a TV industry veteran who was in a position to know. "First of all, he hasn't entirely owned up to her being a disaster. Secondly, I don't see how he can eat the seventy-five million to hundred million dollars he's committed to Katie and still survive in his job with Sumner Redstone. And finally, who could he put in her place now?

"The only person who could move the needle would be [CNN anchor] Anderson Cooper, because he's young and different and appeals to young as well as old," this source continued. "But, as I say, I don't believe

"Les has a plan to replace Katie—unless she has a nervous break-down, or someone talks sense into her to try something else."

AND SO, in the end, it all came back to Katie.

What would she do?

Would she stay at *The CBS Evening News* and tough it out?

Perhaps only another network news anchor could fully appreciate Katie's torment. The Nielsen scoreboard lit up every Tuesday, and few things were more painful for an anchor than being two million viewers behind the leader, as Katie was now.

In July, ten months into Katie's turbulent reign as CBS's evening anchor, Katie's personal publicist, Matthew Hiltzik, apparently convinced her that the best defense was an offense. He urged her to sit for an interview with *New York* magazine writer Joe Hagan. Hiltzik expected Hagan to go easy on Katie and give her the opportunity to launch a PR campaign aimed at persuading viewers to come back to CBS and give Katie a second look.

The results of the strategy proved disastrous. Unleashed by Hiltzik, Katie allowed all her repressed feelings—a jumble of anger and confusion—to spill onto the pages of *New York* magazine and create the impression she was seeking an exit strategy from *The CBS Evening News*.

When asked by Hagan if she would have taken the job if she had known it would have turned out this way, Katie admitted, "It would have been less appealing to me."

Worse, Katie placed the blame for her dismal performance on everyone but herself. The TV audience was "very unforgiving and very resistant to change." The old guard at CBS was stabbing her in the back. And her boss, Leslie Moonves, had betrayed her by luring her to CBS with false promises.

"According to Nicolla Hewitt, Couric's longtime producer and 'really, really close friend' (whom Couric personally authorized to speak for this story), the network began to renege on its promises and stopped giving Couric the support she needed to pursue news or command the news division," Joe Hagan wrote. "Management 'nickel and dimed' her on ambitious enterprise stories and deferred to what Hewitt called the 'old guard' at *60 Minutes* on interviews that belonged to Couric."

As might be expected, Moonves was furious at Katie for trying to make him the fall guy for her failure. He even went so far as to tell Joe Hagan—*on the record*—that he bore no responsibility for how the show had failed.

"Nope," said Moonves. "I really don't."

The spectacle of Katie and Les Moonves at each other's throats left the impression that her days were numbered at CBS News. Some people thought that if Katie's pain became unbearable, she would follow Barbara Walters's example. Nearly thirty years ago, after it became clear to Walters that her co-anchorship with Harry Reasoner was a flop, she declared that it had been "a wonderful experiment," and that it was time for her to go off and do longer, more satisfying pieces for *20/20*.

Katie always had *60 Minutes* to fall back on.

Or did she?

Katie talked wistfully about doing more pieces for *60 Minutes*—or even moving over to that show permanently if things didn't work out for her on the evening news. But that was not going to be so easy. The fact was that the majority of the people at *60 Minutes*, including the correspondents, did not respect her. They thought she was a lightweight, and that she would not be willing to put in the kind of hard, slogging, on-the-road work that was necessary.

Katie was damaged goods. She had spent a lifetime striving to fulfill her father's dream for her—that she sit in the chair once occupied by the great Walter Cronkite. Her father had told Katie that she was destined for greatness, and she had believed him without fully understanding her own limitations.

At heart, Katie was not an anchor—sober, authoritative, and wise. She had reached the heights of TV stardom by being what she had been in her father's house—cute, funny, and girlish. There was no way for her to reconcile her ambition with her personality.

There was no elegant way out for Katie.

Author's Note

AT THE TIME I STARTED RESEARCHING THIS BOOK, THERE WERE MANY unanswered questions about Katie Couric. What explained her extraordinary success in the world of morning television? Who helped her on her way to the top? What lay ahead for her at CBS News?

There was a good reason no one had ever addressed these questions in a book. While Katie was on *The Today Show*, her interviews with authors were so important to book sales that publishers were reluctant to commission a biography that might incur her displeasure.

Her decision to leave *Today* created a long-sought window of opportunity for a book-length, fully textured biography. However, even then, the profile you've just read could not have been written without the assistance of many people.

Chief among those is Leon Wagener, a skilled reporter who has worked with me on my last two books. Others who provided generous support were my agents, Robert Gottlieb and Dan Strone; my editor, Rick Horgan; my photo editor, Melissa Goldstein; and my wife, Dolores Barrett, whose suggestions proved invaluable and whose patience was inexhaustible.

THIS IS THE first unauthorized biography of Katie Couric. "Unauthorized" is often a misunderstood word. In this case, all it means is that Katie did not participate in the research and writing of this book. In fact, she actively discouraged its publication. In what I believe was a misguided effort to protect her image, she refused repeated requests for an interview, and urged her friends and colleagues not to talk to me. She even declined to grant me permission to reproduce photographs of her that she controls.

However, the use of the word "unauthorized" should not be taken to mean that this book was based on a negative premise. On the contrary, in my effort to be scrupulously fair, I spent months researching Katie's life story, and conducted nearly two hundred interviews with people who are both her critics and most ardent supporters.

In addition to those who agreed to speak to me on condition of anonymity, I would like to thank those who spoke on the record. They include: John Baker, Sue Erikson Bloland, Steve Brill, Scott Brittain, Donald Brown, Al Buch, Tom Capra, Jean Carper, Chris Curle, Dini Diskin-Zimmerman, Kathie Dolgin, Sam Donaldson, Don Farmer, Karen Feldgus, Jack Ford, Mary Ford, Tom Freston, Tony Frost, Leon Frohsin III, Ralph Frohsin, Hank Goldberg, Michael Gore, Larry Grossman, Bob Hager, Jerry Inzerillo, Ted Kavanau, Fernanda Kellogg, Sandy Kenyon, Todd Kern, Joe Kett, Suzie Kolber, Marcia Ladendorff, Ira Lazernik, John LeBouttier, Carroll "Cap" Lesesne, Matthew Levine, Stuart Loory, King Mallory, Dave Marash, Jack McCallie, M.D., Jim Van Messel, George Michael, Judy Milestone, Dawson "Tack" Nail, Ed Nardoza, Jim Pinkerton, Frank Radice, Dan Rather, Sam Roberts, Shelley Ross, Jack Schneider, Reese Schonfeld, Tony Segretto, Sandy Socolow, Kathryn Holt Springston, Pruddy Squire, Tom Touchet, Liz Trotta, Andrew Tyndall, Meredith Vieira, Jonathan Wald, Dave Walker, Mike Wallace, Jeannette Walls, Lou Waters, Mardi Waters, Linda Wells, Carole Wendt, Bill Wheatley, and Robert Wussler.

FINALLY, THIS BOOK is the product of my long years as a reporter, editor, and biographer. I trust that it has accomplished my original goal—to say something true and important about a media icon and a watershed moment in American journalism.

EDWARD KLEIN
New York City

Notes

Epigraph

Katie Couric's quote comes from an interview by Tom Junod in "What I've Learned: Katie Couric" in *Esquire* (December 2006). She also told Junod: "You guys even take a shot at me. You have something in the November issue, something about how since I've become an anchor, you don't know me anymore. You don't know me anymore? Bite me."

Chapter One: The Stuff of Legend

The story of how Katie Couric barely escaped from being fired by CNN is drawn mainly from the author's interviews with Katie's friends and colleagues, some of whom asked to remain anonymous. Extensive on-the-record interviews were conducted as well with John Baker, Jean Carper, Donald Brown, Sam Donaldson, Sandy Kenyon, Ted Kavanau, Tom Gault, Dave Guilbault, Don Farmer, Chris Curle, Stuart Loory, Marcia Ladendorff, Frank Radice, Judy Milestone, Reese Schonfeld, Susan Lisovicz, Michael Shore, Mardi Waters, Lou Waters, Candy Stroud, Dave Walker, Dini Diskin-Zimmerman, Robert Wussler, and Mary Ford.

The author conducted not-for-attribution interviews with people who had firsthand knowledge of Katie's relationship with Guy Pepper, although Pepper himself refused to be interviewed.

Additional information about Katie's early days in television came from the following sources: "We Knew Katie When" in *Washingtonian* magazine (December 2006); Reese Schonfeld's *Me and Ted Against the World: The Unauthorized Story of the Founding of CNN* (HarperCollins, 2001); "Katie Couric Talks About Her New Book, Her New Look and Life After Tragedy" on *Larry King Live* (December 18, 2000).

Chapter Two: Family Secrets

The portrait of Katie as a girl and young woman—her experiences growing up in Arlington, her family life, her years in high school and at the University of Virginia, and the journalistic influences on her career—come from a wide variety of sources, including interviews with friends, family members, classmates, and professional colleagues. Among those who were willing to speak on the record: Bob Hallahan, Larry Grossman, Dawson "Tack" Nail, Judy Milestone, Lea Thompson, Kerri Bartlett, Professor Joe Kett, Professor Hal Kolb, Professor Victor Cabas, Robert Lopardo, Jack McCallie, M.D., Michael Matylewich, and Scott Brittain.

The description of Arlington, Virginia, was enriched by a tour of the city given to the author by Arlington historian Kathryn Holt Springston.

Principal published sources include Lesley Stahl's *Reporting Live* (Simon & Schuster, 1999); Richard Campbell's *60 Minutes and the News: A Mythology for Middle America* (University of Illinois Press, 1991); John Baker's *The Peacock vs. the Lite Bulb* (an unpublished manuscript); James Robert Parish's *Katie Couric: TV News Broadcaster* (Ferguson, 2006); Sherry Beck Paprocki's *Women of Achievement: Katie Couric* (Chelsea House Publishers, 2001); *Life with Mother*, introduction by Katie Couric (Little, Brown, 1995).

The following articles were also used: Karen Schneider and Sue Carswell's "Live Wire" in *People* (August 9, 1993); Kimberly Powell's "Your Guide to Genealogy" in About.com; "Katie Couric: Anchor, Today, Contributing Anchor, Dateline NBC," MSNBC.com (November 29, 2005); "The Essential Katie Couric Photo Gallery," Beyond Imagination Web Design, Dallas, Texas; "Katie Couric: Journalist," Power to Learn.com; Jay Sharbutt's "Katherine Couric Returns to Today," Associated Press (September 9, 1991); Roxanne Roberts's "Yipes! It's Katie Couric!" in the *Washington Post* (May 21, 1991); Elisabeth Bumiller's "What You Don't Know About Katie Couric" in *Good Housekeeping* (August 1996); Robin Abcarian's "Celebrities Are Their Own Biggest Fans" in the *Los Angeles Times* (September 12, 2006); "Celebrity Biographies: Katie Couric" (Baseline, 2005); Ken Auletta's "The Dawn Patrol" in *The New Yorker* (August 8, 2005); "How Women Took Over the News" in *TV Guide* (October 9, 1999); "Secret of Katie's Roots" (*Globe*, May 18, 1999); Bruce Weber's "Today Show Co-Host Ridiculously Normal," *New York Times* (April 12, 1992).

In addition, the author drew on a National Broadcasting Company transcript of the May 22, 2001, *Today Show*: "Katie Couric Goes Back to Her Alma Mater, the University of Virginia, to Remember Old Times and See

How Things Have Changed"; "The Washington-Lee High School Year-book" (1973); "The Washington-Lee High School Yearbook" (1974); "The Washington-Lee High School Yearbook" (1975).

Chapter Three: "A Tongue with a Tang"

The narrative of Katie's years at CNN's headquarters in Atlanta is drawn from interviews with several sources who requested anonymity. However, nearly a score of people were willing to go on the record. They are Reese Schonfeld, Stuart Loory, John Baker, Ted Kavanau, Susan Lisovicz, Chris Curle, Don Farmer, Tom Gaut, David Guilbault, Marcia Ladendorff, Sandy Kenyon, Bert Reinhardt, Judy Milestone, Lou Waters, Mardi Waters, Dave Walker, Robert Wussler, Mary Ford, and Dini Diskin-Zimmerman.

Principal published sources include Reese Schonfeld's *Me and Ted Against the World: The Unauthorized Story of the Founding of CNN* (Harper-Collins, 2001); John Baker's *The Peacock vs. the Lite Bulb* (an unpublished manuscript); "Katie Couric Talks About Her New Book, Her New Look and Life After Tragedy" on *Larry King Live* (December 18, 2000); Ken Auletta's "The Dawn Patrol" in *The New Yorker* (August 8, 2005).

The author also wishes to single out Lisa DePaulo's "Killer Katie" in *George* (May 1997) as the single best piece of reporting in magazine form on Katie's early years.

Chapter Four: Shattered Dreams

The account of Katie's time in Miami and her trip for CNN to Havana are drawn from more than a dozen interviews, including those with Brad Marks, Don Farmer, Chris Curle, Hank Goldberg, Al Buch, Ralph Renick Jr., Donald Brown, Suzie Kolber, Ira Lazernik, Alan Perris, Tony Segretto, John Lang, Lu Ann Cahn, and Cori Rice.

For a description of Katie's experience in Havana, the author found a great deal of useful information in Don Farmer and Skip Caray's *Roomies* (Longstreet Press, 1994).

The following articles were used: Tom Jicha's "Couric's Star Started Its Rise in S. Florida; Today Show Celebrity Began On-Camera Career as a Reporter for WTVJ," which appeared in the (Fort Lauderdale) *Sun–Sentinel* (April 6, 2006); "Couric Built Miami-Tough" in *The Hollywood Reporter* (April 6, 2006); Lisa DePaulo's "Killer Katie" in *George* (May 1997); Brian

Donlon's "NBC Has Faith in Dateline Differences" in *USA Today* (March 31, 1992); Michael Greppi's "Roots: Guy Pepper's CNN Sequel" in *Electronic Media* (December 31, 2004); Paul J. Gough's "CNN Hooks Up New Studio" in *The Hollywood Reporter* (October 4, 2006); Bruce McCabe's "Something Completely Different" in the *Boston Globe* (September 11, 1988); Mike McDaniel's "Networks Scramble to Get an Interview with Bush" in the *Houston Chronicle* (April 18, 1992); "Guy Pepper" (www.imdb.com).

Chapter Five: Mother Teresa

The account of Katie's experiences at WRC-TV in Washington, D.C., is based on interviews with several people who requested anonymity, as well as with the following people who were willing to go on the record: Mary Ford, Ike Seamons, Donald Brown, Margaret Murphy, Carl Gottlieb, Tom Gaut, Glenn Garvin, Al Buch, Tom Capra, Sandy Kenyon, Lea Thompson, Bob Hager, Larry Grossman, and George Michael.

Principal published sources include Brandon Tartikoff and Charles Leerhsen's *The Last Great Ride* (Turtle Bay Books, 1992); Lesley Stahl's *Reporting Live* (Simon & Schuster, 1999); Alan Weisman's *Lone Star: The Extraordinary Life and Times of Dan Rather* (John Wiley & Sons, 2006).

The following articles were used: Lisa DePaulo's "Killer Katie" in *George* (May 1997); Patricia Sellers's "Playing with Pain" in *Fortune* (May 1, 2006); "We Knew Katie When" *Washingtonian* magazine (December 2006); Matea Gold's "When Katie Met Jeff " in the *Los Angeles Times* (June 20, 2005); Howard Kurtz's "In the Hot Seat" in the *Washington Post* (May 23, 2004); Judy Flander's "The Two Faces of Katie Couric" in the *Washington Journalism Review* (May 1992).

The author also consulted Janice Lieberman's "Jeff Zucker" in *Lifestyles* magazine.

Chapter Six: The Hardcore

The description of Katie's first meeting with her future husband, Jay Monahan, the events leading up to their marriage, and their early days as a married couple come from both confidential interviews and on-the-record interviews with the following people: Mary Ford, Lea Thompson, Karen Feldgus, Jack Ford, Steve Brill, Candy Stroud, King Mallory, Michael Gore, Raoul Felder, Beth Cook, Pruddy Squire, Jim Campi, and Matthew Levine.

The articles used in this chapter: Jenny Allen's "Taking a Chance on Herself " in *Good Housekeeping* (November 2006); Karen Schneider and Sue Carswell's "Live Wire" in *People* (August 9, 1993); "Newsgal's Death Made Katie Couric Want to Be a Mom" in *Globe* (October 28, 2003); Lisa De-Paulo's "Killer Katie" in *George* (May 1997); "We Knew Katie When" in *Washingtonian* magazine (December 2006).

Principal published sources include Elsa Walsh's *Divided Lives* (Anchor Books, 1995); Tony Horwitz's *Confederates in the Attic* (Vintage Departures, 1988); Margaretta Barton Colt's *Defend the Valley* (Oxford University Press, 1994).

The author also consulted these websites: www.cwreenactors.com, The Civil War Reenactors home page; www.civilwar.org, The Civil War Preservation Trust home page; and www.bellegrove.org, Belle Grove Plantation home page.

Chapter Seven: The Hardest Beat in Washington

The story of how Katie became the deputy Pentagon correspondent for NBC News is based on interviews with several sources, including correspondents and producers who were present in the Washington and New York offices of NBC News at the time; virtually all of them requested anonymity. In addition, the following people were willing to go on the record: Andrew Tyndall, Donald Brown, Mary Ford, Ike Seamons, Hank Goldberg, Al Buch, Lea Thompson, Jack Ford, and Tom Capra.

The following articles were used: "From a Camel to a General" in the *New York Post* (March 11, 1991); "She's Off to the Front Line" in the *New York Post* (August 31, 1990); Jenny Allen's "Taking a Chance on Herself " in *Good Housekeeping* (November 2006); Karen Schneider and Sue Carswell's "Live Wire," in *People* (August 9, 1993); Lisa DePaulo's "Killer Katie" in *George* (May 1997); "We Knew Katie When" in *Washingtonian* magazine (December 2006); "New Producer for Today" in the *New York Times* (January 16, 1990).

Chapter Eight: Doogie Howser

The fall of Deborah Norville and the rise of Katie to the position of cohost of *The Today Show* is drawn from extensive interviews with several people—including cast, crew, and producers—who were directly involved in the story. Most of these people requested anonymity. The following were willing to go on the record: Tom Capra, Carole Wendt, Mary Ford, Andrew Tyndall, Donald Brown, and George Lewis.

The following articles were used: Jill Brooke's "Dropping Anchors" in *Mirabella* (February 1991); John Carmody's "NBC Pays Millions: Couric New Co-Anchor" in the *Washington Post* (April 5, 1991); "Katie Couric Covers Washington for Today" from the (Chicago) Tribune Wire Services (June 1, 1990); Verne Gay's "Katie Couric: Today Savior?" in *Newsday* (June 11, 1990); Lee Siegel's "On Television—Rise and Shine" in *The New Republic* (November 10, 2003); Edward Klein's "NBC's Great Blonde Hope" in *Vanity Fair* (January 1990); Tom Gliatto, Alan Carter, Lisa Russell, and Joanne Kaufman's "With Deborah Norville Switched to the Mommy Track, Today Has Arrived for New Coanchor Katie Couric" in *People* (April 22, 1991); "We Knew Katie When" in the December 2006 issue of *Washingtonian* magazine.

Chapter Nine: Capra-Corn

The story of Katie's early days as cohost with Bryant Gumbel on *The Today Show* is drawn from extensive interviews with people who worked on the program at the time as well as with several non-NBC news and entertainment executives in New York and Los Angeles. Most of these sources requested anonymity. Those who were willing to go on the record include Tom Capra, Donald Brown, Sandy Kenyon, Marcia Ladendorff, and Frank Radice.

There is a voluminous public record of Katie's early years as cohost of *The Today Show*. Principal published sources include Edward Klein's "NBC's Great Blonde Hope" in *Vanity Fair* (January 1990); Tom Gliatto, Alan Carter, Lisa Russell, and Joanne Kaufman's "With Deborah Norville Switched to the Mommy Track, Today Has Arrived for New Coanchor Katie Couric" in *People* (April 22, 1991); "We Knew Katie When" in the December 2006 issue of *Washingtonian* magazine; Karen Schneider and Sue Carswell's "Live Wire" in *People* (August 9, 1993); Judy Flander's "Catching Up with Katie Couric" in *The Saturday Evening Post* (September 1992); Lisa DePaulo's "Killer Katie" in *George* (May 1997); David Zurawik and Christina Stoehr's "The Windbags of War" in *Fineline: The Newsletter on Journalism Ethics* (October 1990); Joseph Cirincione's "The Performance of the Patriot Missile in the Gulf War" in *An Edited Draft of a Report Prepared for the Government Operations Committee, U. S. House of Representatives* (October 1992); Brian Donlon's "Couric Awakens to the Wonders of Motherhood" in

USA Today (September 9, 1991); Brian Donlon's "Her Bright Outlook Catches On" in *USA Today* (April 14, 1992); "Egos" in *USA Today* (May 5, 1992); "Katie Couric: For Boosting Ratings and Feminism at the Same Time" in *Glamour* (December 1992); "Notoriety, Stability Mark Couric's 1st Today Anniversary" in *The Hollywood Reporter* (April 3, 1992); Brian Donlon's "Couric's Fortunate am-Bush" in *USA Today* (October 14, 1992); Tom Shales's "Top of the Morning, Katie!" in the *Washington Post* (September 10, 1991); Edwin Diamond's "The Couric Effect" in *New York* (December 9, 1991); Lisa Schwarzbaum's "Katie Did It" in *Entertainment Weekly* (July 31, 1992); Rick Warren's "From the Bleachers: NBC: No Blacks Competing" in the *Sacramento Observer* (August 19, 1992); Stan Isaac's "Sports: Barcelona" in *Newsday* (August 8, 1992); "Here and Now" in the (Ontario, Canada) *Hamilton Spectator* (August 7, 1992); Howard Rosenberg's "Oh, My! Going for the Gold with Couric" in the *Los Angeles Times* (August 5, 1992); Prentis Rogers's "Morning TV Co-Host Katie Couric Keeping Things Together with a Smile" in the *Atlanta Journal and Constitution* (August 3, 1992); Mike Kern's "Katie Couric and Dick Enberg Are an Odd Pair and Seem Stiff on Camera" in the Orlando (Florida) *Sentinel* (July 29, 1992); Rick Warner's unheadlined article from Barcelona, Spain, in the Associated Press (July 24, 1992); Rick Du Brow's "Today Sends Wake-Up Call to GMA" in the *Los Angeles Times* (June 2, 1992); Joanne Kaufman's "Katie and Chris Go for the Gold" in *Ladies' Home Journal* (August 1992); Judy Flander's "Katie Couric" in the *Washington Journalism Review* (May 1992); Walter Goodman's "Some Today Segments Bigger Than Bite-Size" in the *New York Times* (March 2, 1992); "Katie Couric: Today's Savvy Co-anchor Put Her Show Back on Top by Excelling" in *People* (December 28, 1992); "Zing Him" in *USA Today* (March 9, 1994); Joanne Kaufman's "Katie Couric Today" in *TV Guide* (February 6, 1993); Richard Zoglin's "The Wooing of David Letterman" in *Time* (December 21, 1992); Joshua Hammer (with Joe Seldner), "Exit Laughing" in *Newsweek* (December 21, 1992); Peter Johnson, Matt Rousch, and Alan Bash's "NBC Hopes Today Offer Convinces Zucker to Stay" in *USA Today* (July 25, 1994); Kenneth R. Clark's "NBC's Zucker Has His Hands Full—And He Loves It" in the *Chicago Tribune* (February 28, 1993); Joshua Hammer and Carolyn Friday's "Zucker Unbound" in *Newsweek* (February 1, 1993); Tim Allis and Toby Kahn's "Rookie of the Year: Younger Than the Show He Produces, Jeff Zucker Juices Up Today" in *People* (August 17, 1992); Brian Donlon's "Boosting Today Ratings Child's Play to Zucker" in *USA Today* (June 11, 1992); Charles Fishman's

"Jeff Zucker: A Miamian, Whispering in Bryant Gumbel's Ear" in the *Or-lando* (Florida) *Sentinel* (May 31, 1992); Jane Hall's "Meet Today's New Wake-Up Call; 26-Year-Old Jeff Zucker's Job Is to Take Couric, Gumbel & Co. Back to the Top and Keep Them There" in the *Los Angeles Times* (April 5, 1992); Richard Zoglin's "Miles in the Morning; Jeff Zucker, Today's 26-Year-Old Wunderkind Producer, Turns the Show Into—Surprise!—a Happy Family" in *Time* (March 23, 1992); Susan Bickelhaupt's "Today Is 40, But Producer Is Just 26" in the *Boston Globe* (January 24, 1992); Sonia Murray's "Young and Restless: Can a 26-Year-Old Run Today Show? NBC Thinks He Can" in the *Atlanta Journal and Constitution* (December 27, 1991); Verne Gay's "At 26, Pro-ducer Is Today's Doogie" in the *St. Louis Post-Dispatch* (December 18, 1991); Bill Carter's "Today Producer, 26, Hopes Youth Equals Success" in the *New York Times* (December 15, 1991); Skip Myslenski's "Not Your Average Fact-Finding Tour" in the *Chicago Tribune* (June 17, 1988).

Chapter Ten: Breaking the Mold

The accounts of Katie's relationships on and off the screen are drawn from interviews with members of *The Today Show* cast and crew, many of whom were interviewed repeatedly, and friends of Katie's. Most of these people were unwilling to be quoted by name. Among the sources who agreed to go on the record are Donald Brown, Sandy Kenyon, Marcia Ladendorff, An-drew Tyndall, Karen Feldgus, Michael Gore, Todd Kern, Terry Irving, Elizabeth McClung, Prudence "Pruddy" Squire, Nancy Talley, Jeannette Walls, Judith Martin Woodall, Mary Ford, Terry Irving, Todd Kern, Mike Wallace, Jack Ford, and Dawson "Tack" Nail.

Principal published sources include Lloyd Grove's "Kiss of the Anchor-woman" in *Vanity Fair* (August 1994); John Carmody and Mike Mills's "CBS's Stringer Switches to Bell" in the *Washington Post* (February 24, 1995); Susan Schindehette's "Howard Stringer: The Man Who Won the Great David Letterman War Finds That Making CBS No. 1 Is All in the Stars" in *People* (April 5, 1993); Bill Carter's "The Top CBS Executive Is Leaving" in the *New York Times* (February 24, 1995); Robin Schatz's "Stringer Joins New Media Venture" in *Newsday* (February 24, 1995); Tom Shales's "The Prime Time of a Veteran Broadcaster" in the *Washington Post* (February 24, 1995); Rosemarie Lennon's "It's Bryant v. Katie" in *Star* (November 9, 1999); Adam Buckman's "No Love Lost" in the *New York Post* (October 22, 1999); Michael Hanrahan and Tony Brenna's "The Real Reason Katie & Bryant Hate Each

Other" in *The National Enquirer* (November 9, 1999); Karen Schneider and Sue Carswell's "Live Wire" in *People* (August 9, 1993); Judy Flander's "Catching Up with Katie Couric" in *The Saturday Evening Post* (September 1992); Lisa DePaulo's "Killer Katie" in *George* (May 1997); S. Krum's "The Rise and Rise of Katie" in *People* (December 4, 1994); Tom Shales's "Playboy Interview: David Letterman" in *Playboy* (January 1994); Lawrence Donegan's "Undisputed Queen of Breakfast Shows" in the (Manchester) *Guardian* (January 30, 2002); Dan Mangan and Dareh Gregorian's "Nasty Nanny's Mud Blitz vs. Mom—Au Pair to Stars Sued for Gossipy Letter Campaign" in the *New York Post* (September 22, 2005); Doug Camilli's "Loose-Lipped Nanny Gets the Gate: NBC Anchor Katie Couric Will Hear No Evil About Husband" in the (Montreal) *Gazette* (December 6, 1994); Rick Marin and Yahlin Chang (with Elizabeth Angell) in the article "The Katie Factor" in *Newsweek* (July 6, 1998); Brian Williams's "Katie Couric: I Like to Win So Much I Even Bend the Rules" in *The National Enquirer* (July 4, 1995); Untitled article in *USA Weekend* (April 23–25, 1993); Letter to the Editor in *People* (August 16, 1994); Leslie Lampert's "Katie's Place" in *Ladies' Home Journal* (May 1994); "TV for Two" in the *New York Observer* (February 15, 1993); Gail Shister's "Katie Couric Benefits from Diane Sawyer's Flirtation with NBC" in the *Philadelphia Inquirer* (February 22, 1994); *USA Today* (June 10, 1994); Peter Johnson's "Rumblings at NBC, ABC Over Diane Sawyer's Deal" in *USA Today* (February 21, 1994); "In Mourning" in *People* (February 9, 1998); Sandra McElwaine's "Nice and Tough" in *USA Weekend* (April 23–25, 1993); Rosemarie Lennon's "Katie Couric's 'Odd Couple' Marriage" in *Star* (September 3, 1996); Rosemarie Lennon's "Uptown Girl" in *Star* (October 1, 1996); Pat Gregor's "Katie Couric's a Cheapskate" in *Globe* (March 18, 1997); Sean Broderick's "Katie's Sexy Struggle to Save Marriage" in *Globe* (January 7, 1997); Suzanne Ely, Peter Bloch, and Tony Brenna's "Secrets of Daytime TV's Women" in *The National Enquirer* (December 10, 1996); Roger Hitts and Leon Freilich's "Katie Couric's Long-Distance Marriage Crisis" in *Star* (August 20, 1996); Tony Brenna's "Fear of Olympic Terror Attack Makes Katie Couric Leave Kids at Home" in *Globe* (August 6, 1996); Marie Terry's "Katie Couric's Wacky Hubby Is Civil War Buff Who Loves to Play Bugle in His Undies!" in *Globe* (November 8, 1994); Mary Murphy's "Katie Couric & Matt Lauer: Performers of the Year" in *TV Guide* (December 20, 1997); "Family Viewing" in *People* (March 6, 1995); Ken White's "Broadcasters Honor Today Show" in *Las Vegas Review-Journal* (April 8, 1997); NBC News Transcript of *The Today Show* (April 7, 1997).

Chapter Eleven: "Ego, Ego, Ego"

The account of Katie and Jay's struggle to settle down in New York City, their growing marital strife, Jay's involvement in Civil War reenactments, and Katie's early days on *The Today Show* are drawn from many interviews, including the following that were on the record: Beth Cook, Mary Ford, Peter Cook, Jim Campi, Karen Feldgus, Michael Gore, Todd Kern, Prudence Squire, Cary Tolley, Nancy Talley, Jeannette Walls, Judith Martin Woodall, Jack Ford, and Dawson "Tack" Nail.

Primary publications include S. Krum's "The Rise and Rise of Katie" in *People* (August 29, 1993); "The Reenactment of the Battle of Cedar Creek" in Cedar Creek Battlefield Foundation website (October 19, 2003); Lloyd Grove's "Kiss of the Anchor Women" in *Vanity Fair* (August 1994); Lawrence Donegan's "Undisputed Queen of Breakfast Shows" in the Manchester *Guardian* (January 30, 2002); Karen Schneider and Sue Carswell's "Live Wire" in *People* (August 9, 1993); Dan Mangan and Dareh Gregorian's "Nasty Nanny's Mud Blitz vs. Mom" in the *New York Post* (September 22, 2005); Doug Camilli's "Loose-Lipped Nanny Gets the Gate" in the Montreal *Gazette* (December 6, 1994); Rick Marin and Yahlin Chang with Elizabeth Angell's "The Katie Factor" in *Newsweek* (July 6, 1998); Marie Terry's "Katie Couric's Wacky Husband" in the *Examiner* (October 1, 1996); Brian Williams's "Katie Couric: I Like to Win So Much I Even Bend the Rules" in *The National Enquirer*; *USA Weekend* (April 23–25, 1993); Nancy Poznek's Letter to the Editor in *People* (August 2, 1994); Leslie Lampert's "Katie's Place" in *Ladies' Home Journal* (May 1994); Gail Shister's "Katie Couric Benefits from Diane Sawyer's Flirtation with NBC" in the *Philadelphia Inquirer* (February 22, 1994); Peter Johnson's "Rumblings at NBC, ABC Over Diane Sawyer's Deal" in *USA Today* (February 21, 1994); Sandra McElwaine's "Nice & Tough" in *USA Weekend* (April 23–25, 1993); Rosemarie Lennon's "Katie Couric's 'Odd Couple' Marriage" in the *Star* (September 3, 1996); Pat Gregor's "Katie Couric's a Cheapskate" in *Globe* (March 18, 1997); Sean Broderick's "Katie's Sexy Struggle to Save Marriage" in the *Globe* (January 7, 1997); Suzanne Ely, Peter Bloch, and Tony Brenna's "Katie Couric: Inside Her Zany Marriage" in the *National Enquirer* (December 10, 1996); Robert Hitts and Leon Freilich's "Katie Couric's Long Distance Marriage Crisis" in the *Star* (August 20, 1996); Marie Terry's "Katie Couric's Wacky Hubby Is Civil War Buff Who Loves to Play Bugle in His Undies!" in the *Globe* (November 8, 1994); Mary Murphy's "Katie Couric & Matt Lauer" in *TV Guide* (December 20, 1997); "Nanny Woes Hit 'Today's'

Couric" in *USA Today* (December 3, 1994); "Family Viewing" in *People* (March 6, 1995); Ken White's "Broadcasters Honor *Today* Show" in the *Las Vegas Review-Journal* (April 8, 1997); NBC Transcript, *The Today Show* (April 7, 1997).

Chapter Twelve: Coming of Age

The account of Katie's rise to number one in daytime television, the story of Bryant Gumbel's dismissal by NBC (which is told in this book for the first time), and the description of Jeff Zucker's cancer are drawn from a score of interviews, both on and off the record. Those who spoke for attribution include Howard Smith, Jack Ford, Andrew Tyndall, and Jeannette Walls.

Principal published sources include Rick Marin and Yahlin Chang (with Elizabeth Angell) in the article "The Katie Factor" in *Newsweek* (July 6, 1998); "We Knew Katie When" in the December 2006 issue of *Washingtonian* magazine; Jenny Allen's "Taking a Chance on Herself " in *Good Housekeeping* (November 2006); "Cheeky Katie Spanked Over Fan-ny Mail" in *Globe* (April 29, 1997); Jeannie Williams's "Katie, Bryant" in *USA Today* (April 20, 1997); Jay Bobbin's "Today Gets Room with a View" in the *New York Daily News* (June 19, 1994); "Katie Couric Weeps for Cancer-Stricken Boss" in *Globe* (November 12, 1996); "Couric Happy Now, But Fuzzy About Future on Today" in the *New York Daily News* (April 4, 1996).

Chapter Thirteen: No "Woe Is Me"

The account of Katie's reaction to her husband's battle against colon cancer and his death is drawn from interviews with a number of her friends, family members, and colleagues. Out of respect for Katie's privacy on this subject, all these sources requested anonymity.

It is important to note that, from this point in Katie's life—when her power reached its zenith—fewer and fewer people were willing to speak on the record. However, there was no shortage of people with special knowledge who were willing to speak on background. The information provided by these people was double-sourced by the author.

The author drew on voluminous published material, which includes Beth Potier's "School of Public Health Honors Couric; After Tragedy, TV Host Takes Up Cause of Colon Cancer" in *Harvard University Gazette*

(October 23, 2003); Joanna Powell's "Katie's New Life" in *Good House-keeping* (November 2000); CNN Transcript of *Larry King Live,* "Katie Couric Talks About Her New Book, Her New Look and Life After Tragedy" (December 18, 2000); "We Knew Katie When" in the December 2006 issue of *Washingtonian* magazine; Rick Marin and Yahlin Chang (with Elizabeth Angell) in the article "The Katie Factor" in *Newsweek* (July 6, 1998); Jenny Allen's "Taking a Chance on Herself " in *Good Housekeeping* (November 2006); CNN Transcript of *Larry King Live,* "Katie Couric" (May 4, 2004); "Brave Katie Couric Vows to Keep Smiling for Kids' Sake" in *Star* (June 10, 1997); Larry Haley, Michael Hanrahan, and Tony Brenna's "Katie Couric Heartbreak" in *The National Enquirer* (February 10, 1998); Rosemarie Lennon's "Katie Couric Sobs on Set as Hubby Battles Cancer" in *Star* (June 17, 1997); "Funeral Mass for John Paul Monahan III, St. Ignatius Loyola Church, January 28, 1998"; "Couric Takes Timeout as Her Husband Reportedly Battles Cancer" in the *Milwaukee Journal Sentinel* (June 7, 1997); "Couric's Commentator Husband Has Surgery" in the (Cleveland) *Plain Dealer* (June 7, 1997); "Couric's Husband Falls Ill" in the *St. Petersburg* (Florida) *Times* (June 7, 1997); John Carmody's "Katie Couric's Husband Has Cancer Surgery" in the *Washington Post* (June 7, 1997); "Couric's Spouse Undergoes Surgery for Colon Cancer" in the (Salt Lake City) *Desert News* (June 6, 1997); CNBC News Transcript of *Rivera Live,* "Search Warrants Re-leased in Investigation of JonBenet Ramsey's Murder Brings More Unan-swered Questions" (September 29, 1997); "Couric Back After Spouse Has Surgery" in the *Chicago Sun-Times* (June 17, 1997); "Couric Back, Stays Mum on Husband" in the (Fort Lauderdale) *Sun-Sentinel* (June 17, 1997); John Car-mody's "The TV Column" in the *Washington Post* (June 17, 1997); "Few Use Ratings for Kids" in the *Charleston* (West Virginia) *Daily Mail* (June 9, 1997); "Couric Takes Leave to Nurse Husband" in the *New York Daily News* (June 7, 1997); Roger Friedman's "Will Katie Kiss Today Goodbye?" in FOXNews.com (June 9, 2001); Jeff Samuels's "Katie's Amazing Courage" in *Globe* (June 24, 1997); "In Mourning" in *People* (February 9, 1998); "A Coura-geous Katie Says Sad Farewell to Husband" in *Star* (February 17, 1998).

Chapter Fourteen: Hand-to-Hand Combat

The author drew on interviews with people throughout the television industry for the narrative of Katie's return to *The Today Show* after her husband's death, her well-publicized negotiations with NBC that resulted in a $7 million contract, her crusade against colon cancer, and *Good Morning America*'s ratings' challenge.

Principal published sources include "10,000 Cards Later, A Host Returns" in the *New York Times* (February 25, 1998); "Widowed Couric Talks of Tragedy" in the *New York Daily News* (June 13, 1998); "Step by Step" in *People* (October 4, 1999); "Couric Returns with Grace, Then Gets Right to Work" in *USA Today* (February 25, 1998); Patrice Baldwin's "Katie to Matt: I'm the Boss" in *Globe* (December 15, 1998); Charles Krupp's "Dressing for Two" in *In Style* (January 1996); Elisabeth Bumiller's "What You Don't Know About Katie Couric" in *Good Housekeeping* (August 1996); Tom Gliatto and Anne Longley's "Kiss Today Goodbye" in *People* (January 20, 1997); Samantha Ettus's "How Couric, Jackson, Hanks Manage Their Brands" in Scripps Howard News Service (August 12, 2004); Rick Marin and Yahlin Chang (with Elizabeth Angell) in the article "The Katie Factor" in *Newsweek* (July 6, 1998); Monica Collins's "Couric Rebounds with Grace" in the *Boston Herald* (March 3, 1998); Vicki Ward's "Growing Into Glamour" in *Vogue* (March 2005); Rebecca Traister's "The Cruella Syndrome" in Salon.com (March 18, 2004); CNN Transcript of *Larry King Live,* "Katie Couric" (March 4, 2004); Mike Drew's "NBC Will Pay to Keep Couric in Play" in the *Milwaukee Journal Sentinel* (March 16, 1998); Jennifer Tung's "TV's Katie Couric Bounces Back" in the *New York Post* (March 11, 1999); "Host Seeks More Pay for Today" in the *New York Daily News* (June 18, 1998); J. Max Robins's "Suitors Courting Couric" in *TV Guide* (January 24, 1998); Verne Gay's "Katie Couric: Contract Negotiations" in *Newsday* (June 17, 1998); Peter Johnson's "Report: Couric May Be Shopping for Other Offers" in *USA Today* (June 17, 1998); Kyle Pope's "Today Co-Anchor Expected to Enter TV Bidding Wars" in the *Wall Street Journal* (June 17, 1998); David Bauder's "NBC Inks Couric $7M Deal" in the *Boston Globe* (June 29, 1998); "One Day at a Time for Katie Couric" in *New York Magazine* (March 16, 1998); Michael Starr's "Katie's Cashing In" in the *New York Post* (June 17, 1998); Chris Petrikin and Josef Adalian's "Berger Ankles ICM for AMG" in *Variety* (October 31, 1999).

Chapter Fifteen: High Voltage

The accounts of Katie's rivalry with Diane Sawyer, her efforts to become more glamorous, her divalike behavior, and her on-air colonoscopy are derived from several dozen interviews with current and former correspondents and producers at NBC and ABC. Many of these people were granted anonymity.

The author owes a special debt of gratitude to one of those who spoke on the record: Kathie Dolgin, aka High Voltage.

Principal published sources include "Couric Leads Cancer Crusade" in *USA Today* (March 1, 2000); "Today to Air Cancer Test" in the *New York Daily News* (March 6, 2000); Joanna Powell's "Katie's Crusade" in *Good Housekeeping* (October 1998); Howard Rosenberg's "Couric's Crusade Is a True TV Public Service" in the *Los Angeles Times* (March 10, 2000); Christine Gorman's "Katie's Crusade" in *Time* (March 13, 2000); Lisa de Moraes's "NBC Tests Viewers' Intestinal Fortitude Today" in the *Washington Post* (March 8, 2000); Jonathan Storm's "Couric Joins Long Tradition of Celebrities with a Cause; Today to Show Host Being Tested for Colon Cancer" in the *Philadelphia Inquirer* (March 5, 2000); Hal Boedeker's "When TV Journalists Get Too Up Close and Personal" in the *Buffalo News* (March 17, 2000); Joanna Powell's "Katie's Haven" in *Good Housekeeping* (September 1, 1999); Rick Marin and Yahlin Chang (with Elizabeth Angell) in the article "The Katie Factor" in *Newsweek* (July 6, 1998); Peter Johnson's "Inside TV: NBC's Couric Reflects on the State of TV News" in *USA Today* (February 19, 1997); Page Six's "Rough Wake-Up Call for Couric" in the *New York Post* (February 1, 1999); "Katie Couric's Wacky Disco Diet" in *Star* (February 2, 1999); "Exposed! Shocking Past of Katie's Fitness Trainer" in *Globe* (February 16, 1999).

Chapter Sixteen: Columbine

The accounts of Katie's coverage of the Columbine school shooting massacre and the departure of Jeff Zucker from *The Today Show* are drawn from interviews with many industry sources who asked to remain anonymous.

Principal published sources include Peter Johnson, Gary Levin, and Robert Bianco's "Katie's Moving Moments" in *USA Today* (April 22, 1999); Robert Bianco's "Couric's Skill, Care Did This Story Justice" in *USA Today* (April 22, 1999); "Sobbing Katie Breaks Down" in *Globe* (May 11, 1999); Mike Williams's " 'We're Going to Get Through This' " in the *Atlanta Journal and Constitution* (April 23, 1999); Dusty Saunders's "A Time to Talk, a Time to Heal" in the (Denver) *Rocky Mountain News* (April 23, 1999); Jeff Simon's "Inside the Media Machine, the Human Face of Tragedy" in the *Buffalo News* (April 27, 1999); Matea Gold's "When Katie Met Jeff " in the *Los Angeles Times* (June 20, 2005); Kurt Anderson's "The Rise and Rise of Jeff Zucker" in *New York Magazine* (October 3, 2005); Verne Gay's "Off Camera: Is Couric Looking Beyond Today?" in *Newsday* (December 20, 2000).

The author also consulted "NBC's Jeff Zucker" on the website extratv.com (August 22, 2001).

Chapter Seventeen: The Big Makeover

The story of Katie's makeover and her new life as a dating single mom is drawn from interviews with her friends, ex-boyfriends, and colleagues. One of those ex-boyfriends—Cap Lesesne, M.D.—was willing to go on the record. The others refused to comment for publication.

There are voluminous published sources, principally Dr. Cap Lesesne's *Confessions of a Park Avenue Plastic Surgeon* (Gotham Books, 2005); Joanna Powell's "Katie's New Life" in *Good Housekeeping* (November 2000); Clarissa Cruz's "Dressed to Thrill" in *Entertainment Weekly* (October 20, 2000); Vicki Woods's "Growing Into Glamour" in *Vogue* (March 2005); CNN Transcript of *Larry King Live,* "Interview with Katie Couric" (March 4, 2004); J. D. Reed and Anne-Marie O'Neill, K. C. Baker, Michelle Caruso, and Lyndon Stambler, and Brian Karem and Margery Sellinger's "Katie's New Life" in *People* (November 27, 2000); "Katie's Ex Spills the Beans" in *Globe* (October 24, 2005); Michael Hanrahan and Alan Butterfield's "Katie's Boyfriend Was Arrested for Wife-Beating" in *National Enquirer* (November 23, 1999); Hallie Levine's "Katie's Doc" in *USA Today* (November 18, 1999); Bill Hoffmann's "Scandal Cutting Katie's Love Ties to Face-Lift Doc" in the *New York Post* (November 12, 1999); Martha Frankel's "Candid Katie" in *McCall's* (April 2000); "Katie Goes from Gloom to Glam!" in *Globe* (November 3, 1998); "Wow! Katie's Got Sizzling New Look" in *Star* (May 4, 1999); "Katie Couric Starts New Life as a Single Mom" in *National Enquirer* (May 19, 1998); "Katie Couric Sells Piece of Her Heart" in *Globe* (May 12, 1998); "It's Makeover Katie!" in *Globe* (April 14, 1998); Joanna Powell's "Katie's Haven" in *Good Housekeeping* (September 1, 1999).

The author also consulted the following websites: "The Curious and Kinky Case of Katie Couric's Legs" in www.tunc.biz/athina_simonidou .htm; Rebecca Traister's "The Cruella Syndrome" in Salon.com (March 18, 2004).

Chapter Eighteen: The Greatest Aphrodisiac of All

The story of Katie's romantic relationship with Tom Werner, much of it published here for the first time, is drawn from several of the author's longstanding confidential sources in Hollywood, as well as with people who had direct, firsthand knowledge of the events described. As with all not-for-attribution material, the author double-sourced the information for accuracy.

The author found that the following published sources conformed to his personal interviews: "Katie's Secret Affairs" in *The National Enquirer* (January 8, 2007); "Top of the Morning" in *People* (January 14, 2002); Elizabeth Kastor's "Katie, Today" in *Good Housekeeping* (May 1, 2000); Mitchell Fink's "New Love May Be Real for Katie" in the *New York Daily News* (August 11, 2000).

Chapter Nineteen: "The Charm Ran Out"

A person intimately familiar with Katie's family, who requested anonymity, provided the author with a great deal of the exclusive information for this chapter.

Principal published sources include Emily Couric's *The Divorce Lawyers* (St. Martin's Press, 1992); *Women Lawyers*, edited by Emily Couric (Harcourt Brace Jovanovich, 1984); Emily Couric's *The Trial Lawyers* (St. Martin's Press, 1988); Emily Couric's "Seasons" in *The Virginia Quarterly Review* (Summer 2002); Elizabeth Kastor's "Katie, Today" in *Good Housekeeping* (May 1, 2000); J. D. Heyman's "Brave in the Face of Loss: *Today Show* Host Couric Pays Tribute to Her Late Sister and Husband" in *The Vancouver Province* (November 4, 2001); Jen Michaels's "Couric Loses Battle with Pancreatic Cancer" in *The Cavalier Daily* (October 19, 2001).

Chapter Twenty: The $65 Million Woman

The description of Katie's contract negotiations, which resulted in her record-breaking salary, is derived from interviews with numerous sources— television agents, producers, and on-camera talent (many of them personal friends of the author's)—who spoke on condition of anonymity.

In addition, the author would like to acknowledge his debt to Shelley Ross, Dan Rather, and Frank Radice for speaking on the record.

Principal published sources include Jason Gayu's "Everybody Loves Katie . . ." in the *New York Observer* (August 20, 2001); Karen S. Schneider, K. C. Baker, Rachel Felder, Rebecca Paley, Diane Herbst, and Elizabeth

McNeil, Jenny Hontz, Frank Swertlow, and Robyn Flans, and J. Todd Foster's "Top of the Morning" in *People* (January 14, 2002); Brian Lowry and Elizabeth Jensen's "Courting Katie" in the *Chicago Tribune* (August 14, 2001).

Chapter Twenty-one: The Queen of Sheba

The description of Katie's relationship with Matt Lauer and other members of *The Today Show* and the account of Tom Touchet's firing are drawn from extensive interviews with television industry sources and several of the principals in the story. All of them requested anonymity.

Principal published sources include J. D. Reed and Anne-Marie O'Neill, K. C. Baker, Michelle Caruso, and Lyndon Stambler, and Brian Karem and Margery Sellinger's "Katie's New Life" in *People* (November 27, 2000); Bill Carter's "Sports Producer Named by NBC to Run Today" in the *New York Times* (April 21, 2005); Steve McClellan's "At Today, What Happens Tomorrow? Off-Camera Tensions, Tighter Ratings Race Make Morning News a Battleground" in *Broadcasting & Cable* (February 23, 2004); Tom Shales's "Katie Kicks It Like the Big Boys" in *TelevisionWeek* (May 2, 2005); J. Max Robins's "Viacom's Big Daddy" in *Broadcasting & Cable* (October 9, 2006).

Chapter Twenty-two: The End of the Affair

The descriptions of Katie's trip to Hawaii with Tom Werner, the story of their subsequent breakup, and the details of Katie's romance with Chris Botti are drawn from a wide variety of confidential sources, several of whom have firsthand knowledge of the events described in this chapter. As the author indicates in the text, one of these sources is a tabloid reporter, whose notes were carefully scrutinized and doublechecked by the author; a second is a ranking executive in Tom Werner's office; a third is a longstanding Hollywood friend of Tom Werner's.

The section on Leslie Moonves's decision to court Katie for the *CBS Evening News* anchor chair is drawn from the author's interviews with a number of people who formerly or currently occupy prominent positions at CBS News, including producers and on-air talent.

The author would like to express his gratitude to Andrew Tyndall, Larry Grossman, Sandy Socolow, Dan Rather, and Jack Schneider for their analyses of the past and present state of broadcast news.

Principal published sources include Elizabeth Kastor's "Katie, Today" in

Good Housekeeping (May 1, 2000); Gayle Fee and Laura Raposa's "Couric and Werner About to Strike Out" in the *Boston Herald* (October 14, 2004); CNN Transcript *of Larry King Live*, "Interview with Katie Couric" (March 4, 2004); Stephen M. Silverman's "Katie Couric's New Squeeze Speaks Out" in *People* (November 9, 2004); " 'Kiss Me' Katie! Prim Today Host Tarts Up" in *Globe* (February 7, 2005); "Plastic Surgery Secrets of TV News Stars" in *Globe* (August 15, 2005); Roger Hitts's "Katie's Hot New Romance Blows Up" in *Globe* (March 14, 2005); Jeff Samuels and Miki Taylor's "Katie's $1M Dream Wedding" in *Globe* (October 25, 2004); Julia Etherington's "Hollywood Botox Backlash" in *The National Enquirer* (August 29, 2005); Alexander Hitchen's " 'Moaning' Katie Ditched by Lover" in *The National Enquirer* (July 25, 2005); Greg Lindsay's "Ready for Her Close-up" in *Women's Wear Daily* (February 17, 2004); Jeff Samuel's "Katie Did It!" in *Globe* (June 3, 2003); Valerie Kuklenski's "Jay Today, Katie Tonight" in the *Daily News of Los Angeles* (May 12, 2003); Allison Romano's "A New Era in Network News" in *Broadcasting & Cable* (April 10, 2006); "Interview with Leslie Moonves" on *Charlie Rose* (September 15, 2006); Josef Adalian's "Anchor Touts News Chops" in *Variety* (June 1, 2006); Andrew Tyndall's "The Anchor's Job, in Minute Detail" in *Broadcasting & Cable* (April 10, 2006); Peter Lauria's "Moonves' Moves" in the *New York Post* (April 9, 2006); Edward Klein's "Winning Diane" in *New York Magazine* (March 13, 1989); Edward Klein's "True Grit" in *Vanity Fair* (June 1992); Edward Klein's "Eye of the Storm" in *New York Magazine* (April 15, 1991); Peter J. Boyer's *Who Killed CBS?* (Random House, 1988); Bill Carter's *Desperate Networks* (Doubleday, 2006); Rebecca Dana's "What If CBS News Is Calling Diane, Not Katie Couric" in the *New York Observer* (January 30, 2006); Jeff Samuels's "Katie Wooed for Rather's Anchor Seat" in *Globe* (January 10, 2005); CNN Transcript of *Larry King Live,* "Interview with Dan Rather" (July 12, 2006); Peter Bart's "Hands-On Honcho" in *Variety* (January 8–14, 2007); Alan Weisman's *Lone Star: The Extraordinary Life and Times of Dan Rather* (John Wiley & Sons, 2006); Brandon Tartikoff and Charles Leerhsen's *The Last Great Ride* (Turtle Bay Books, 1992); Lynn Hirschberg's "Giving Them What They Want" in the *New York Times* (September 4, 2005).

The author also consulted several websites: www.journalism.org, "The State of the News Media: An Annual Report on American Journalism"; wwd.com, a correction to Greg Lindsay's February 17, 2004, article, "Ready for Her Close-Up" in *Women's Wear Daily* (May 27, 2004); FoxNews.com, Roger Friedman's column (February 13, 2004).

Chapter Twenty-three: Miracle Worker

The portrait of Dan Rather's relationship with Leslie Moonves is drawn, in part, from the author's interview with Dan Rather, as well as confidential interviews with agents, producers, and on-air talent at CBS News.

Principal published sources include CNN Transcript of "Reliable Sources: Schieffer on Rather" (June 25, 2006); Allison Romano's "A New Era in Network News" in *Broadcasting & Cable* (April 10, 2006); "Interview with Leslie Moonves" on *Charlie Rose* (September 15, 2006); Josef Adalian's "Anchor Touts News Chops" in *Variety* (June 1, 2006); Andrew Tyndall's "The Anchor's Job, in Minute Detail" in *Broadcasting & Cable* (April 10, 2006); Peter Lauria's "Moonves' Moves" in the *New York Post* (April 9, 2006); "Katie Dumps Her Trumpeter" in the *New York Post* (February 20, 2005); Edward Klein's "Winning Diane" in *New York Magazine* (March 13, 1989); Edward Klein's "True Grit" in *Vanity Fair* (June 1992); Peter J. Boyer's *Who Killed CBS?* (Random House, 1988); Bill Carter's *Desperate Networks* (Doubleday, 2006); Rebecca Dana's "What If CBS News Is Calling Diane, Not Katie Couric" in the *New York Observer* (January 30, 2006); Edward Klein's "Eye of the Storm" in *New York Magazine* (April 15, 1991); Jeff Samuels's "Katie Wooed for Rather's Anchor Seat" in *Globe* (January 10, 2005); CNN Transcript of *Larry King Live,* "Interview with Dan Rather" (July 12, 2006); J. Max Robins's "Big Bucks for What" in *TV Guide* (April 19, 2006); Bryan Burrough's "Sleeping with the Fishes" in *Vanity Fair* (December 2006); Bill Carter's "Anchor's Chair Was an Irresistible Lure for Couric" in the *New York Times* (April 6, 2006); Peter Bart's "Hands-On Honcho" in *Variety* (January 8–14, 2007); Alan Weisman's *Lone Star: The Extraordinary Life and Times of Dan Rather* (John Wiley & Sons, 2006); Brandon Tartikoff and Charles Leerhsen's *The Last Great Ride* (Turtle Bay Books, 1992); Bill Carter and Jim Rutenberg's "With No Knockouts, NBC's Champ Faces Jabs" in the *New York Times* (September 15, 2003); Meg James's "Zucker Wraps a Good Run" in the *Los Angeles Times* (January 5, 2004); Lynn Hirschberg's "Giving Them What They Want" in the *New York Times* (September 4, 2005); Rachel Smolkin's "Hold that Obit" in *American Journalism Review* (June/July 2006).

Chapter Twenty-four: Damaged Goods

The discussion of Katie's reputation as a "transparent liberal" and her other perceived shortcomings is drawn from extensive interviews with agents, producers, and on-air talent at both CBS News and NBC News. No one was willing to speak on the record.

Prominent published sources include Alessandra Stanley's "Today Seeks Yesterday's Glory" in the *New York Times* (April 25, 2005); Eric Deggans's "All Eyes on Katie" in *NewsMax* magazine (September 2006); David Bauder's "Katie Couric Heads to Evening News as Poll Shows Viewers Prefer Her in the Morning" in the Associated Press (April 5, 2006); Rebecca Dana's "Katie Go-Nightly" in the *New York Observer* (January 10, 2007); Dusty Saunders's "Katie's Tour: A Matthew Hiltzik Production" in the (Denver) *Rocky Mountain News* (May 14, 2006); Josef Adalian's "Couric Takes on Crix" in *Variety* (June 2, 2006); Howard Kurtz's "Up Close and Too Personal" in the *Washington Post* (August 15, 2006).

The author also consulted the following websites: www.front pagemagazine.com, Lowell Ponte's "Katie Couric" (April 5, 2006); www .nationalreviewonline, Tim Graham's "Central Perk" (April 10, 2006); www.slate.com, Rebecca Dana's "The Katie Show" (March 7, 2007); www.poynteronline.org, Jim Romenesko's "Why Do Reporters Insist on Describing Couric as 'Perky'?" (April 17, 2006).

Chapter Twenty-five: Wooing Meredith

The narrative of Jeff Zucker's decision to replace Katie with Meredith Vieira is drawn from an on-the-record interview that the author conducted with Vieira on May 20, 2006. The description of Katie's "mixed feelings" about Meredith Vieira and the story of the anchor shakeup at all three broadcast networks are based on confidential interviews with television agents and prominent figures at the networks' news divisions.

Chapter Twenty-six: "A Celebration of Moi"

The description of Katie's "nervous agitation" during her contract negotiations with Leslie Moonves is drawn from a confidential interview with a source directly connected with this matter. Moonves's comment that "Katie probably paid for herself in the first week of our upfront" was made at a public meeting of stock analysts in June 2006. The quotes from Katie's farewell appearance on *The Today Show* were taken from a transcript of that show.

Prominent published sources include Marc Peyser and Johnnie L. Roberts's "The Katie Factor" in *Newsweek* (April 17, 2006); Howard Kurtz's

"Katie Couric, Thinking About Tomorrow" in the *Washington Post* (May 30, 2006); Alessandra Stanley's "A Sentimental Send-Off for Katie Couric, with a Touch of Sendup" in the *New York Times* (June 1, 2006); Adam Buckman's "NBC Lays It on Thick With 'Mourning' Show" in the *New York Post* (June 1, 2006).

Chapter Twenty-seven: Great Expectations

The description of behind-the-scenes preparations for Katie's debut on the *CBS Evening News* is drawn from a number of sources inside CBS News, including executives, producers, and on-air talent, who requested anonymity. The narrative of Katie's romance with James Reyes comes from confidential interviews with people intimately familiar with the story.

Prominent published sources include Jeff Freeland's "Katie Couric Correction: Anchor Would Consider War Zone" in the *National Ledger* (July 22, 2006); David Bauder's "7 Months Into Job at CBS News, the Rebuilding Continues for Sean McManus" in the Associated Press (July 2, 2006); Howard Kurtz's "Up Close and Too Personal" in the *Washington Post* (August 15, 2006); "Katie's New Billionaire Boyfriend" in *The National Enquirer* (February 12, 2007); "Katie Couric Lets Off Steam" in Page Six, the *New York Post* (September 14, 2006).

The author also consulted these websites: www.marketwatch.com, Jon Friedman's "Katie Couric's Listening Tour Is Just a Gimmick" (July 19, 2006); www.latimes.com, Ann Midgette's "Katie Couric's New Groove" (September 7, 2006); www.filmmusicsociety.org, Jon Burlingame's "Horner, Williams TV Themes Debut" (September 14, 2006)

Chapter Twenty-eight: Katie Golightly

The description of Katie's fiftieth birthday party at Tiffany is based on an on-the-record interview with the store's head of public relations (Fernanda Kellogg) and with participants who requested anonymity. The account of Katie's romance with Brooks Perlin comes from a confidential interview with a friend of the Perlin family.

Prominent published sources include Karen Schneider, K. C. Baker, Diane Clehane, Liz Hamm, Jason Lynch, Tiffany McGee, and Jennifer Liebrum's "Katie's New Romance" in *People* (April 30, 2007); "Meet Katie Couric's Young Boyfriend" in *People* (April 20, 2007); Rebecca Dana's "Katie

Go-Nightly" in the *New York Observer* (January 10, 2007); "Couric Enjoys 'Tiffany's' Birthday Party" in UPI (January 14, 2007); "Katie Couric's Tiffany Ice-Capade *for* Charity" in *Radar* (January 17, 2007); " 'Gender' Blamed for Katie Couric's Low Ratings" in *NewsMax* (January 30, 2007); David Bauder's "CBS Correspondent Makes Plea for Airtime" in the Associated Press; "Climber's Widow Tells Her Story," *CBS News* (December 21, 2006); Ben Grossman's "CBS News Boss: Gender Bias Hurts Couric" in *Broadcasting & Cable* (January 2007); Phil Rosenthal's "CBS Refuses to Be Interrupted by Ford's Death" in the *Chicago Tribune* (December 30, 2006); "Couric Challenges Rice: 'To Quote My Daughter, "Who Made Us the Boss of Them?" ' " in *NewsBusters* (September 24, 2006); Jacques Steinberg's "Under Couric, Ratings Race Is Once Again, Well, a Race" in the *New York Times* (September 19, 2006); Melanie McFarland's "On TV: After the Hype, Couric Needs More Than Fluff to Get Viewers" in the *Seattle Post-Intelligencer* (September 16, 2006); Alessandra Stanley's "For the New Face of CBS News, a Subdued Beginning" in the *New York Times* (September 6, 2006); Gail Shister's "Big Bucks for Couric, But Still Third Place for CBS News" in the *Philadelphia Inquirer* (October 18, 2006); CNN Transcript of *Larry King Live*, "Interview with Katie Couric" (November 1, 2006); Linda Stasi's "Not Necessarily the 'News' " in the *New York Post* (October 6, 2006); Howard Kurtz's "The Couric Difference" in the *Washington Post* (September 6, 2006); Tad Friend's "Her Debut" in *The New Yorker* (September 18, 2006); Gail Shister's "Couric's Ratings Down, But Be Patient, Trio Urge" in the *Philadelphia Inquirer;* James Wolcott's "Courage, Katie!" in *Vanity Fair* (January 2007); Howard Kurtz's "Couric's Journey" in the *Washington Post* (December 4, 2007); Peter Johnson's "On CBS News, Couric Is Out of Her Interviewing Element" in *USA Today* (January 15, 2007); Gail Shister's "A Big Opening, Then Some Drift in Couric's Ratings" in the *Philadelphia Inquirer* (September 12, 2006).

The author also consulted these websites: www.freerepublic.com, "Debate Over Katie Couric's Mt. Hood Widow Interview" (December 23, 2006); www.broadcastingcable.com, "Women Scarcer on CBS Evening News" (October 23, 2006); www.washingtonpost.com, "Lara Logan, Rapid Riser" (May 18, 2006); www.cbsnews.com, "Couric & Co.: Katie: A Woman at the Table" (January 18, 2007); www.harddrivelife.com, "Katie Couric Plays the 'Chick' Card (January 17, 2007); www.washingtonpost.com, Steve Gorman's "Ratings Tell Mixed Story About Couric's Success" (October 5, 2006); www.washingtonpost.com, Tom Shales's "Getting a Read on the Speech

Makes for Quite a Snapshot" (January 24, 2007); www.townhall.com, "CBS Chief Moonves High on Katie Couric" (September 12, 2006); www.mediamatters.org, "Couric Fails to Challenge 'Scary Smart,' 'Girly and Fun' Rice on a Host of Issues" (September 27, 2006); www.washingtonpost .com, Tom Shales's "No News Not the Best News for Katie Couric's Debut" (September 6, 2006); www.marketwatch.com, Jon Friedman's "Couric's Woes Were the Media Story of the Year" (December 11, 2006).

Chapter Twenty-nine: No Way Out

The account of Katie's disappointing ratings is based on a score of interviews with sources in the broadcast news business, all of whom requested anonymity. The description of Rick Kaplan's "maturity" is drawn from a close associate who has known him for more than twenty years. Katie's "pain factor" was described to the author by a prominent network news figure. The description of the anti-Moonves atmosphere at CBS News comes from confidential conversations with several current and former CBS News correspondents.

Prominent published sources include Tom Jicha's column in the *South Florida Sun-Sentinel* (November 16, 2006); Gail Shister's "New Producer Brought In for 'CBS Evening News'" in the *Philadelphia Inquirer* (March 9, 2007); Matea Gold's "CBS's New Script: Just the Facts, Couric" in the *Los Angeles Times* (March 8, 2007); excerpt from CNN's *Reliable Sources,* "CBS Chose to Make Katie Couric 'Anchormom,' and That Was a Bad Decision" (December 25, 2006); James Poniewozik's "Here's the News: Old Is In" in *Time* (March 22, 2007); Bill Carter's "CBS Producer Goes Around, Comes Around" in the *New York Times* (March 9, 2007); Adman Buckman's "Couric Picks Up Speed" in the *New York Post* (March 15, 2007); Gail Shister's "Jeff Greenfield Defends His New Colleague Katie Couric" in the *Philadelphia Inquirer* (April 4, 2007); "Couric's Guy Quick to Switch" in the *New York Post* (April 15, 2007); Alessandra Stanley's "Amid Chaos, One Notably Restrained Voice" in the *New York Times* (April 19, 2007); Gail Shister's column in the *Philadelphia Inquirer* (April 24, 2007); "Katie's 'Kid' Beau Has a Gent-le Touch" in the *New York Post* (May 8, 2007); "Katie Cougar: New Love Is 17 Yrs. Her Junior" in the *New York Post* (April 12, 2007); Bill Carter's "Is It the Woman Thing, or Is It Katie Couric?" in the *New York Times* (May 14, 2007).

The author also consulted the following websites: www.huffingtonpost .com, Nora Ephron on Katie Couric (November 8, 2006); www.tvweek.com,

Michael Greppi's "CBS Taps Kaplan to Turn 'News' Around (March 12, 2007); www.worldnetdaily.com, Joe Kovacs's "'Balloon Animal' Couric Scorched by AOL Users" (March 14, 2007); www.the hollywoodreporter .com, Paul J. Gough's "Kaplan In at 'CBS Evening News'" (March 8, 2007); www.usatoday.com, P. Johnson's "Six Months, Third Place for Couric" (March 7, 2007); www.theatlantic.com, William Powers's "Trading Places" (April 3, 2007); www.huffingtonpost.com, Nora Ephron's "Some People" (March 26,2007); www.motleyfool.com, Steven Mallas's "Should CBS Be Patient With Katie?" (April 11, 2007); www.slate.com, Timothy Noah's "The Deeper Fakery of Couric's Plagiarism" (April 12, 2007); www.televisionweek.com, "Top 10 Most Powerful People in TV News 2007" (April 16, 2007); www.foxnews.com, Roger Friedman's "Katie Couric's Enemies Are CBS Insiders" (April 25, 2007); www.jossip.com, "The Katie Couric Agenda: Why There's Another Hatchet Job, and Why They Might Keep Coming" (April 27, 2007); www.seattlepi.com, David Bauder's "Poll: Couric Gets More Negative News" (May 3, 2007).

Index